Codermetrics

Codermetrics
Analytics for Improving Software Teams

Jonathan Alexander

O'REILLY®

Beijing · Cambridge · Farnham · Köln · Sebastopol · Tokyo

Codermetrics

by Jonathan Alexander

Published by O'Reilly Media, Inc., 1005 Gravenstein Highway North, Sebastopol, CA 95472.

O'Reilly books may be purchased for educational, business, or sales promotional use. Online editions are also available for most titles (*http://my.safaribooksonline.com*). For more information, contact our corporate/institutional sales department: (800) 998-9938 or *corporate@oreilly.com*.

Editors: Andy Oram and Mike Hendrickson	**Indexer:** John Bickelhaupt
Production Editor: Kristen Borg	**Cover Designer:** Karen Montgomery
Proofreader: O'Reilly Production Services	**Interior Designer:** David Futato
	Illustrator: Robert Romano

Printing History:

August 2011:	First Edition.

ISBN: 978-1-449-30515-4

[LSI]

1312293148

Table of Contents

Part II. Metrics

Part III. Processes

Preface

Is there a rational way to measure coder skills and contributions and the way that software teams fit together? Could metrics help you improve coder self-awareness, teamwork, mentoring, and goal-setting? Could more detailed data help you make better hiring decisions, help make performance reviews fairer, and help your software teams become more successful?

Whether you are a coder, team leader, or manager, if you are interested in any of these topics or in how metrics can be applied in a variety of other ways for software development teams, then this book is designed with you in mind. The ideas in this book are a departure from how metrics have been applied to software development in the past. The concepts and techniques presented here are meant to help you think differently about building software teams and to help get you started on your own journey using metrics in new and better ways as part of the software development process.

As a manager of software teams, I myself am on that journey. I believe the techniques in this book have helped "turn around" troubled software teams and have helped good software teams become even better. Gathering metrics on a wider set of activities and outcomes isn't the only path to success, of course, but it has worked for me, and I believe it can work for you, too.

Maybe you measure success by the number of people who use your software, or by how efficiently you deliver releases, or by how few errors you have. Will the use of metrics improve your teams and your success by 5%, 10%, 25%, or more? You will only know by testing these ideas yourself. But even if it's just 5% (though I think it can be much more), how much is that worth? Even if using metrics simply helps the coders on a team become more self-aware and become better teammates, how much is that worth? At the very least, I believe the potential benefits justify the small amount of time and effort it takes to start gathering and using the kind of metrics described in this book. And if you don't decide to gather metrics, I believe there are many concepts here that you can still learn from and apply to your own teams.

Organization of This Book

This book is written in three parts, designed to be read in order, although you may find specific parts of the book more useful for later review if you are putting metrics into practice. Part I, "Concepts", provides a more detailed introduction behind the thinking of codermetrics, the variety of analyses that metrics can enable, and the data that can be measured for coders and software development teams. Part II, "Metrics", is set up as a kind of metrics reference guide, with each metric explained with examples and notes. Part III, "Processes", covers techniques to introduce metrics in your teams and put them to use in the development process, as well as how to use metrics to improve and build better software teams.

Part I, "Concepts", consists of the following chapters:

> Chapter 1, Introduction, provides a more detailed explanation of the thoughts, motivations, and goals behind this book.
>
> Chapter 2, Measuring What Coders Do, talks about the general concepts behind metrics, measuring coders, and analyzing teamwork and team performance.
>
> Chapter 3, The Right Data, discusses what constitutes useful data, how to obtain it, and the detailed data elements that will be used for codermetrics.

Part II, "Metrics", consists of the following chapters:

> Chapter 4, Skill Metrics, covers metrics for a wide variety of coder skills and contributions.
>
> Chapter 5, Response Metrics, covers metrics that measure various types of positive and negative user response to software.
>
> Chapter 6, Value Metrics, covers metrics that highlight the value that coders bring to a team.

Part III, "Processes", consists of the following chapters:

> Chapter 7, Metrics in Use, provides a multistep approach to test and introduce metrics in an organization, and offers techniques to use metrics in the development process and performance reviews.
>
> Chapter 8, Building Software Teams, describes how to use metrics to determine team needs, and how to apply them in personnel planning, hiring, and coaching of current team members.
>
> Chapter 9, Conclusion, provides final thoughts on the value of metrics, how to deal with key qualities that are hard to quantify, and how metrics might be improved or expanded in the future.

Safari® Books Online

Safari Books Online is an on-demand digital library that lets you easily search over 7,500 technology and creative reference books and videos to find the answers you need quickly.

With a subscription, you can read any page and watch any video from our library online. Read books on your cell phone and mobile devices. Access new titles before they are available for print, and get exclusive access to manuscripts in development and post feedback for the authors. Copy and paste code samples, organize your favorites, download chapters, bookmark key sections, create notes, print out pages, and benefit from tons of other time-saving features.

O'Reilly Media has uploaded this book to the Safari Books Online service. To have full digital access to this book and others on similar topics from O'Reilly and other publishers, sign up for free at *http://my.safaribooksonline.com*.

How to Contact Us

Please address comments and questions concerning this book to the publisher:

O'Reilly Media, Inc.
1005 Gravenstein Highway North
Sebastopol, CA 95472
800-998-9938 (in the United States or Canada)
707-829-0515 (international or local)
707-829-0104 (fax)

We have a web page for this book, where we list errata, examples, and any additional information. You can access this page at:

http://oreilly.com/catalog/9781449305154/

To comment or ask technical questions about this book, send email to:

bookquestions@oreilly.com

For more information about our books, courses, conferences, and news, see our website at *http://www.oreilly.com*.

Find us on Facebook: *http://facebook.com/oreilly*

Follow us on Twitter: *http://twitter.com/oreillymedia*

Watch us on YouTube: *http://www.youtube.com/oreillymedia*

Acknowledgments

The ideas in this book were inspired by Michael Lewis's writing on sabermetrics and sports statistics, which led me to the writing of Bill James. They are the epitome of informed, informative, and entertaining writers. Although they'll never have a reason to read this book, my initial thanks is to them.

My thanks also goes to all the excellent coders I've worked with over the years, and the fine managers and executives. I've been very lucky and I can't really think of a single professional situation where I didn't learn a tremendous amount. Particular thanks to Wain Kellum, CEO, and the entire team at Vocalocity, who supported my efforts in writing this book.

I want to thank Andy Oram, my editor at O'Reilly, who helped me through this process and to whom a great deal of credit goes for making this far better than it would have been otherwise. It was a pleasure to work with you, Andy. Also, thanks to Mike Hendrickson at O'Reilly who originally supported and encouraged this idea. And to the entire O'Reilly Media production team, thanks, too.

For the feedback and reviews they provided on this book during the process, I want to thank Brian Jackson at Google, Nagaraj Nadendla at Taleo, and Ben Wu at Zuora. They are all excellent leaders and managers themselves. Thanks guys.

To my dad, thanks for giving me a love of sports, which has become a love for statistics too. To my mom, thanks for encouraging me to write a book.

Most of all I want to thank my wife, Barbara, who did the most to support my efforts in writing this book, not the least of which was using her excellent editorial skills to proofread this book, catch a number of flaws, and point out a number of improvements, even though she's a lawyer so she can't write a line of code (OK, maybe a line). Thanks honey! And to my two beautiful daughters, Naomi and Vivian, because they make every day special, my loving thanks.

PART I

Concepts

This section covers general concepts about metrics, pattern analysis, data gathering, and data elements.

CHAPTER 1

Introduction

Let's not be too sure that we haven't been missing something important.

—Bill James, baseball statistician and author, from his article "Underestimating the Fog"

This is a book about coders, software development teams, metrics and patterns. The ideas in this book originated a few years ago when I started to think about the makeup of software teams, both good and bad, and all the subtle contributions and unsung heroes that are a critical part of success. For almost two decades now, I've been responsible for building and managing teams of designers, coders, and testers. Over this time I've realized that software teams, similar to sports teams, require a variety of players and skills to succeed. I've also learned that there are patterns to success and failure that are not necessarily what I assumed before.

Here's a simple pattern I've seen, and maybe you've seen it too: every successful software team I've been on has always had at least one person who uncomplainingly does the little things, like creating the installer, improving the build scripts, or fixing other people's bugs to get features done. The projects never would have been done, or at least not done well, if someone hadn't taken on these smaller but detail-oriented tasks.

Another pattern: many seasoned software teams I've seen had one or two coders who were the clear technical leaders, the go-to people, although they may not necessarily have had the titles to match. These go-to coders not only solved problems, but they exerted a strong influence on others, such that the skills of the other coders often evolved rapidly, closer to the level of the technical leaders. As a result, one or two great coders raised the level of the entire team.

Here's a pattern I've observed on some of the longer projects I've been a part of, especially with small teams in start-up environments: the project team hit a "wall" when the project was about 80% complete. Like a marathon runner at the 20-mile mark, after months of pushing hard, everyone is suffering from real mental and physical fatigue. Sometimes when the teams hit the wall, we broke down and never really recovered. The final 20% of the project seemed to go on forever, and we basically limped to the finish line. But sometimes the team went through the wall, recovered, and picked up the pace again. In every case, this recovery happened because someone on the team had the personality to lighten the load, tell jokes, lift spirits, and make everyone feel better. Thanks to the "joker" on the team, everyone got back to a (mostly) positive mindset, ready to sprint to the finish.

Patterns of success seem obvious once we see them, but to see them we must learn where and how to look. Once I started to think about this, I began to wonder whether we could create a set of metrics that would give us a clear and objective way to identify, analyze, and discuss the successes or failures of our software teams and the full range of coder skills and contributions. Not as a way to rate performance, but as a way to help us better understand and foster the keys to success, and where and how we might improve. In my own teams I began to experiment, and the positive results have me very encouraged that these methods could be useful for others, too.

This book is my attempt to share some of these ideas and practices. To this point, there is very little material written or otherwise available regarding metrics that can be used to analyze coders and software teams. We have thoughtful books on interviewing, skills-testing, project estimation, project management, team management—and on Agile and other methodologies that make the development process more effective. But we have never had much discussion or explored a quantitative and analytical approach to understanding the skills and work of individual coders to improve software teams.

Our metrics, to the extent that most software teams use them today, are commonly a simple set of counts that we use in project estimation or in ongoing project management. We use bug counts, task counts, time increments (hours/days/weeks)—and with Agile, some of us use story points and velocity. There are also more advanced systems and tools for project estimation that make use of sizing metrics such as KLOCs and Function Points.

But the metrics we commonly deal with don't provide enough insight to answer many key questions that we have, such as:

- How well is our software team succeeding?
- How are individual team members contributing to the team's success?
- What capabilities can be improved to achieve greater success?

These are simple but profound questions. If we can't answer these questions, or lack a clear way to discuss and think about the answers, then as individuals and team members, we are not doing all we can to succeed. Of course, we must fundamentally explore what we mean by success and how we measure success for software teams, but assuming this can be sufficiently settled, then the above questions remain. In the pages that follow, I will try to suggest new and different ways for us to achieve greater understanding and perhaps answers, too.

I'm a big sports fan, and so in many parts of this book, I've chosen to use sports analogies. It's not necessary, however, for you to like or understand sports to understand the concepts in this book. Like all analogies, the purpose is just to help make the ideas quicker to grasp and easier to remember. Personally, I think using sports analogies to discuss software teams is apt—and fun.

I think of software development as a team sport. Software products are typically not produced by an individual but by a team, and even in the case where one coder works alone, that coder must fill the various roles of a larger team. In sports, we know that successful teams require players that complement each other, and not everyone needs nor should have the same skills. A football team needs players who can block and tackle as well as those that can run, pass, and catch. Not everyone is good at the same thing. In fact, a team where all players have the same strengths, no matter how strong, is in many cases worse than a team where players have different and contrasting skills. In the end, every player on the team matters, and every player must do their part if the team is going to succeed.

My first thoughts about applying quantitative analysis to coders came from the attention that statistical analysis has recently garnered in major organized sports. Computers and software have contributed to enormous changes in how professional sports teams analyze player statistics, and how they determine the player skills that most directly contribute to winning teams. Bill James and other noted analysts have created a discipline around statistical analysis of baseball players referred to as "sabermetrics". And author Michael Lewis has popularized these newer approaches to sports team management in his books *Moneyball* and *The Blind Side*, and in his articles in *The New York Times Magazine* and other publications.

Many of the people who have pioneered these new approaches in sports management have training in more analytical fields, such as Daryl Morey (GM of the NBA Houston Rockets) who majored in computer science at Northwestern, and Paul DePodesta (VP of the MLB New York Mets and former GM of the Los Angeles Dodgers) who majored in economics at Harvard. This "new" approach in sports is often depicted as a reaction to and move away from the more subjective, gut-feel approach of talent evaluation and team-building. Major sports teams are now very big businesses, with huge amounts of money involved. In this new era, managers responsible for these teams spend more time gathering and analyzing metrics, to help them build winning teams in a more rational and predictable way (and as *Moneyball* illustrates, in a way that can be more cost-effective and profitable, too). This doesn't eliminate individual intuition and creativity, but augments it with better knowledge. The key steps followed in this new approach are:

- Find a way to measure the differences between winning and losing teams.
- Find a way to measure the contributions of individual players to their teams.
- Determine key player characteristics that are highly correlated with winning or losing.

The process of finding meaningful metrics and formulas in sports is not static, but continuously evolving. It's well understood that there are many important but subtle skills that are hard to measure and analyze, such as a defensive football player's instinct to find the ball carrier or a player's ability to perform under pressure. Bill James, for example, publishes regular articles and annual books on baseball in which he introduces new metrics and ideas, some of which others adopt and use, some of which others improve, and some of which turn out to be less useful and eventually fade away.

And metrics evolve privately as well as publicly. The actual statistics and formulas that sports teams favor are secretly guarded, since sports is, of course, a competitive field. Many analysts who write publicly also work as private consultants for individual teams. Theo Epstein (GM of the MLB Boston Red Sox) and Billy Beane (GM of the MLB Oakland A's) may share some information with each other, and they may both benefit by the metrics known to the wider community as a whole—but in the end they are trying to win against each other, so there are some elements about their approach that will never be known outside their organizations.

Our field of software development is less public, with different competitive pressures than major sports leagues, and most coders are not in the public eye. We don't and probably never will have fans poring over our statistics or putting our poster on their wall (now there's a scary thought). But it seems a little ironic that those of us who work in a field that in many ways enabled deeper statistical analysis in sports (as well as in other industries), have not yet embraced or fully considered the potential benefits of quantitative analysis in our own domain of software development.

Naturally we, like any workers, might be suspicious about whether good metrics can be found and tell an effective story, and we might be worried that statistics can be misused by managers in performance reviews and such. It is the premise of this book, however, that within our discipline there are a variety of skills and results that we can indeed measure, and from which we can obtain meaningful and useful insights about ourselves and our teams. These numbers are not black and white, and individual numbers never tell the whole story. Knowing Derek Jeter's batting average or Tim Duncan's shooting percentage tells you only a very small part of how effective they are as players and teammates. But when we look at a range of statistics, we can begin to identify patterns for individuals and teams, and sometimes what we find is surprising, even revelatory.

As an example, let me tell you about one of the software teams I managed for many years.

 A note about the stories in this book: these come from my own experience. However in many cases, the stories have been simplified or generalized to convey the key points. I will not use names in order to protect the innocent and the guilty alike, including me.

This example was at a venture-backed start-up, with a team of six coders and three testers (we are focusing on coders in this book, so I will focus on them in this example). There were three key phases that we went through in the first two years: initial development of our 1.0 product release, which took nine months; the period after release when we supported the first customers and developed our 1.1, which took six months; and the development of our 2.0 product release, which took another nine months. The team itself had three senior coders, each with more than ten years of experience and excellent domain knowledge, and three junior coders each with excellent educational backgrounds and about two years of commercial coding experience. During this two year period, all the senior coders remained, but two of the junior coders left after the first year and we brought on two more.

Our executives and our investors thought our initial 1.0 release was a great success. We won a major award at a key industry show and received multiple positive product reviews. We had a large amount of reseller interest, and the number of customer evaluations were double our expectations, so our sales staff was incredibly busy (this was an on-premise enterprise software solution). Revenues in the first quarters after release were also well ahead of plan.

There were plenty of reasons for our software team to feel good, and everyone was patting us on the back. But was our 1.0 release really a success?

It took us a while to realize it, but a deeper look at the numbers at the time would have revealed some serious problems. The key and troubling facts were this: while we had succeeded in generating public awareness and solid customer interest, every customer trial was generating, on average, seven calls to customer support—despite the fact that each customer received installation and setup assistance. These seven calls were resulting in an average support time of three full days to work with the customer and investigate issues, and on average it turned out that every customer was identifying three new bugs in the product that had not been previously found. Coder time to support every customer trial, including the time to assist support and the time to fix significant product issues, was measured in weeks, not hours or even days.

And the seemingly positive revenue results were also misleading. We were ahead of our early revenue plans thanks to a few bigger deals, but our overall rate of converting evaluators to real customers and the time it was taking for conversion were much worse than we required to build a successful business. This was at least in part due to the usability and quality issues that were reflected in the support load and bugs found.

In other words, while outsiders might have thought that our initial release was very successful, in reality it was only a partial success at best. The data shown in Figure 1-1 reveals how bugs and support issues were vastly outweighing new users.

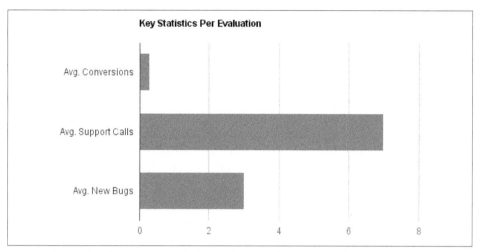

Figure 1-1. A look at key metrics of this 1.0 product reveals serious problems

There was another big issue, too. As time went on, certain coders on the team were having trouble getting along. The decreased amount of time spent working on more "exciting" new features, and the increased time spent on less glamorous investigation and bug fixing, combined with the stress related to support in a start-up environment, began to reveal cracks in individuals and in our software team. Personality differences were exacerbated, to the point that certain coders were avoiding each other, and we even had a few incidents of people yelling in the workplace.

The six months following the 1.0 release, during which the team provided support and worked on the 1.1 release, were filled with turmoil and were a near disaster, even though those outside the team still thought everything was fine. Most of each coder's time went into bug fixing, and we had to delay most of our incremental product improvements. The 1.1 release fixed all the critical bugs—but there were still so many issues remaining that even after the release, the support load and conversion rates did not materially change.

Then, suddenly, everything got much better inside the software team. Even though the support rate remained constant, the team started handling issues much more efficiently, with less people involved on every issue. More time was freed up for new features and major improvements in the most problematic areas. The 1.1 release, which had almost no feature improvements, took six months. The 2.0 release, which had multiple new features and major product improvements, took only nine months with the same size team. Following the 2.0 release, the conversion rate and issue rate noticeably improved, to the point that we could clearly say that the 2.0 release was a much greater success.

So what happened? Was it that everyone got used to handling the issues, or that the issues became repetitive or less severe? To a certain extent that was true. But the key change was that two junior coders left the team, and two other junior coders joined.

The two coders who left did so of their own accord. While they had been mostly happy during the work on our 1.0 release, they were the ones who disliked the post-release support work the most. They were the ones who most regularly wanted or needed others, specifically the senior coders, to help them if they weren't familiar with a problem or an area of code. And one of them was the one who had a temper and fought increasingly with other team members over time.

The new coders who joined the team were not measurably different from those who left in terms of education, experience, or aptitude. Where they were different, however, were in two key skill areas that became highly critical and useful following our first product release: the desire and willingness to solve problems independently and the ability to handle somewhat stressful situations calmly, even happily. Figure 1-2 shows how one replacement outperformed their predecessor.

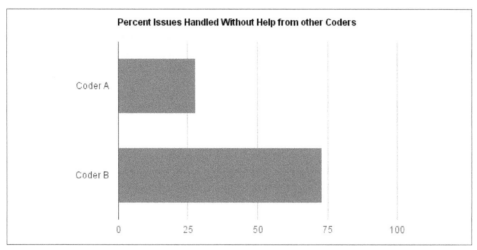

Figure 1-2. A comparison of Coder A to their replacement Coder B shows an important factor in team success

Because the new coders possessed the right skills, they were able to take on and finish more problems themselves. It wasn't necessarily that we were putting less time into support or fixing specific issues, but we were able to get less people involved and have less interruptions, so that other team members were able to stay focused on other work. In the end, we got lucky. Since we had some personality conflicts with the two coders who left, we consciously favored and selected job candidates who had very different personalities. But we didn't realize the full benefits this would bring to our overall productivity and team success.

At the time all this occurred, we did not pay close attention to our metrics. Looking back, I realize how focusing the team on key metrics could have helped us react more quickly and effectively after the first product release. It's hard to make everyone believe there are problems or understand the magnitude when they are being congratulated by outsiders for all the good things they've done. It is easy for a team to develop a false sense of complacency—or in the reverse case, to develop poor morale when they don't get the praise they feel they deserve. Looking at a full range of product and team metrics can balance the adulation or criticism you receive, and provide much-needed perspective around where you're really at and what needs to be done. Measuring and discussing skills such as self-reliance and thoroughness can help foster those skills, and help ensure that coders with those skills receive the credit and recognition they deserve for their contributions to the team.

The objective of this book is to present a method and a set of metrics—that is, coder-metrics—that cover a variety of areas related to individual coders and software development teams. This method is designed to challenge our assumptions, in hopes that we can better discover what is knowable about the patterns that lead to success. To make them easier to understand and remember, the metrics in this book are named after analogous sports statistics. These metrics are designed to give us some terminology to better communicate, and hopefully to make us think generally about how these types of metrics can be useful in our field. In the end, their value can be measured by how well they help us answer the key questions that we face as to what it means to "win" and how we can better ourselves and our teams.

It is my hope that the concepts in this book will lead to further productive dialog between coders, team leaders, and managers, both within and across organizations. There is no doubt that many individual metrics introduced here can and will be improved; and that some of the ideas here will be dismissed, and even better metrics will be found. Personally, I have seen great value within teams in working to define a wider variety of items to measure, in figuring out how to measure and relate individual and team activities to organization goals, and then in sharing the data and discussing it among the team. Even for those of you who never actively use metrics, I hope that you can find value here and that some of the ideas in this book will positively affect how you think about coders and software development teams. If others begin to consider these concepts and perhaps use some of the approaches outlined in this book, working towards a broader and deeper rational analysis of coder contributions and software team-building, then I will feel this book is a success.

It should be noted, in case it's not obvious, that there are many participants and skills in the software development process that are outside the scope of this book. This is partially because the full scope of participants and skills is too much to cover in a single book, and mostly because I personally have not defined a set of metrics for other skills. Perhaps in the future we will develop metrics for designers, testers, managers, or others —and maybe there will be writing on these, too.

CHAPTER 2

Measuring What Coders Do

Never mistake activity for achievement.

—John Wooden, UCLA men's basketball coach, 1946–1975

What are metrics about? How can they help? How are they used elsewhere and how might they be applicable to coders and software development teams?

This chapter begins to explore the general purpose of metrics, and the qualities that make certain metrics relevant and useful, and others not. I will discuss various patterns and noteworthy information that metrics can help you identify and understand. I'll also look at various types of data you can use, along with ways you can gather the data and ensure that it is as accurate and consistent as possible. The concepts covered here provide a basic introduction to the key concepts of metrics and will serve as a basis for further discussions through the remainder of this book.

The Purpose of Metrics

There are three reasons to gather and use metrics. Of course there may be more reasons too, but in this book I will focus on three.

The first purpose of metrics is simply to help you track and understand what has happened. The subjective observation of situations, while sometimes insightful, is often colored by personal biases and experiences. It is dominated by the details you notice and are attuned to, and it misses the things you don't see or recognize.

For example, if you attend a baseball game, and at the end someone asks what you remember, you will describe some of the plays that stood out. Maybe a big hit, or an exciting defensive play. But there will be a lot of details you forget, even though they just happened in the last few hours. Some you just won't remember, maybe some you didn't notice, maybe others you didn't even see because you were at the hot dog stand. Also, how much you remember and what you describe will depend on how familiar you are with baseball, how many games you've seen before, and how much you know about different aspects of the game.

Alternatively, if you look at a box score of key statistics from a game, you can tell a lot about what happened in the game, whether or not you attended. And if you look at a complete statistical breakdown, with full offensive and defensive statistics and details on all scoring, then provided that you know what the statistics mean you can tell a great deal about the game, the players' contributions, and the key factors that went into winning or losing.

Statistics, or metrics, are the detailed documentation of what has occurred. They provide a historical record that allows for a more "scientific," empirical analysis of what players and teams have done, and why they've won or lost.

Metrics also preserve the past. Week by week, month by month, time inevitably colors and clouds what you remember and what you think was significant. The more statistical data you have, the less you are likely to forget or distort the past. For example, when I was young my dad took me to many UCLA basketball games. I remember that Brad Holland was one of my favorite players in the late 1970s, and a great scorer, but I can't remember specific details. If I go to a book or website with player statistics, however, many details come flooding back. The same forgetting can occur for things that happened last year as for those that occurred 30 years ago. Having a statistical record allows us to review and in some sense relive what happened, and balances our selective memories.

The second purpose of metrics is to help people communicate about what has happened. The metrics themselves become part of the terminology, allowing a group of people to discuss situations with some level of confidence that they are talking about the same thing. Defining and naming metrics forces you to clarify the language that you use to communicate. Without such definition and clear terminology, you are more apt to have misunderstandings or, more typically, you may fail to discuss certain issues that might in fact matter a lot.

In baseball, for example, a well-known pitching statistic is Earned Run Average (ERA). The "earned run" refers to a run for the opposing team that did not result from an error, and ERA represents the average number of earned runs a pitcher gives up for every 9 innings pitched (meaning for every complete game). That's a lot to understand and describe. But if you just say that "the pitcher's ERA is 4.29", then for someone familiar with baseball, you have quickly and concisely conveyed a rich set of information.

The third purpose of metrics is to help people focus on what they need to improve. Metrics document what you have done and accomplished, and that gives you a point of comparison to what you hope to do and achieve. Without points of reference, it's very difficult to know where you stand, how far you might have to go, and whether you've arrived.

American football players measure their performance on and off the field. They measure yards gained, touchdowns, and tackles during games. But they also measure their times in the 40-yard dash and repetitions when bench-pressing 225 pounds, which are not actually part of a football game. They do this because they know that speed and strength are important factors to success in their sport. They also have years of data to show the range of speed and strength that is required for different positions such as cornerbacks, linebackers, running backs, and linemen. Taking measurements to show where they stand allows players to focus on what they most need to improve.

Metrics Are Not Grades

In grammar school, high school, and college, you receive grades for your work. Grades are supposed to reflect your mastery of a subject and your relative ranking to others in the class. They may be strictly correlated to your performance on objective tests, although in most cases either the tests or some other element of the grade involves subjective evaluation by the instructor. In your earlier years, grades provide feedback to help identify the need for improvement, but in your later years the grades become increasingly competitive, with ranking and rewards. For reasons both institutional and traditional, for better or worse, the school system is not only responsible for teaching students, but also for ranking them.

If you are going to embrace metrics, it is important to establish and understand that metrics are not grades. Metrics measure specific individual skills and contributions, and as I will examine in this book, there is often no fixed scale of what is "good" or "bad." Successful teams can and will have many individuals whose personal metrics vary widely. It's similar to a football team, where linemen are slower than running backs, and great cornerbacks often have less tackles or passes defended because quarterbacks don't throw towards them.

The purpose of metrics, as discussed above, is to provide a clearer picture of what happened, to improve communication, and to help you identify and develop useful skills. Later in this chapter and in this book I will explore how metrics may come into play in recruiting, performance reviews, and other aspects of team management. However, in all cases this will only work if the metrics are not seen or used as grades, but as a fair reflection of each coder's current skills, strengths, and weaknesses.

Team Dynamics

While metrics should not be thought of strictly as grades, there is no way to avoid the fact that any good system of metrics will identify the inevitable differences between people. And as such, in any organization where people are paid for labor and their pay scale is tied to their contributions and skills, good metrics will have some correlation to pay scales and other perks. This should not, however, cause you undue concern about capturing and utilizing metrics, or make you believe that people will seek to distort the data in untruthful ways.

As James Surowiecki points out in his book *The Wisdom of Crowds*, people mainly expect there to be a true and equitable relationship between accomplishments and rewards. Most people don't expect to be rewarded equally for unequal accomplishments, and in fact most people are content when the reward system is seen as fairest and most in line with their relative contributions. In the sense that metrics provide greater detail and more accuracy in understanding people's relative skills and contributions (and this can help you make sure that people are fairly compensated), the use of metrics can therefore result in increased satisfaction among individuals and teams. People just want to be treated and recognized fairly—ask yourself whether fairness is even possible without a rational, metrics-based approach.

In professional sports, players statistics are scrutinized endlessly, and their annual salaries are generally known to the public as well. For leading players, their personal contract negotiations are closely followed and discussed in the media. But while some negotiations are stickier than others, in the end both the players and teams typically seek contracts that are "fair" and in line with their industry standard and other players of similar skills. Many sports contract disputes are now settled in arbitration where an independent party determines the fair salary through a comparison process. Player statistics play a large role in arbitration.

Jed Lowrie, a utility infielder for the Boston Red Sox, does not expect to be paid the same as second-baseman Dustin Pedroia, who is one of the team's proven stars. While we can assume Lowrie would be happy to receive more money, we also believe he and other players like him are satisfied as long as they feel that their compensation is fair. And, of course, they are still very important to the team's success. If anything, the use of statistics in salary negotiations makes the process more fair, so that players no longer feel mistreated in the way they did in the past when someone like Dodgers GM Buzzie Bavasi just told Sandy Koufax how much money he would make despite how well he performed, and that was that.

In software development you don't typically make salaries public, and you certainly don't have reporters following your salary negotiations. Even if you did, you can assume not all team members would expect the same salary. But you can also assume that everyone would want the system to be as fair and objective as possible.

All of this is not to say that you should base your salary discussions and performance reviews solely on metrics, which would be tantamount to treating the metrics as grades. This is only to say that the open exposure of metrics related to people's skills and achievements is not anathema to creating a healthy and cooperative team environment. Rather, metrics can directly contribute to a healthier environment if they are used to help the team improve and succeed—and if they result in better understanding of individual contributions that might not have been fully appreciated before.

Connecting Activities to Goals

Coders are players on a software team that itself is part of a bigger team, namely the business or the organization. At least some of the goals of the organization are also the goals of the software team (and therefore the goals of the coders too). The most meaningful and useful metrics will allow you to connect and relate coders and teams to their organizational goals.

To do this, you must define those organizational goals that the software team shares and how those goals can be exactly or approximately measured. Then you need to determine the coder and team skills that can be measured, and finally, you must create models or metrics that relate the skills to the goals.

You could say that sports teams have one clear goal, to win games (and in the end, to win championships). They might have other goals, like making money, but clearly winning games is one key goal, and it's easy to measure and track. The trick is determining which player and team skills are most relevant to winning games. This can only be done by gathering individual statistics and then analyzing the historical record in light of past wins and losses. From there, team managers can spot trends that reveal key insights—for example, that bases on balls are more critical to winning than stolen bases.

The evaluation of the historical record and how the bottom-up metrics connect to the top-down goals is an ongoing process. New insights are discovered over time, and findings evolve as your understanding grows and circumstances change.

Good Metrics Shed a Light

While metrics will not tell you which skills are good or bad, individual metrics themselves can definitely be good or bad. Bad metrics waste your time with details that aren't useful or don't really matter, distracting you from deeper understanding. Good metrics help you pull back the curtain and shed a light on things that matter, particularly things you might have missed, forgotten, or otherwise failed to fully appreciate over time.

The problem is that you can't always tell good metrics from bad until you try to use them. Metrics can turn out to be bad if they are either too hard to gather, or too abstract and confusing. To evaluate whether a metric itself is good or bad, you can ask yourself the following questions:

- Is the metric relatively easy to describe and understand?
- Can the metric show me something I don't already know?
- Does the metric clearly relate to a goal I care about?

If the answer to any of the above questions is clearly no, then the metric either needs more work, or it should probably be discarded.

Individuals and teams will naturally choose the metrics that make the most sense to them and that provide them the most value. Over time there's no need to hang on to less meaningful, less useful metrics if better ones exist or can be found. You want descriptive metrics and metrics covering a wider variety of skills, but too many metrics are just confusing and impractical.

Literally hundreds of statistics have been devised to track all kinds of details on baseball players, including such creatively named gems like Vultured Runs, Ghost Runs, the Component ERA (CERA), and the Defense-Independent Component ERA (DICE). No one regularly uses or understands all of these. Maybe at one time someone thought each of these metrics might be good, but over time some of them have proven to be useless. Each analyst and each team, through a process of trial and error, examines the statistics that are most meaningful for specific player positions and situations, and the good metrics remain in use.

Good metrics do more than track activity. The quote at the beginning of this chapter from John Wooden notes that activity does not equal achievement. Good metrics can be directly related to achievement or outcomes. Tracking how many hours someone worked, for example, is not a useful metric by itself. In basketball, no one keeps statistics on how many times someone dribbles the ball because to do so would just track activity that isn't related to the outcome of games. But people do keep track when someone loses the ball dribbling (a turnover), since change of possession can be critical to winning or losing games.

In baseball, Saves and Blown Saves are two examples of good stats. When a relief pitcher enters a close game that their team is leading, if they successfully preserve the lead then they are credited with a Save. If they lose the lead then it is a Blown Save. These stats meet the criteria for good metrics presented above: namely, they are relatively easy to understand, they show us something that we otherwise wouldn't easily track, and they relate directly to key goals for players and teams (wins and losses).

You could imagine a metric similar to baseball saves, but for coders. A coder could get credit for fixing critical issues at the late stages of a project or after release. Having such a metric would allow you to track these special "saves," which in turn allows you to communicate with each other about it, discuss its value, and possibly identify when the team has missed opportunities for "saves." You could make sure that a coder with many "saves" is properly recognized and appreciated. Finally, as you begin to understand the metrics on good teams, you might begin to identify if your software team is lacking "saves" and needs to improve focus or skills in this area.

Examining Assumptions

The truth is not always obvious. For this reason, it's healthy to question your assumptions about what matters and what doesn't when it comes to the factors of success. In the search for useful metrics, you should look beyond the obvious and consider possibilities both large and small. Sometimes where others have failed to look, new data may help you find hidden truths. You can gather and use metrics to challenge your assumptions, and if that only ends up proving your assumptions that's helpful too, because then you really know.

In American football for almost 100 years, it was an accepted coaching philosophy that if your team failed to gain a first down (advancing the ball 10 yards) after three plays, and you were too far away to kick a field goal, then you should punt the ball. That way, if the punt is successful, you back the other team up. If you try to convert the first down and you fail, you would give the other team the ball in a better position to score, so the punt seemed to be the safer approach.

But about 10 years ago, a group of statisticians began to analyze data on fourth-down conversions, punts, and the likelihood of scoring when you have the ball on first-down from different positions on the field. What they determined is that, statistically speaking, if a team has short yardage remaining and they have the ball around mid-field, their likelihood to convert on fourth down combined with the resulting opportunity to score makes it a superior choice to go for it on fourth down instead of punting. Open-minded coaches such as the New England Patriots' Bill Belichick began to put this thinking into effect, and now it has become pretty standard for teams to try and convert fourth down in certain situations, because it directly increases their chance to win. If someone had not taken the time to examine the assumption that punting was the best choice, based on data gathered from previous outcomes, this old-school philosophy might never have changed.

How many assumptions do you have about what it takes to deliver successful software that might similarly turn out to be wrong? As an example, here are some statements about coders and software development that you might consider:

- Adding development time will increase quality and customer satisfaction.
- Larger teams are less efficient.
- Difficult tasks will be done better by more experienced coders.

Whether you assume the above statements are true or false, without good data and proof, you don't really know. Metrics give you the data to examine your assumptions.

Identifying the key assumptions that you would like to investigate more closely, especially those that drive key decisions in your daily work, is also a great way to determine what kind of metrics you should gather and use. For example, if you want to examine the assumption that "difficult tasks will be done better by more experienced coders," you need to gather metrics on the complexity of tasks, the experience level of coders, and the relative quality of completed work.

Timeout for an Example: The Magic Triangle (Partially) Debunked

A lesson from one set of projects provides a thought-provoking example of how metrics can challenge your assumptions. This example involves a team that worked on a rapid product schedule, typical for an early stage start-up, meaning that we were delivering quarterly releases with new features, enhancements, and bug fixes. There were ten coders working on the project.

I had an assumption about the contents of each release. Looking back, I'm not really sure where or when I arrived at the assumption. I guess it just seemed like common sense, but it's one of those oft-repeated assumptions that you come to believe is based on objective fact and experience, when really it is based on something someone told you.

Given the hard deadlines, I assumed that the more we tried to cram complex features in the release, the less quality we would get. Following this logic, I believed that a quarterly release with more complex features would also have more bugs. My belief was based on a concept that you probably have heard of, the software development "magic triangle." This adage says that, among the three choices of more features, tighter schedule, and higher quality, you can pick two and the other one has to give. Since we were already committed to a tight schedule with many features, I assumed if we added more features, then lower quality would result. Makes sense, right?

To measure the contents of each release, I rated every coder task (feature, enhancement, or bug fix) on a scale from 1 to 4, from easiest to most complex. The average complexity of a release was determined by the average complexity of the tasks, and the total amount of work was calculated as the sum of all the task complexities. To measure the quality problems of each release, I ranked all the bugs found post-release on the same scale, and performed similar calculations.

Well, here's the surprise. Over six releases in a period just under two years, as shown in Table 2-1, after normalizing the data for the actual time on each release, the two releases with the highest complexity and most work did not have lower quality, measured by the bugs found post-release. In fact, the best quality results came from one of the releases where we packed the most stuff in, and when looking at issues found relative to the amount of work done in each release, the two most complex releases had better relative quality.

Table 2-1. *Quality on the most complex releases was better than other releases*

	Avg. Complexity (all work items)	Total Complexity (sum of all work)	Quality Problems (total complexity)	Release Quality % (100 - Problems / Complexity)
Release 1	1.2	272	86	68%
Release 2	1.6	248	77	69%
Release 3	1.5	274	109	60%
Release 4	2.8	318	69	78%
Release 5	2.4	347	88	75%
Release 6	1.4	261	92	65%

How could that be? First, it should be noted that although we packed more into certain releases, we did plan carefully and did began each release believing we had at least a chance to get all the work done. The releases with more complexity, however, had schedules that were much tighter, with more risk and much less room for error. The second thing to note is that we had an excellent team that worked together very well. The final note is that we did not allow any meaningful feature creep in any of these releases, since we were already working on a tight schedule, so the team knew the complexity target at the beginning of each release.

One explanation would be that our planning was too conservative, so we actually had room to deliver more complexity in the releases. Maybe what we thought was a stretch really wasn't. But that wouldn't explain why the quality of the more complex releases was higher. If our less complex releases were too conservatively planned, the quality on those should have been even higher, not lower.

You could theorize other potential explanations. For example, perhaps the quality of certain areas was just improving over time. Suffice to say that there are multiple potential explanations, and that more data could be gathered and studied to prove or disprove them. My personal theory, however, based on my intimate working knowledge of the team, is that there is another more interesting story here.

Here's what I believe the data illustrates. Good teams like to be challenged, and when challenged they rise to the occasion. If you give them more to do, if you set the bar higher, they get more focused, more motivated, and they actually do better work. So it is possible to add more work and more complexity to a release with a tight schedule and not give way on quality. In fact, you may even gain quality if your team reacts well under pressure and is well motivated. The concept of the magic triangle does not consider this aspect of human behavior. In some sense I think this is reflective of many false assumptions we have in our planning methods, where we base plans and schedules on the belief that coders produce a consistent level of quality all the time.

Much more real-world data would be needed to say anything more authoritative about this. But, at the very least, examples like this show that the magic triangle is potentially an oversimplified concept, and one that could lead to incorrect assumptions (like mine).

Because of what I learned, I am no longer quick to dismiss the idea that adding more complexity to an already difficult release—maybe even stretching a team's previous limits—could be a good thing.

Patterns, Anomalies, and Outliers

The longer you gather and keep metrics, generally speaking, the more useful they become. Analyzing metrics is a process of pattern recognition, which means finding repetitive patterns that provide insight. While a single set of metrics taken from a single time period might reveal interesting information, and possibly allow you to form interesting hypotheses, it takes multiple metrics over multiple periods of time to improve your theories, or to convert your theories to knowledge.

While you are looking for patterns, it is important to realize that not all patterns are simplistic. You should be careful to not just focus on the obvious, because the patterns and explanations found in combinations of metrics may far exceed the power and usefulness of individual metrics. For this reason again, it is useful to have metrics gathered at discrete intervals over longer periods of time, and to have a good variety of metrics to examine together.

Although voluminous, for thought-provoking material on complex pattern recognition and the richness of patterns, it is worth reviewing Stephen Wolfram's *A New Kind of Science*. His studies focus on computer models and the natural world, but his point that what appears chaotic or extremely complex may actually be based on discoverable patterns is directly applicable to statistical analysis in any field.

In baseball, one of the most widely used and powerful statistics is OPS, which stands for On Base Percentage plus Slugging Percentage. After decades of close examination by hundreds of statisticians, this formula is now considered one of the best at identifying a batter's effectiveness and overall value to the offense of a team. OPS is more descriptive than just looking at single statistics such as Home Runs (HR) or Runs Batted In (RBI). Without going into all the details here, suffice to say that the complex formula [OPS = AB(H + BB + HBP) + TB(AB + BB + SF + HBP) / AB(AB + BB + SF + HBP)] was only discovered through a process of complex pattern analysis, utilizing years and years of data.

As you look at metrics over time, you should also try to distinguish between anomalies and outliers. Numbers that appear "unusual" or outside the norm have a tendency to be discarded or overlooked. For example, if Coder A typically completes a certain amount of work every few weeks, but then during one period has an extreme drop-off or a big spike, you might just ignore it. If you mainly review averages over time, the fact that this even occurred might soon be forgotten or lost. But there is a big difference between an "anomaly" that is an aberrant occurrence with no future explanatory power or likelihood to recur, and an "outlier" that represents a significant departure from the norm that might recur over time, perhaps even following some "predictable" pattern. Here are definitions:

anomaly (noun): an incongruity or inconsistency, a deviation from the norm

outlier (noun): a person or thing that lies outside, a point widely separated from the main cluster

In his noteworthy book *The Black Swan*, Nassim Nicholas Taleb explores the power of outliers, as does Malcolm Gladwell in his book *Outliers*. In both cases, the authors introduce examples where outliers play a significant role in large successes. In *Outliers*, we see, however, that when studied more closely there are often explainable patterns behind these seeming exceptional successes. And in *The Black Swan*, we see that outliers can be viewed as a probable occurrence in complex systems. One fact is clear: to overlook outliers is to limit our understanding about the patterns of success.

The first thing we should do when we see particularly unexpected or unusual results is try to determine whether it is an anomaly or an outlier. For example, if a sudden drop-off in Coder A's results is attributable to the fact that the coder had personal problems during the measured period, then this can be seen as an anomaly. A rule of thumb to approach this is:

- If there is a clear explanation for a one-time occurrence, the result is an anomaly.
- If there is no clear explanation for what appears to be a one-time occurrence, the result is an outlier and should be examined more closely and watched over time to determine if it is meaningful or part of a pattern.

From 1993 through 2007, Ivan Rodriguez was a remarkably consistent catcher in Major League Baseball. Signed as a 16-year-old phenom in 1988, he was eventually voted to the All-Star team 14 times. The dips in his statistics over that period can mostly be explained by injuries or being on worse teams (which affected Rodriguez's opportunities and, therefore, his stats), so these were anomalies.

Mike Piazza was the other great catcher during the same period, with 12 All-Star appearances and similarly consistent statistics. Both Rodriguez and Piazza will undoubtedly end up in the Baseball Hall of Fame. However, Piazza was also noteworthy in baseball history because he was the 1,390th player drafted in 1988 when the Los Angeles Dodgers picked him in the 62nd round. He was overlooked because he did not fit the pattern that baseball scouts looked for. Although he broke school hitting records in high school, he had an unremarkable college career. He didn't have the physical appearance of a star, not like Ivan Rodriguez, and his name and ethnic background were unusual for baseball at the time. The bottom line is that these superficial analyses of what makes a great ballplayer were dead wrong. This nearly undrafted player is now a sure Hall-of-Famer and the top home run hitter among catchers all time.

Mike Piazza and players like him are outliers. In software development, you can apply a lesson here to your own methods of recruiting and hiring. Does your recruiting process allow you to find the Mike Piazzas, the future Hall-of-Famers whose background doesn't fit your expectations or the pattern of great coders you've seen before? Do you have objective methods you use to help you understand what skills your team really needs, and to find those coders who can meet or exceed those needs, even though they might not have the background or appearance you typically expect? Metrics are not the entire answer here, but they certainly can be part of the answer.

You tend to see what you are looking for, biased by what you believe and what you think you know. As so many success stories show, surprises that "break the mold," that almost no one predicted, happen regularly enough to show that such stories will continue to happen time and time again. When these surprises occur, they provide a chance to learn, and maybe to discover that they really weren't surprises at all. If you had just known more or had a deeper understanding about the patterns of success, then you might have predicted the result and it wouldn't have been a surprise.

Outliers are the surprises and unexpected results in the data. As you gather metrics and analyze patterns, it behooves you to study outliers carefully.

Peaks and Valleys

As metrics allow you to spot patterns over time, they also reveal peaks and valleys. Like outliers, these can be extremely significant and therefore are worth examining.

Sometimes the high points and low points in any particular time range are merely part of the normal variance in activity and achievement, but sometimes they can reveal useful insights. The "local maximum" and "local minimum" values are worth studying to see if they can be explained.

A baseball player who is an average hitter may have one great game every few weeks or every month, and conversely a baseball player who is a great hitter will still have bad games. In many cases, this is just part of the normal ebb and flow in performance and outcomes. But, in some cases, there could be an explanation. Maybe the hitter does particularly well or poorly against a specific pitcher, for example, or in a specific ball-park. If the hitter's surges or dips in performance are dismissed and not studied, then the instances where explanatory reasons exist will be missed.

When particularly high or low metric values are seen, you should track and examine them, and look for patterns that emerge over time. You are hoping to find the reasons and the causes behind the higher or lower results. Discovering these explanations, either for individuals or for teams, might help you adjust circumstances to improve the results as you like.

Even more significant than infrequent peaks or valleys are sustained peaks and valleys. In sports, these are referred to as "hot streaks" and "cold streaks" or "slumps." Over longer periods of time (such as entire seasons), these are referred to as "peak years", "career years," and "down years." In sports, when someone is on a hot streak, teams seek to get them more opportunities (particularly in significant situations—giving them the ball more or getting them more at bats), in order to maximize the team's success.

And if a player is having a cold streak, teams try to change the player's circumstances, possibly with a new assignment or even a few days off, in order to shake the slump.

In software development, isn't it possible that coders have hot streaks and cold streaks, too? If you could spot these more sustained highs and lows, then just like sports teams you might take further advantage of hot streaks or look for ways to shake slumps.

Ripple Effects

Another important pattern that metrics can help you identify is the impact or influence that one person has on other members of the team. A great coder, for example, can "rub off" on others, or may help others more rapidly advance their own skills. These kind of ripple effect patterns are among the hardest to identify and confirm, but when found, can be among the most valuable. The positive or negative effects of individuals on teams are the factors that make a team either greater or less than the sum of its parts.

A related pattern you can examine and that is equally important is the result of specific people working together. In this case you are not looking so much at the impact one individual has on others, but whether specific combinations of people are more or less effective. The obvious intention here is to identify relationships that demonstrably flourish or flounder, so you can use that information to successfully align your teams.

Basketball and hockey statisticians over the past decade have put much time and effort into analyzing the results when specific players are in the game or out, and the results of specific combinations of players together. The analysis focuses on the team results, offensively and defensively, during the game and at specific points in a game, such as in a basketball game during the all-important final four minutes known as "crunch time." These statistics are considered very important both in analyzing player effectiveness but also in making coaching decisions related to who should play together at specific times.

It's likely that in any human endeavor involving teams, there are ripple effects related to the specific impact of individuals or combinations of people. And the effects may not be what individuals themselves believe, since their judgment is most times biased by personality traits, meaning with whom they feel most compatible and whom they don't. But sometimes the most effective combinations of people are not necessarily the ones who like each other the most.

Within software development teams we can expect to find the same patterns. Some coders make everyone around them better, and some combinations of coders turn out to be particularly effective together, while others are not. The hard part is figuring out how to objectively identify and measure ripple effects, especially knowing that the individual perspectives of team members might not reflect the truth.

Repeatable Success

While metrics can increase your understanding and provide benefits in many ways, among the top things you are searching for are the patterns of repeatable success. If found, these patterns indicate what your team needs to maximize its chance of success and minimize its chance of failure.

An oft heard quote is that "it's better to be lucky than good." In the short term, that might be true. But luck is not some innate factor that remains consistent (although many gamblers wish it was). Highly skilled individuals or teams might appear to be lucky, but it's their hard work and planning that makes them a consistent success. Someone might get a "lucky break" or go on a "lucky streak." But over time, luck of this sort evens out—which is to say that over a longer period of time, an individual or team (in any area involving skill and teamwork) will normally achieve the level of success it deserves.

In sports, you see many instances where players or teams have one-time or short-term success, but that success doesn't last over the long term. Many teams might have a week or two (or even a month) where they get "hot" and go on a winning streak. But over the course of a season, if those teams don't really have the elements to win consistently, the hot streaks don't last and are often offset by "cold" streaks. You also see players whose isolated results benefit from circumstances. A baseball pitcher can win a game when they pitch badly, if their own team scores a lot of runs to win. Should the pitcher get credit for the win? In baseball they do, which is why wins and losses are not a great measurement of a pitcher's skills or value to their team, and are not a great indicator of repeatable success.

In software, the way you define and measure success needs careful thought. Sometimes, for example, the software team might succeed but the business fails, or the other way around. Success or failure of the business is not necessarily reflective of a software development team. I will discuss this in much more detail later.

Once you have defined success, then the software teams that achieve a consistent level of such success become models you can analyze. You can also analyze those teams that achieve success for a period of time, but aren't able to maintain that level. Finally, there are teams that never achieve success, and you should look at those, too. Examining all the cases you are exposed to, you can begin to identify the factors and patterns of success, and better understand all the skills and contributions that make for successful teams.

The more data you gather from more projects, the better chance you have to identify the patterns of repeatable success. Finding metrics that correlate to success, and metrics that correlate to failure, adds to your knowledge. Your data may not be conclusive, but it can provide enough insight that you can make improvements.

As a simple example, you might see that on more successful projects, your teams had many coders who helped each other—and on less successful projects, your coders interacted less. If this was true, it would be very useful for everyone on the team to understand, in order to improve projects in the future. Metrics are the means to help you identify such patterns and to communicate your findings to others.

Understanding the Limits

The use of metrics and statistical analysis is a practice, a methodology, useful to find patterns, examine assumptions, and increase understanding of the past in hopes that you can improve the future. It is not a science, and clearly the explanatory capability of metrics is abstract and imperfect. Practically speaking, the metrics you gather will never provide a complete picture of all that coders do, or of the complex team dynamics and all the elements that lead to success.

While baseball's WHIP statistic (walks plus hits per inning pitched) may help identify what makes pitchers effective, it cannot fully describe what made Sandy Koufax unique and special. No stats can fully measure his ability to focus and his desire to compete. And while victories and team stats are clear indicators of winning teams, those and individual stats cannot fully explain why the 1975 Cincinnati Reds stand out in fans' minds as the greatest team of their era—because of their personalities and charisma.

This shouldn't discourage you or make you believe that metrics aren't useful, simply because there is so much they don't capture. Instead you should be encouraged to use metrics for what they can provide, while accepting their limitations. You can continue on in the pursuit of better metrics in the happy knowledge that perfect understanding will never be achieved, and there will always be more you can measure and learn.

Timeout for an Example: An Unexpected Factor in Success

Here is a story about a surprising metric that I've come to believe indicates a greater likelihood of success for coders and software teams. This example involves a software development team working inside a large organization, with about 500 total employees of this company located on a single floor, in an open floor plan mostly made up of cubicles.

I have always been a big believer in the "closed door" policy. That is to say that I have been an advocate of coders getting extended "quiet" time, without interruptions, so they can remain focused once they get in the flow of their work. For this reason, I am always very careful to avoid lots of meetings in the middle of the day, and, personally, I try not to interrupt coders when they are working. I don't like to be interrupted myself. My theory used to be that an increase in uninterrupted work time would translate to an increase in productivity and high-quality results.

There is a reason I say that "used to be" my theory.

This is just something I happened to notice, not something I was looking to find. As I said, I was already biased. If I had my preference, every coder would sit in an office and could close their door. As it was, in this company everyone was in a cubicle, and was subject to random walk-by interruptions any minute of the day.

In the middle of one of our release cycles, while the coders were working hard on product enhancements and new features, a few team members began to complain to me that they were being interrupted too much. Support people were asking them about issues, sales engineers were asking about how new features worked, and product managers and product marketers were asking for answers to questions from customers, analysts, and the press. I was getting many of these interruptions, too, so I knew what they were talking about. Part of it was a direct output of our product's success, but that didn't make it seem less aggravating or counterproductive. Based on the complaints, I started thinking about what we could do. Maybe we could come in one weekend with bricks and cement and just build a big wall.

But then, as time went on, I noticed something else. The coders who were getting interrupted the most, and were complaining, were producing great software: new features, key improvements, and bug fixes. They were proactively tackling stuff that had sat dormant for a long time before, and there was a noticeable increase in innovation. These were some of our top team members, which was why they were getting interrupted more than other coders. But even though they were complaining, their work wasn't really suffering. Their work, in fact, was better than ever before.

I realized that even though the increased interruptions were annoying the coders, they were actually helping them. It was causing them to think more about the real customer problems, to learn more about what people were interested in, and it made them more sensitive to quality and craftsmanship. The frequent interactions with others outside the development team was healthy and educational. Following interruptions, it would take time to return to the flow of coding, but they might know something that they didn't before. The result was better software and more innovative solutions. Since that time, once I started looking for it, I have seen this pattern over and over again.

I used to think that interruptions were a bad thing, and I tried to shield myself and coders during times of work. Today I still avoid meetings in the middle of the day. But now I actually include "interruptions" as a key metric I like to track. I don't do it to make sure the coders aren't getting too many interruptions. I do it to make sure they are getting interrupted enough. Now I want coders to be interrupted. I want them to interact spontaneously with people outside the development team. For coders who are not getting interrupted, once they have sufficient experience, I try to get them in the flow of the interruptions as well. I now prefer departments to be co-located, with open floor plans and open doors.

Whether interruptions are valuable or have the same effect for coders who work at home or remotely, I don't know. I'm not talking about the interruptions they get from outsiders in their remote workplace, for example if their kids interrupt them at home.

But perhaps if they receive emails or calls from people inside and outside the software development team, and they deal with those, the interruptions might have the same effect as in-person. In my metrics, I track email and phone call interruptions the same as in-person, but all the coders I've worked with are normally co-located, so I don't have good data on remote workers. What I can say is that I believe email and phone interruptions appear to have much the same effect as in-person for coders who work together in an office, so I believe they would have the same effect for coders working remote.

Having a metric for interruptions helps us track the effects, but also it creates a means to communicate with coders about the value of these interactions. It may not make the moment of interruption less aggravating, but when you understand how interruptions can positively educate team members and positively influence the software, they are easier to put up with.

Useful Data

Later chapters of this book will cover a variety of specific codermetrics. Some of these will be fairly simple, based on atomic data elements such as production bugs, and some will be more complex, based on formulas leveraging and combining multiple elements of data.

Before I delve into specific metrics, however, you might consider all the types of data you could use for coders, and think about the data that might be useful or not. You want to think broadly and contemplate new and interesting data elements that could make for more meaningful metrics. You can also think about how to identify data that would measure how coders and software teams are doing relative to team and organization goals.

Below is a list of example data that I have found to be useful and that will be discussed more in later sections. This list is just meant to be illustrative and, as such, describes the type or category of information, not the specific numeric data (such as counts or averages) that will be discussed later:

- How long a coder has been part of a team
- Size, growth, and contraction of a team
- Tasks completed by a coder, categorized by complexity
- Tasks where coders worked together, or where one coder helped another
- Tasks that had extreme urgency, such as fixing severe production issues
- Tasks where a coder demonstrated exceptional creativity, innovation, or initiative
- Tasks that were delayed, failed, or cancelled
- Projects, products, and product areas a coder worked on
- Time spent on tasks

- Time in meetings or dealing with in-person interruptions
- Issues found by customers, categorized by severity and complexity
- Customer contacts (calls, emails, or chats) in need of support
- Customers who buy or use a product or feature
- Customers who try a product or feature, but decide not to use it
- Customers who cancel or stop using a product or feature
- Customers maintained, gained, or lost by direct competitors
- Existing customers who benefited by a product or feature change
- Internal employees who benefited by a product, feature, or other completed task

These are just examples of the type of data I will suggest using for metrics. Beyond the data I cover in this book, there are undoubtedly many other types of data that may prove useful for codermetrics, too. Given all the possibilities, it's a good bet that most of the potential data I probably haven't fully examined or thought about. There are some data types, however, that I have personally tried or contemplated, and for various reasons decided they were not extremely useful or that there were better options, so they will not be used in this book. Below are a few examples and my reasoning in regards to some of these *excluded* data types:

KLOCs

It seems reasonable to think that lines of code (KLOC stands for 1,000 lines of code) could be useful as a way to measure coder productivity, and by many accounts KLOCs have proven useful in estimation techniques and tools designed to reduce project estimation errors, especially on larger projects. But in general, I believe KLOCs are indicative of activity more than identifiable accomplishment, and I think it is hard to relate this metric to specific team goals, such as customer adoption or satisfaction or product quality. Another issue with KLOCs is that they are not uniform across different programming languages. For example, 1,000 lines of Java takes a different amount of time and requires a different level of capability than 1,000 lines of Javascript or XML or PHP or Ruby (although theoretically, we could figure out a way to normalize KLOCs across languages). Finally I think coders themselves have difficulty in feeling that "lines of code" is an important or meaningful metric in relation to their achievements and successes or failures—and if coders don't embrace a metric, then it's hard to use it effectively as a means to discuss their skills and contributions. Therefore, for the purposes that are discussed in this book, I've found that focusing on tasks and categorizing the tasks by complexity is more meaningful than using KLOCs.

Development bugs

Bug count is certainly a metric to look at to evaluate code quality. But unlike post-release "production" bugs, in my experience, there is too much variability around bugs found during development to make "development bug count" a highly useful metric. The number of bugs found in development will fluctuate based on the number of testers, the depth of testing, and the maturity or immaturity of the code in development. If you start in-depth testing on a complex piece of code early in the development cycle, you'll find many bugs, but that tells you very little about the progress made to that point. You could argue that there are certain sets of development bugs, such as those found after a coder has deemed a feature complete and unit-tested, that could make for useful metrics. But personally I've found in practice it's too inconsistent and too hard to pin down. In the end, I think we can get the meaningful information we need by just keeping metrics around the complexity of tasks and the time it takes to complete those tasks. That should include the time it takes to fix the development bugs sufficiently so that the code can be released. If a coder creates a lot of bugs, then the effect is that their tasks will take much longer to complete. That coder will typically take longer than another coder, working on similarly complex tasks, who is methodical but who creates less bugs.

Product revenues

Product revenues (gross or net) are a critical part of business planning and product planning. Which products you build, which features you add, and which problems are worth spending time on all require financial analysis. Your budget for software development is also in most cases directly tied to product revenues. This is all as it should be. However, as a metric to be used in the software development process, to measure the success and relative contributions of coders and teams, I think product revenues are problematic. One issue is that a lot of software has no revenue (open source and internal projects are two examples). Where revenues do exist, they are not always tied directly to the software and the work of the software development team. They may vary wildly based on discounting, the ability of various sales people, and many other factors including the national or global economy. Another significant issue is that using money as a metric can be distracting and misleading. Everyone tends to focus too much on the money and not enough on the "purpose" or meaning of the metric. For example, if you charge $2 for a new iPhone app, and 1,000 people purchased it today, in many ways the customer count provides more clarity and meaning (and sounds more positive) than the $2,000 gross revenue (which doesn't sound as impressive). Conversely, if your company made just one $100,000 sale this week, the dollar figure might sound very impressive but adding just one customer in a lot of businesses would be cause for concern. My feeling is that it's useful for the software team in general to be aware of how product revenues and revenue forecasts are driving product planning decisions, but as metrics for the progress of a software team's work I would rather measure features delivered, conversion rates of trial user to customers, production bugs, and keep a close eye on the number of users and the amount of usage.

Overall, however, there is very little to lose by exploring new data types and trying them out. You should be willing to test new ideas. You can expect that highly useful and reasonably obtainable data will stand out, and you can throw away the rest.

Choosing Data

Finding good data for metrics is a little bit science, a little bit art, and a lot of trial and error. You face many choices when deciding on which data to use, clearly you can come up with a variety of measurements that aspire to the same result or equate to nearly the same thing. As an example, to determine how well a coder does on quality testing, you could choose to measure the number of test cases written, the amount of code covered by tests, or the number and severity of bugs found. Or you could measure all the above.

Generally speaking, when I have to choose among multiple measurements that might be used, I apply the following rules of thumb to decide which is "best":

- Choose the data that is most easily obtained.
- Choose the data that is easiest for non-coders to explain and understand.

While the first rule of thumb might be obvious, the second rule of thumb might seem more curious. Why should you care if non-coders can explain and understand the measurements and data? This rule suggests a specific test for clarity and simplicity, namely that a non-coder, such as a tester or a technical writer, should be able to understand the data and how it relates to software development. Since a key benefit of good metrics is their descriptive power, along with their ability to improve communication and to help drive desirable behaviors, it is essential that metrics and the data behind them be easy to grasp. This rule could be rewritten as "choose the simpler measurements," or just "keep it simple," but I like the litmus test of non-coders being able to explain and understand the measurements and the data.

Consider, for example, how to measure code complexity. One way to do it would be through a statistical analysis of the source code, which could produce a variety of data for you to analyze, such as keyword frequency, method lengths, nesting levels, and loop complexity. Or you could measure the complexity of the code by how long it takes a coder to change a feature, fix a bug, or by the rate of bugs in the code over time. Personally, I have favored measuring complexity by time involved and post-release issues rather than via automated code analysis. This is because the data is generally easier to obtain and is more "explainable and understandable" by non-coders and coders alike. In my view, such data will result in metrics that are also more explainable and understandable, and therefore will be more powerful and useful, too.

Obtaining Data

There are a number of systems you can tap into to gather data elements. Some may provide easy access to useful data, especially the development-related systems that you directly interact with or control. One of the most useful systems for metrics can be your actual product itself, which if properly instrumented and monitored can provide a wealth of data on customer adoption and the use or success of specific features and product changes.

Some systems may be hard to access, usually because they belong to other parts of the business that you are not normally authorized to use. My experience is that if you explain the usefulness and purpose of the data to the system owners or administrators, along with the fact that you don't need any security-sensitive data, you should get cooperation. Sometimes you can pull the data directly from the systems, or you may get it indirectly through regularly generated reports or other documents such as departmental or financial summaries.

In most cases, weekly or monthly collection of the target data will be sufficient, and most modern systems have the capability to schedule reports and exports. For the data obtained from systems used to track coder work, such as project or bug tracking systems, you may choose to obtain data weekly, and you will want to obtain data for individual coders, teams, and product areas. For the data obtained from business systems outside development, such as a customer support system, it may be fine to get monthly summaries, but you will still want data broken down by product areas. Here are some systems that may provide key data elements:

Project tracking systems

>Examples: VersionOne, Greenhopper, Rally, Microsoft Project Manager
>Useful data: task counts, task durations, task complexity
>Granularity: weekly by coder and product area

Bug tracking systems

>Examples: Bugzilla, JIRA, FogBugz
>Useful data: post-release bug counts, bug severity, bug complexity
>Granularity: weekly by coder and product area

Sales lead tracking systems

>Examples: Salesforce.com, Microsoft Dynamics, Siebel
>Useful data: opportunity count, opportunity loss count, deal close count
>Granularity: monthly by product (and feature where applicable)

Customer support issue tracking systems

>Examples: Salesforce.com, Microsoft Dynamics, RightNow, Zendesk
>Useful data: support contact counts, support case counts, case severity
>Granularity: Weekly by product area

Your software product (instrumented for appropriate monitoring)

>Useful data: user activations, logins, feature usage, user errors, performance
>Granularity: weekly by product

As you obtain data, you will need to decide how to store it. If you have time to put it into an actual database, that is great and certainly would help in analysis over time. My suggestion, however, is to not worry too much about the storage mechanism to start with. Simply putting the data into spreadsheets—and possibly generating monthly summaries in presentation slides or documents—is a great place to start. Don't let storage concerns stand in your way. Just accumulating the data and putting it to use will provide a great advantage, even if it is dispersed each month over a set of spreadsheets and documents.

Spotters and Stat Sheets

Where data cannot be obtained from existing systems, the best way to get it is to use the same method as professional sports teams—namely spotters and stat sheets.

Pro teams use assigned stat-keepers, called spotters, to watch games and fill out stat sheets on individual players and on the teams. In some sports, such as baseball, there may be an official scorer who tracks a number of statistics and who is responsible for judgment calls when necessary, such as determining if a certain play was a hit or an error. But even in these cases the scorer usually has spotters assisting them, and in addition, the teams have their own spotters assigned to keep track of the statistics that the scorer does not keep. Technology has in some cases automated the statistics collection process, but humans are still needed for many tasks.

Spotters use stat sheets designed by the teams, which are usually just simple forms or spreadsheets. They mark stats down on their computers, or in the cases where they use paper (since these sheets are certainly simple enough to use on paper) then they enter them into computers later. The spotters are trained to know about all the statistics they track and how to spot them, and they are trusted to enter accurate stats. In some cases multiple spotters are used, just to ensure or increase accuracy.

This same approach can easily be applied for coders and software teams. First, you need to identify the data you want to track that is not easily obtained from existing systems, such as when a coder helps another figure out how to complete a task or when a coder works extended hours to solve a critical production issue. Second, you need to set up a stat sheet, which may just be a simple spreadsheet.

Finally, you need to choose your spotters. These assigned team members need to have enough visibility to track the chosen items, such as a team leader, a project manager, or a scrum master. They can fill in stat sheets at your desired granularity, for example weekly by coder and by team. Then this data gets combined with the system-extracted data that contributes to your overall codermetrics data set. For smaller teams, having one assigned spotter should be fine. For larger teams, having multiple spotters might increase accuracy, the same as in pro sports.

It is also certainly possible to have coders act as their own spotters and fill in their own personal stat sheets daily or weekly. In very small teams this may be the best or only alternative. Where coders do act as their own spotters, they can be trusted to provide accurate information, since they know that the data may eventually be shared with the whole team. In general, you can expect the use of spotters to provide very accurate data as long as the resulting metrics are not used specifically as grades, and as long as the metrics are seen as a fair and accurate representation of the work coders are doing and the achievements of the software team. Overall, using spotters and stat sheets can be a highly efficient and effective way to gather the data you need.

Fairness and Consistency

One legitimate concern you should have when using metrics is that they are fair, which means that as far as possible they are accurate and consistent. It's not necessary to be perfect, but it's necessary that the numbers are a fair representation of the truth. If a basketball player is told he scored six points when he really scored sixteen, then that isn't fair and the player or anyone else would quickly ignore such inaccurate stats. But if a player is credited with a steal in a situation where two players helped knock the ball loose and a judgment call was made as to which one got the steal, that is fair enough and small issues like these won't affect the overall usefulness of the stats.

Data accuracy is generally addressed by making sure your systems are reliable and your spotters understand what they are supposed to record. It is not that hard to keep track of accurate production bug counts, for example, or how long certain tasks took to complete. As far as "judgment calls" go, you can define guidelines for decisions and adjust them over time.

Consistency in some cases may prove more difficult to ensure. Data can be inconsistent for a variety of reasons, including general inflation or deflation of a common range over time, or the differences between teams in subjective ratings such as severity or complexity. As development tools improve or coders use higher-level programming languages, for example, the time it takes to complete more complex tasks goes down. And one person may decide that a specific task is medium complexity while another person thinks the same task is high complexity.

Normalization and calibration are two techniques that you can use to improve the consistency of your data. Calibration is the process of removing "subjective" inconsistencies introduced by people's ratings, and normalization is the process of removing "non-subjective" inconsistencies that occur between groups or over time.

A product that has 1,000 users might naturally have many fewer calls to customer support than a product with a million users. If you want to analyze the support incident metrics across these products, rather than using the raw count of customer calls you might instead normalize the data by looking at "calls per 1,000 users". As another example where normalization might be used, consider a development team that has large productivity gains over a period of years due to the evolution and maturation of libraries used. A new product feature might take one-quarter of the time than it did before thanks to better libraries or code reuse. If you want to compare productivity metrics over time, you can normalize the data based on the average productivity for each time period. Table 2-2 shows an example.

Table 2-2. Data normalization helps us make better comparisons across projects

	Total Users	Total Support Calls	Total Bugs Reported	Calls Per 1K Users	Bugs Per 1K Users
Product A	57,850	518	86	8.95	1.49
Feature 1	12,378	187	31	15.11	2.50
Product B	6,582	54	28	8.20	4.25
Feature 2	758	22	8	29.02	10.55

This is similar to the way statisticians compare different eras in sports. In baseball's "dead ball" era of the early 1900s, it was much rarer for players to hit home runs than it is today. There were multiple reasons including the use of more worn balls, the size of ballparks, and rules of the game that have since changed. Knowing this, and knowing that 30 home runs in a season was almost unheard of at the time (Babe Ruth set the league record with 29 home runs in 1919), statisticians can compare home run hitters of different eras by normalizing the data. For example, rather than raw home run counts they can look at ranking among peers, or they might treat every home run in the dead ball era as the equivalent of two in more recent years.

Calibration can be used to correct inconsistencies that may arise when some element of subjective ratings is included in your data. Many organizations use a calibration process in performance reviews (which in the end contain much subjective content), and a similar process can be used here. One typical approach is to conduct an in-person meeting, where all the people handling the ratings convene to review each other's ratings, and to decide whether any of the ratings should be adjusted to make them fairer and more consistent across all groups. The goal is not to review individual ratings, but to review the criteria and rating scale that each group is using, and finally to "calibrate" to a common scale.

For example, if you have three agile software teams and each one rates the complexity of tasks using t-shirt sizes (Small, Medium, Large or X-Large) you might have the scrum masters and team leaders meet to review the current and upcoming task ratings. If one person or team has a tendency to categorize tasks on an easier or harder scale, such as listing tasks as X-Large when other teams would typically call similar tasks Large, then these meetings should identify these differences. The group can discuss the differences and decide how to adjust so that everyone tries to use the same criteria and scale. Even one session of calibration might be enough to establish a common scale.

Timeout for an Example: Metrics and the Skeptic

The grizzled, seasoned coder on our team gave me that look. Just a little eyebrow raise and a smirk. Sure, that look said, go ahead and tell these young guys about metrics, and how they are going to help us improve as a team. I won't spoil it, his silence foretold, I won't say anything, but his raised chin let me knew that he wasn't buying it. He was a skeptic.

One month passed. We had a team meeting, and I showed everyone a set of company and product metrics. It showed how our product was doing, how we compared to the competition (as far as we knew), and how individual features were being received. We focused on the features we had implemented in the last six months. Everyone was very engaged. It was the liveliest team meeting we'd had the whole year. Our grizzled coder even made a couple of comments.

Another month passed. We had another team meeting. This time we looked at updates of company and product metrics, but we also looked at team metrics taken from our recent sprints (we used agile methodology so we worked in incremental "sprints"). We had just released a new feature. We speculated about how our team metrics might correlate to the reception of the new feature and which metrics we thought might be significant and why. The grizzled coder said the complexity of the work that we did on the feature in the final sprint probably was too high, that he expected our testing probably had missed issues, and so we would probably see a decent influx of issues found in production. Our QA Manager pointed out that we had completed all our planned tests and a full round of regression, but we all agreed that there was likely cause for some concern.

Two more months passed. Now we had good data on the customer reception for the new feature, which was solid although not spectacular, and the issues found in production. Our coder had been right. The rate and complexity of issues on the feature was clearly higher than on other features we tracked. Most of those issues had been fixed by that point, but still the team took note for future consideration. For the first time, we also started looking at individual coder metrics. We looked at complexity of work done in sprints, including feature development and product bug fixes. We looked at interruptions that each coder dealt with, and we looked at how many different parts of code everyone worked on. We looked at how many times a coder helped someone else, which we called "assists." We also looked at these metrics aggregated by team. We discussed how these might correlate to team goals, team success, product success, and company goals. We agreed in coming months we would continue to watch these metrics to see what we could learn.

Some interesting metrics stood out, and some team members commented on them. For example, a few coders had very high total workloads, but the average complexity of items they worked on was low. Other coders had the opposite, meaning smaller workloads but high average complexity. No conclusions were drawn from these, we just found it interesting and some wondered aloud whether this seemingly uneven distribution of task complexity was a good thing for the team. Another fact that stood out was that some coders had a very high number of "assists," while other coders had none at all. We talked about how we had measured this, letting team leaders act as spotters. No one seemed to have a problem with that. The seasoned coder didn't say anything at all.

Two days later, however, he walked into my office. "Dang," the coder said. "A bunch of the guys are helping the younger guys a lot. I didn't have any assists—I wasn't helping out. I just wanted you to know I got it. I'm definitely going to do my part." And that was it.

Another skeptic converted.

CHAPTER 3

The Right Data

The big challenge is to measure the right things.

—Michael Lewis, from his article "The No-Stats All-Star"

Before you have metrics, you need data. For "good" metrics, you need the "right" data. This chapter will help you choose the data you want to collect and use to improve the performance of your software team and the people in it. I'll start by helping you decide what questions you want to ask, which in turn will help you determine the data you need to collect.

The first section of this chapter covers key questions that you might ask about coders, software teams, and software projects or releases. These are the questions that you would want metrics to help you answer. The second section of this chapter dives into the data sources and data elements that can be used to create metrics that will, at least in part, answer the key questions. All of this is to lay the groundwork for the specific metrics that will be covered in detail in the coming chapters.

Questions That Metrics Can Help Answer

The first step in building metrics is to think about the key questions that you want to answer for coders and software development teams. To create meaningful and useful metrics, you need to have an idea of what you are looking for. Some of these questions are obvious, some are not. Once the set of questions are determined, you can determine what data is available, and among the available data which elements would be the best to help create meaningful metrics and to serve the overall purpose of helping you to learn about the patterns of successful teams.

How Well Do Coders Handle Their Core Responsibilities?

Sports statistics begin with the basics. In baseball, this means measuring individual accomplishments such as Hits, Home Runs, Runs Batted In, or Runs Scored. For pitchers, it means tracking Hits and Runs Allowed. In basketball, we begin with basic offensive statistics such as Points Scored or defensive statistics such as Blocked Shots.

How well do coders write code?

The most obvious thing that coders do, of course, is write code. Some code may be excellent, some may be poor. Some might be beautiful, and some might be just good enough. Some coders might write a lot of code, and some might write a little, maybe because that's all they were required to do. Some coders follow a certain style, some don't, and some edit their code after the first draft to make it better. Some may write code every day and some only once in awhile. But if you don't write code at all—well then, you're not a coder.

How well do coders design their code?

Coders also design code. Even if they are not explicitly identified as designers or architects, every coder makes design decisions in nearly every line of code they write, from variable names to syntax. And certainly when creating new objects and methods, design is central to the coding process. The design of the code may conceptually stand prior to and apart from the code, but in the end it is a part of the code itself. So it too may be excellent or poor, beautiful or maybe just good enough. Some coders are required to do more design than others, but every coder must do design.

How well do coders test their code?

And so too with testing—the coder who never tests code probably never was a coder, or isn't anymore. If the code is compiled, there's a syntax test every time the compiler is run. Beyond that, every coder tests at least some part of their code at least once. Some coders make test development and writing tests a key part of their work, an extension of the coding itself. Some coders use analysis and simulation tools. Some coders are detailed and thorough testers, while others do very little or just enough.

How Much Do Coders Contribute Beyond Their Core Responsibilities?

Beyond the obvious, there are many other things that coders do that are important to the success of projects and the software development team. These less obvious things are equally important to consider as the basics of code, design, test. In sports, the less obvious statistics have proven very valuable in determining key ways that players contribute to team success. For example, in baseball it is very useful to know how selective a hitter is in the pitches they swing at, or how much range fielders have in getting to balls hit near them.

How many areas do coders cover?

Some coders are required to demonstrate "range" when they need to move from one area of code to another or from one type of work to another. For most coders this happens at a gradual pace, over longer periods of time. For example, a coder may work on a specific area of code for a few months, then move on to another while perhaps still maintaining the previous area of code. Some coders, however, must juggle multiple areas simultaneously. For instance, a coder might be bug-fixing for multiple features while also improving build scripts and updating the installer code.

How effectively do coders take initiative?

Another important thing some coders do is take initiative. If there is a problem or an opportunity, they see it and they take it on themselves to address it and get it done. Often these actions may be unplanned and unscheduled. A different type of initiative, but also important, is when a coder makes the effort to point out something that is wrong, or about to go wrong, to other members of the team. This could be coming forward proactively to point out a piece of code that someone else has written that needs work, or it could be telling a team leader or manager about some problem, maybe even a personal problem with another team member. When coders do take such initiative, it is noteworthy, so it is worth mentioning here as something you should consider measuring.

Do coders innovate?

Closely related to initiative is innovation. Coders often come up with unique solutions or improvements, or new capabilities that weren't thought of before. Sometimes the benefits are small or marginal, but sometimes they are great. As with initiative, sometimes innovation comes from one coder alone, and sometimes from multiple coders working together. Innovation can obviously be a strong contributor to project success.

How well do coders handle pressure?

Coders also sometimes have to deal with pressure and stress. This may be in the form of looming deadlines or having to fix critical production issues. In different environments the fluctuations and frequency of stress differs, so what is considered "high stress" versus "normal stress" will be relative. For example, in a bootstrapped start-up, what is considered normal stress might drive some coders crazy. But from time to time many coders do have to deal with pressure, and these situations can be especially critical, much like the last two minutes of a basketball game, the fourth quarter in football, or the bottom of the ninth in baseball.

How well do coders deal with adversity?

Similar to pressure situations, but worth calling out on its own, is adversity. Lucky coders will never have to deal with adversity, which can come in many forms. The failure of a product. Financial troubles at a company that result in layoffs on the software team. The illness or death of a team member. Some coders do have to deal with adversity, and to succeed they will need to make it through or bounce back. This is worth noting as an item to consider for metrics, too.

How Well Do Coders Interact With Others?

The other aspect to consider about coders is how they interact with others, including other members of the team, team mangers, and people outside the team such as support personnel or customers. How well members of the team interact and help each other is an important part of success. In basketball and hockey, the statisticians pay close attention to teamwork, such as tracking assists and measuring how well certain combinations of players do together. Tracking and measuring teamwork is a way for you to better understand which interactions are most meaningful for team success, and to help you focus individual team members on the positive interactions that you want to encourage.

Do coders demonstrate leadership?

Leadership on any team is important. To lead means to help others see the goal, the way to reach the goal, and to help them along the way. Some coders may be assigned leadership responsibilities, and some coders may just provide leadership within the team. In some cases, they may lead an entire project or sometimes just a particular task. Many forms of leadership are subtle, such as when a coder influences others by working hard during a period of adversity. Whether you measure it directly or indirectly, you want to pay attention to times when coders provide leadership—and the results.

Do coders inspire or motivate their teammates?

Sometimes leadership also involves inspiring and motivating others or lifting team morale. Some coders also lift others' morale even though they are not typical leaders. They might do this by telling jokes, keeping a happy attitude during stressful times, or by demonstrating passion about a project in team meetings. They might help arrange a beer bash, a foosball tournament, or some other type of team outing or party. It might be something they do from time to time, or it might be a constant effect that comes from their personality. The effect that a coder has on team morale is another type of interaction to keep in mind as we think about what we measure.

How well do coders mentor others?

A different form of leadership, worth noting by itself, is when a coder mentors others. Again, for some this may be an assigned role, and for others this may be something they just choose to do, or that they do as a matter of course in their regular work. Most of us think of a mentor as a seasoned veteran who transfers knowledge to younger coders to help them progress quickly. But mentoring does not always follow traditional patterns. In our line of work, with ever-changing technologies and programming languages, in many cases it may be the younger coders who mentor the seasoned veteran. Mentoring and the results of mentoring, in its various forms, is another important factor in team success and, therefore, something to address in metrics.

How well do coders understand and follow directions?

While some coders may never be leaders or mentors, every coder must be able to take direction. Accepting a defined role and completing assigned tasks is fundamental to coders working within a software development team. Implicit in being able to take direction is the ability to understand direction, to grasp the bigger picture and how one's individual role and tasks fit into that. A coder who lacks such understanding is more likely to misinterpret direction or to make individual decisions that are not consistent with the intended direction. The resulting work is unlikely to meet the intended goals. It is well worth considering how to capture this in metrics, because following direction and understanding goals is certainly critical to success.

How much do coders assist others?

Every member of a team has opportunities, from time to time, to help others on the team. A coder, for example, may assist another coder by helping them find the cause of a bug or by discussing implementation alternatives and helping to choose the right one. There are also opportunities—and sometimes needs—to assist people outside the team. A coder might help a support person or salesperson understand how a new feature works, or they might help someone diagnose a product configuration problem. This in turn might help the coder learn about ways to improve the software. Assistance that coders provide within the team or outside the team often improves the team's chance for success, and therefore these are important interactions to track and measure.

Is the Software Team Succeeding or Failing?

Unlike sports, where every team strives to win and the definition of success is clear and precise, in software development we lack exact measurements of success. The best strategy I have found is to triangulate the success of software development teams based on three factors: customer response, quality indicators, and efficiency. Each of these can be measured, release by release and feature by feature, and evaluated against prior levels, team targets, and organization goals.

What is the user response to each software release?

To start, you might measure that customer adoption of a new release is up 20% over a three-month period. You can compare that to established goals. Performing this type of examination for customer response, quality indicators, and efficiency, provides the team an objective and well-rounded way to analyze team success. Historically, product managers have been tasked to gather some this kind of data, and in fact you may obtain some or all of the data from your product management team. I believe, however, that this data should be examined more regularly and carefully by the software teams themselves, and that you should seek to gather it whether or not you have product managers to assist. Establishing a way to measure progress and success is fundamental to being able to identify the patterns and contributing factors that lead to software team success.

The first part of measuring success or failure, then, is to measure response. Customer or user response includes clear demonstrations of interest, as when a customer tries or tests a product or feature. It includes adoption, as when a customer registers for a product, or chooses to buy or actively use a product or feature. It's also important to measure negative responses, such as when a customer chooses to discontinue use of a product or feature, or when a customer tests a product or feature but then decides not to use it. Obviously, some customer choices are not directly reflective on the software development team, for instance a customer may choose not to buy the product based on price or some other factor outside of the product itself. However, because we lack more precise ways to measure product success, customer interest and customer adoption, or lack thereof, is the best indicator most of us have. Customers may be people who pay for the service, or they may be non-paying users. They may also be internal users, in a situation where the software development team is delivering tools or projects for use within their own company.

Many people associate product success with product revenues. Current and estimated product revenues are clearly important for establishing budgets and for product planning, and to a certain extent it can be very healthy for coders to be aware of these revenues and forecasts so they know why business decisions and product planning decisions are being made. But in terms of regular metrics that the software team itself will track and refer to, I don't like using product or feature revenues. Obviously, there are certain cases where revenues cannot be used, because certain products or features may not be charged for. But even in cases where revenues exist, I believe that it is better to focus on the number of users and the amount of usage. I feel that when looking at revenues, people tend to focus too much on the cash amounts (which can also cause them to overfocus on revenue-related metrics instead of other equally or more important data). Also, people are overly impressed by large revenues and underwhelmed by small revenues, but neither may be an accurate indicator of success or failure. For example, if a product makes $10 million, that sounds really impressive and the software development team might feel pretty good about itself regardless of anything else that's discussed. But if this represented a 10% decline in customer adoption and was 33% below organization goals, the team should be concerned. Just looking at the large revenue figure might cause coders to not fully appreciate how poor the results really are. Or take the alternative case where a product only earned $5,000. The team might not feel too good about itself or the results, regardless of whatever else you might say. But if this represents a rapid increase in customer adoption (maybe it's a mobile phone application that sells for $2) then this might be a great result. By focusing on the number of users rather than the revenues, you eliminate or at least reduce some of these sub-jective side effects. There are certainly times when discussing revenues can be useful, but as a metric that a software team will review frequently, I think it is distracting.

How is the software doing versus competitors?

While I don't suggest using product revenues, I do recommend trying to figure out how your product ranks versus competitors. This is another way to evaluate how your product is doing in terms of customer interest and response. To the extent that you can obtain the data, you might rank your product versus competitors on features or user adoption. There might also be third-party competitive analyses you could use. How you rank, of course, is not only attributable to the coders and the software development team. Marketing, sales, and many other external factors including the size of your business and how long you've been in business may affect your product's competitive position. Competitive ranking, therefore, should not be your only measure of success, but one more input for you to evaluate when determining your relative level of success.

What is the quality of each software release?

Another part of measuring success is to measure software quality. Typically you will have one very good measure of this, which is the number of bugs found in production releases. The amount and frequency of customer support issues can also provide you an indirect measure of product quality, as well as of customer sentiment. Success or failure will be determined by examining the trends of these quality measurements, and comparing them to your goals. Over time, the trend of quality measurements reveals not only a lot about the success of each subsequent release, but also the success of the software architecture and design.

How efficiently does the team deliver new software releases?

The last factor to measure in determining the success of software development teams is efficiency, meaning how much functionality the software team is able to deliver in a specific time period, working within budgetary constraints. The team's efficiency and speed of delivery can be measured against past performance and against team goals to determine the level of success. A team that is very inefficient may not be considered successful even if it achieves good quality and positive user response. And a software team that delivers releases on time, but has poor customer response or bad quality is also not a success. This is why I suggest looking at all three areas: response, quality, and efficiency.

Timeout for an Example: An MVP Season

In sports, there is an award called Most Valuable Player (MVP). It may be awarded within a team or judged across all players in a league. The concept is simple—to award the player at the end of a season who was determined most valuable in helping their team win. When judged for a league, the award may go to the player who was considered the best overall in the league.

I have wondered whether it would be worthwhile to award an MVP on software development teams. Maybe awarded on an annual basis, it could be used as a way to highlight and reward team-oriented skills. Designating an MVP might reinforce the value of measuring coder contributions to the team, since these metrics would be emphasized in making the case for the recipient. I could imagine giving out some sort of plaque, maybe even a monetary award. But I've never done this. I've never been completely comfortable with individual "public" awards, since I worry about creating resentment or other issues that would actually be detrimental to the team. Still, team-oriented awards like MVP are worth considering.

Although I've never given out an MVP award, I do have a story to share about one coder who clearly would have deserved the award if it existed. In this case, it was so clear that I don't think it would have generated any controversy or jealousy within the team, but would have been seen as a well-deserved and positive reward.

We were a one-product start-up, and we had just finished our second release. In the six months following that release, this coder I am thinking of did not work on a single new feature or enhancement. That's because there wasn't time, since during that period the coder had to:

- Spend approximately 15 hours per week responding to emails or handling support calls with new customers and prospects, including calls to far regions in different time zones at strange hours.
- Travel five times to customer locations to assist in large-scale deployments.
- Diagnose and fix over 30 serious product bugs.
- Make our product work with "older" technologies that key customers still had running.
- Tune performance on key backend processes that were dealing with many more records and more complex interactions than we expected to hit so soon.

There were a number of reasons why this particular coder took all this on. The coder was the lead on the configuration and backend integration elements that were critical to large deployments, and that area required the most support. Many of the bugs fell into this area too because the integrations dealt with many unforeseen and untested scenarios. Also, this coder was particularly good at working with our support team and our field engineers, partially because the coder had a great personality, and partially because the coder enjoyed providing support. Finally, the coder was young and single, so working strange hours and making last-second trips did not cause any personal problems—and again in some sense, was something the coder enjoyed.

During this time, we converted more than two dozen prospects that this coder directly helped with, and the vast majority became long-term, satisfied customers. All the bug fixes and related improvements that the coder implemented were an important part of enabling the product to go on to further success, and in general the coder's work during this time shielded other team members, allowing them to continue on with product enhancements.

There is no doubt that this coder was the team MVP for that "season." While, as I said, I have never actually given out an MVP award, I've found it a useful concept to keep in mind when evaluating the breadth and depth of metrics. My theory is that any system of metrics I use should be descriptive and accurate enough so that it could be used to make the case for team MVPs. Applying this theory, it is clear that there should be metrics that track support activities, and make special note of exceptional effort, such as off-hour work or travel. Also, in my mind I can't identify the MVP if I don't have metrics that cover post-release work, such as production fixes and product tuning. And since any MVP must be measured by the contribution to the organization, clearly there should be metrics that appropriately track and value the assistance that coders provide in converting opportunities to deals, and in enabling future product adoption for customers who have similar needs.

The MVP in my example clearly stood out among the team in his value to support, value to his teammates, value to the customers and value to the business. Whether or not you choose to give MVP awards to coders, you can check that your metrics are inclusive and meaningful enough that, were you to choose an MVP, the data you're collecting would help support your choice.

The Data for Metrics

Having explored the key questions that metrics can help you answer, the next step is to determine the specific data elements and the means to gather them. You want to find the key data elements in each area that meet the goals of being obtainable and understandable and of providing explanatory power. These data elements will be the building blocks for the subsequent metrics.

Data on Coder Skills and Contributions

To measure coder skills, you want to obtain data and key indicators for all of the obvious and not-so-obvious things coders do, as well as the variety of ways that coders interact with each other. The data should provide a full and well-rounded picture of all the skills that individual coders may possess and measure the key ways that coders contribute to software projects and software teams.

Productivity

By productivity, I mean specifically the amount of work done, which is separate from the speed or quality of the work (both of which I'll examine later). For coders, basic productivity will focus on the obvious things that coders do, namely coding, design and testing.

There are a number of ways you could try to measure coder productivity. As it pertains to writing code, for example, you could measure lines of code written (LOCs) or non-comment source statements written (NCSSs). You could track objects, functions, or methods implemented, or you could track other individual items created such as servlets or database tables. You could measure version control submissions.

Among the options for measuring productivity on work completed, I believe the easiest and clearest way to track is by counting the individual coder-assigned work tasks that were completed. A task may equate to a feature or enhancement, or part of a feature. A task may also equate to other work, such as design, investigation, writing tests, or bug fixing (although you may choose to group different types of tasks under different metrics). The "task" is the unit of work that is used to organize, plan, and manage coder work and software projects.

To differentiate among the amount of work contained in each, I believe it is also necessary to rate every task for complexity. Complexity ratings can be assigned in planning, but they can also be assigned or adjusted after the completion of tasks. Since they are an important part of the productivity data used for metrics, it is important that the ratings be consistent, meaningful, and fair. The complexity rating is based on an evaluation of the size and difficulty of the task broken down into a straightforward categorization system, such as Small, Medium, or Large. The complexity should be evaluated and defined independently of the coder who is assigned the task. So if you rate a task as high complexity, that rating should remain the same whether it is assigned to a very experienced coder or a novice. For this reason, it is best to not use "estimated time" or "actual time" as the complexity rating, since coders will complete tasks in different amounts of time based on experience and skill.

Each task must fit within the defined complexity scale. For example, if I am using a complexity rating system based on a scale of one for very simple to five for very complex, then all tasks must fit within the range. Tasks assigned a one should be of similar complexity, and tasks assigned a five should have a similar level of difficulty. If my team has smaller tasks, meaning tasks that are less than a one in complexity, then I will combine such tasks together with others to create a single task that meets the minimum complexity rating of one. If my team has defined tasks that are much larger and therefore exceed the level of difficulty normally assigned a rating of five, I will break those down into smaller tasks so that no single task exceeds the maximum complexity rating of five.

Utilizing this higher level concept of "coder tasks" rated by "complexity," is the most consistent way I've found to measure productivity across projects and across different types of work and various programming languages. Part of what makes this true is that it fits the way many teams already manage projects today. Many of us already have a system for defining, rating, and managing tasks. For example, if we are using Agile methodology, we probably have a project management system where tasks are entered and tracked (as stories) and are rated for complexity (using story points, t-shirt sizing, or some other method). Some teams keep track of development tasks in a central database or bug-tracking system, where new features, enhancements, and bugs are all tracked together.

The critical factor is to make sure that all development tasks are defined and that they are rated for complexity in a reasonably consistent manner. Once the tasks are identified and the results are recorded, then it becomes possible to measure productivity among coders on different projects, or between coders who do different types of work (although certain types of work may turn out to have inherently different rates of productivity). You might see, for instance, that Coder A completed twenty user interface development tasks on a project with an average complexity of two, and Coder B completed ten backend development tasks on the project with an average complexity of three. I will later inspect in more detail how we might use such data. But the point I want to make here is that, personally, I have found this provides more plentiful and useful data on productivity than aforementioned options like LOCs or NCSSs.

If multiple coders work on a task, I prefer to simply divide the task into multiple tasks, one for each coder. In this case the complexity is also divided. I prefer to divide complexity equally, since it is usually difficult to accurately assess the proportion of complexity handled by each coder. So, for instance, if two coders are working together on a task that has a complexity rating of four, for tracking and measurement I would treat this as two tasks, one assigned to each coder, each with a complexity rating of two.

In my view, bugs found and fixed during development do not need to be separately tracked. If a coder is working on task A, and prior to release the coder fixed ten bugs found during development, from a metrics perspective that work can be treated as part of completing the task. Bugs found post-release, in production, are a different matter. For those that are deemed serious enough to fix, they will need to be assigned to coders for investigation and fixing. These can and should be tracked with appropriate complexity ratings just like any other coder tasks.

I suggest tracking coders' work on design and investigation in exactly the same way as their work writing code. Tasks can be defined for design and investigation activities and rated on the same scale of complexity as other coder tasks. I believe this is highly appropriate, because in the end it is often impossible to separate design and investigation work from the actual coding tasks themselves. Even in cases where design is done prior to the coding tasks, many times coders will spend additional time on detailed design elements and further investigation once they begin the actual coding. For smaller tasks, coders often plan them exactly this way, assuming that the design and the coding will be done together.

Measuring coder productivity in testing is a trickier matter, particularly because different coders often have widely different approaches to testing and test development. Despite the best intentions and management directions, in my experience some coders are more consistent in testing and in developing automated tests than others. Schedule pressures may also come into play with coders spending less time on testing when deadlines loom.

I suggest two ways to track the work that coders do for testing. For work that will be done at the same time as a coding task, the testing and test-development effort should just be factored in to the complexity rating for the task. If your team is following test-driven development principles, or if coders are responsible for certain automated tests or other testing, then this work and effort does not need to be tracked separately from the tasks themselves. Again, the main issue is that complexity ratings for tasks remain consistent and meaningful. If all tasks have a consistent amount of test effort involved, then this should be straightforward. In cases where the test development or testing effort is particularly complex itself, I suggest taking this into consideration and then adjusting the overall complexity rating of the task accordingly.

In the case where testing or test development work is done separately (as a standalone effort), then these should be tracked as separate tasks, rated according to the complexity of work involved. For example, if an area of software does not have sufficient automated testing, and you decide to go back and develop the tests, then this should be tracked and rated just like any other code work.

Using this method, tracking productivity and work done for coding, design, or test-related activity, becomes a process of tracking the tasks and the complexity of tasks completed by each coder and each software team.

The other thing to consider is what to do when a coder fails to complete a task. Failure could be outright never completing a task, or it could be that the coder only partially completed a task. In either of these cases, the task may remain incomplete, or another coder may complete the task. First of all, I have found that it's useful to keep track of how many tasks each coder fails to complete. This is simply a count of "failed tasks," with no complexity rating. The other adjustment is that if a task is partially complete, then the complexity rating should be adjusted at the end. For example, if a coder completes the main work on the task but fails to complete the expected automated tests, then the complexity rating for the task might be reduced to Medium from High.

To summarize, these are my recommendations for gathering data on coder productivity:

- Track design, coding, and testing as individual tasks.
- Establish a complexity rating scale for tasks, and rate every task.
- If tasks don't fit within the complexity scale, then combine or divide tasks accordingly.

- Adjust the complexity ratings after tasks are completed, for accuracy and consistency.
- If multiple coders work on a task, divide the task equally among them for tracking purposes.
- Do not track bugs found and fixed during development.
- Track production bug fixes separately, the same as you would for any other tasks.
- Design, testing, and test-development done concurrent with coding should just be combined within each task.
- Track standalone design, testing, or test-development separately, the same as you would for any other tasks.
- Keep track of how many times a coder fails to complete a task.
- Adjust the complexity rating (down) if a task is only partially completed.

Speed

Speed is a coder skill that may be good or bad (faster work is not always better work), and I suggest measuring it independently. When you look at speed metrics along with qualitative metrics, you can analyze whether speed correlates to certain outcomes. For example, you can see whether coders who work faster are delivering software that has more problems or maybe the other way around. Individual speed and the results of speed will of course vary for coders and that may be instructive in itself.

Once you have decided how to track productivity, measuring speed is a simple matter of keeping track of how productive a coder is during a specific period of time. If Coder A, for instance, completes five tasks over four weeks with an average complexity rating of three for each task, then you could say that the coder's average speed per week was 1.25 tasks, and .75 complexity of work.

I suggest tracking speed in weekly or biweekly increments, making sure you have recorded the amount of work done (productivity) by each coder during that time. Hourly tracking is too small and too onerous for many tasks, and daily is probably more detailed than necessary. If you have a regular schedule for planning and review, such as weekly planning, or two-week agile sprints, then it may be easiest to track coder speed at these "built-in" checkpoints. Like all things with metrics, what really matters is that you pick a measurement duration and stick with it consistently.

The following, then, is what I suggest for measuring coder speed:

- Track speed weekly or biweekly, or using some other consistent time interval.
- Measure speed as the work done (tasks and complexity) by each coder during each time interval.

Accuracy

Accuracy is obviously a highly desirable coder skill. It is a critical element of quality that reflects directly on the design, coding, and testing done. Measuring accuracy serves as a key quality metric, although it's not the only quality metric. It's certainly possible to produce software that has no bugs and meets all the defined requirements but that no one likes. To gather a more complete picture of quality, therefore, you must also look at user response, as I'll discuss more later.

To measure accuracy, I like to focus on post-release production issues and bugs. As discussed in the previous chapter, I don't believe development bugs serve as a useful metric. There is too much variance in development bug counts based on timing and depth of testing. I believe the best way to account for development bugs from a metrics perspective is to make sure that tasks are not considered complete until development bugs are fixed.

Production issues can range from dramatic problems like crashes or downtime for hosted systems, to very small problems like misspelled error messages. Each issue should be tracked, and as far as possible, each product area and individual coders assigned to each area should be identified. Each issue should be rated for severity on a consistent scale, based on the impact to the customers and users. Many software teams already have such a rating system for bugs—but if you don't, I suggest a simple scale such as one to five, where one is Very Low impact and five is Critical.

Of particular note are "regression" bugs, which are production issues where something that worked before is partially or fully broken. Regression bugs can be particularly harmful to the perception and confidence of existing users, and therefore even though the actual issue may be trivial the overall effect may be more severe. In general, you want coders to be particularly careful about avoiding regression bugs. I suggest that you consider rating regression bugs with a higher level of severity than they otherwise might receive. For example, if a product issue is discovered that would normally be rated Medium severity, you might actually rate it as High severity if it is a regression.

It is also useful to keep track of how many customers (or what percentage of customers) are affected by a particular issue. A crash bug is a severe issue but it is even more severe if all customers are experiencing it as opposed to just one. I suggest you rate the severity of issues in respect to the customers who are reporting the issue, but that you also separately track the estimated percentage of customers experiencing (or assumed to be experiencing) each issue. This percentage may get adjusted as you learn more.

It may not be possible, especially at the time that issues are found or reported, to determine the exact product areas involved or the specific coders who have responsibility. This is understood, but in my experience this is not a major problem. Only a relatively small percentage of issues will be unclear or unassigned, so this will not introduce significant errors in the data. Over time, the more important issues will get investigated and assigned, at which time you can make sure the metrics are adjusted to reflect the findings. So, in the end, at least for the higher priority and more severe product issues, it should be possible to gather good data.

In some cases multiple coders may be responsible for a product issue, and the coder assigned to fix the issue may not be the one (or only) coder responsible for the problem in the first place. If multiple coders are responsible for a product area that has an issue, then bugs in that area should be tracked for all of them and divided equally among them, regardless of who will be responsible for fixing the bugs (which will be tracked separately using productivity metrics). When coders work together on product areas, it can be hard to pin down the exact percent of responsibility each coder has for a particular bug. So unless you can clearly determine that a specific coder has full responsibility for the code related to an issue, I suggest you simply tally the issue equally for each coder who works on that area. For example, if you find a bug in the backend that reveals a structural problem in the object-relational mapping area worked on by three coders, I suggest you track that as an issue for all three coders, where each coder is responsible for one-third. The ideal is to define a very granular list of product areas and to identify the coder or coders responsible for each product area. Then making sure that issues are assigned to specific product areas, you will be associating the issues to the coders. If three coders are assigned to the object-relational mapping system and that system has nine bugs with an average severity of three each, then I would track each coder as having a total of three bugs (total nine bugs in the area divided by three coders) and total severity of nine (total severity of twenty-seven divided by three coders).

Product issues include configuration problems, scalability problems, or performance problems as well as outright coding errors. If the system runs too slow or crashes under load, then those are product issues that you should track. Again, you will need to define the product areas involved and the coders responsible.

There is a gray line here, too, since in some cases a customer or user may request an enhancement or feature change that might be interpreted as a product issue, or you might realize that there is a system limitation or design flaw that needs to be corrected before it causes bigger problems. For tracking accuracy, I suggest you focus on issues that are clearly cases where something that was supposed to be working isn't. That means that anything that was in scope on the original task requirements, or should have been implicit and was overlooked (which might be a design or planning error), should be included. Anything that was not in scope and was not part of the explicit or implicit requirements should not be tracked as a product accuracy issue. If, for example, a customer sees that a page is missing a help link, it is an accuracy error if other pages have a help link and that page should have had one too. But it is not an accuracy error if all such pages in the product do not have a help link and were not intended to have one. As another example, if the product is performing slowly under an anticipated load, then that is definitely a coder accuracy problem. But if the product is only showing performance problems under a load that was much higher than anticipated, then that probably is not something you should track as coder inaccuracy. As the examples indicate, this line is subjective. However in my experience, I have found that there are generally only a small number of issues that are hard to categorize. Fair assessments that also allow for team feedback should result in negligible mistakes in your coder accuracy data.

Once you decide to fix a product issue, it will be assigned as a work task and rated for complexity. I don't believe it's necessary to rate product issues for complexity before they are assigned to be fixed. One reason is that it is often hard to determine complexity until someone investigates or actually works on the fix. While you might argue that an issue that is Critical severity and Very High complexity to fix is much worse than an issue that is Critical severity but Low complexity to fix, from the perspective of tracking coder accuracy I would argue that they are the same. Rating issues based on complexity to fix can be misleading. For example, if the area that Coder A worked on resulted in three Critical severity production issues, but all were Low complexity to fix, while Coder B's area had two Medium and one Low severity production issues, but all were High complexity to fix, which coder would you say was more accurate in their work? Personally, I would say Coder B had greater accuracy because that coder's "mistakes" had a less severe effect on users, although in fact it may be that Coder B has more work to do to fix the issues. Many times, the complexity of a fix is directly related to the complexity of the area that a coder works on, which again I believe means that rating product issues by complexity is a potentially misleading way to weight them, and one that can make it hard to compare accuracy across product areas and coders.

Here, then, are the steps I suggest to track coder accuracy:

- Keep track of all post-release production issues where something that was supposed to be working isn't, or the system isn't performing as expected.
- Rate every product issue on a consistent and simple scale for severity to the users, and consider increasing the severity for regression bugs.
- Keep track of the estimated percentage of customers experiencing each issue.
- Define granular product areas, assign each product issue to the appropriate product area, and identify the coders who worked on each area.
- If a product issue is assigned to an area with multiple coders, for tracking purposes divide the issue equally among them.
- Do not rate issues for complexity of the work involved to fix them.

Breadth

In helping to understand what each coder is doing, and how the team is functioning, I find it very useful to keep track of the breadth of items that each coder works on. Breadth is a key indicator of the overall complexity of the software that a particular team is responsible for and the utility that each coder provides. Having coders to cover all the necessary areas is critically important to the success of any software development team.

Some coders are better at this than others and some coders are just more willing to handle multiple areas, so I consider this another coder skill.

The easiest way to track this, I have found, is to use the same granular definition of product areas that you use to track bugs and to make sure that you track all tasks according to the product area. This applies to all types of tasks, including design, coding, testing, or bug fixing. The range of work is thereby tracked along with the tasks themselves. The breadth of any coder is the count of product areas involved in tasks they complete.

A different way to track breadth would be to keep track of coder check-ins to your version control system and to either keep count of the number of source files touched, or to have a system (automatic or manual) that equates the source files to specific product areas. My concern, however, about just tracking source files is that it may not be, by itself, a real indicator of breadth. For example, one product area may have many small but similar files, and a coder who updates these might touch more files than another coder who works in two truly distinct areas. If you can equate source files to product areas, then that provides the same result as my suggestion above. If fully automated, it would be even more reliable. In my experience, however, manually tracking product areas with tasks has just proved the easier approach.

To measure the breadth of coders, I suggest:

- Define granular product areas, preferably the same ones as defined for issue tracking.
- Make sure that every coder task is assigned to one or more product areas.
- Use this data to keep track of how many product areas each coder works on.

Helpfulness

As I discussed previously, there are a number of ways that coders can help others inside and outside the software development team. The amount of help that people ask for or require can tell you a lot about the current status of a software product and a software team. Helpfulness in its many forms is a coder skill, one that some coders may possess more or be called on for more than others. The amount of help that coders provide to others can tell you a lot about them as individuals, what they are doing that might not otherwise be easily noticed, and how they are contributing to the overall success of the team.

Helping others can include, but is not limited to: assisting another coder in figuring out how to solve a problem or how to handle a specific task; mentoring a team member; assisting customers; assisting support, sales, or marketing personnel; coordinating a team outing or event; helping a team member deal with a personal issue that might interfere with work; inspiring others; or improving morale. Helpfulness can be defined as anything a coder does or is called on to do to help the team meet its goals but that was not part of an assigned or planned task.

I believe it is useful to track two pieces of data here. First, I like to track the number of times that a coder receives a request and in turn helps someone. These are essentially interruptions in the flow of a coder's planned, assigned tasks. These may come in the form of emails, text messages, phone calls, or in-person visits. No request is too small to count, so any request for help that applies to a coder's work qualifies as long as it is not related to a currently assigned task.

The best way I have found to track this data is the simplest, which is to ask the coders to report at specific intervals (weekly for example) the number of requests they've received and responded to. Using this approach, the numbers are not going to be completely accurate. Coders will not track the exact number of requests, so they will estimate, rounding up or down. Yet these self-reported counts will still provide an order-of-magnitude measurement of the number of requests that each individual and the team as a whole receives. Sharing these numbers publicly (with the entire team) will encourage everyone to be reasonably accurate and to self-normalize the reported numbers with their peers.

The second piece of data I like to track is the number of times a coder proactively helps someone without having received any request. As with requests, no help that a coder provides outside of his assigned tasks is too small to count. To track this, I've found it works to ask team members to act as spotters and to notify the data-recorder (me or someone else gathering metrics data) when they observe a coder providing help to someone. In many cases the best person to report, in fact, is the person who received the help. As described above, help can come in many forms, including problem solving, pitching in, mentoring, motivation, team-building, and personal support. Since tracking the proactive positive acts of assistance is probably something you want to encourage, there are a variety of ways you could implement reporting these acts to make it more visible and fun. For example, you could have a group mailing list like *team-assists@myorg.com* or a blog or wiki where team members can cite others for their acts of helpfulness. Making them public provides encouragement for the acts themselves, and the reporting thereof. It also makes tracking simple, since you can just tally the number of messages or threads citing each coder.

You might wonder whether it's worth capturing more data about these interactions. My own experience is that there is surprisingly little benefit in trying to pinpoint who coders are interacting with (within the team or outside the team), or in trying to identify the reasons, or in trying to track the exact amount of time involved.

First, I've found that more detailed data can be hard to gather. When data is being self-reported or reported by spotters (team members), asking for more granular data can backfire, resulting in less data. People are willing to gather and report data as long as it is easy to do and they understand its potential usefulness. If you ask a coder to give you a weekly count of the times they were asked for help and the times they see others providing proactive help, that is easy enough. But once you start asking them to keep track of where the requests are coming from, who they are helping, and how long they're spending, the difficulty of gathering the data is much higher. For many people, if they can't do it right or it takes too much time, then they'd rather not do it at all.

Even if gathering greater detail was possible, in this case I don't think there are things you would learn that you wouldn't already see through other means. For example, you might think that more detail about the coder's "helpful" interactions would tell you more about specific quality or team problems. But any real product quality problems should quickly turn into bugs or tasks, and team problems (such as a coder having trouble learning a new technology) will also show up as incomplete or delayed tasks. In the end, my theory is the things that you'd learn from more detail will show up in your metrics data in other ways. The helpfulness data is unique, however, in that it shows you another element of coder skills and team dynamics that is highly relevant for success.

Therefore, I recommend the following to measure coder helpfulness:

- Have coders report weekly how often they receive work-related requests that they respond to (above and beyond their assigned tasks).
- Have other members of the software development team report if they receive proactive assistance from a coder, or if they observe a coder proactively helping someone else.

Innovation and Initiative

Like helping others, when coders innovate or take initiative to solve problems they can help the team immensely. I can think of many project I've worked on where one or two innovations, or one or two instances of coders taking initiative to tackle unassigned areas, became the keys to success. I believe it is very important for codermetrics to include analysis of these sorts of contributions, under the theory that teams where coders exhibit these skills are more likely to succeed.

But, just as with helpfulness, innovation and initiative are not usually identified or tracked in any consistent fashion. So you need to get creative in thinking about how to measure these. In this case, I believe that team leaders and managers are in the best position to evaluate which coder actions are significantly innovative and to see when coders demonstrate notable initiative in taking on unsolved problems or opportunities. Asking your team leaders to act as spotters, they can report each time a coder demonstrates noteworthy innovation or initiative.

What qualifies as innovation or initiative? I like to use the "happy surprise" heuristic. If a coder does something that leaves you or others happily surprised, then chances are they did something innovative or took initiative in some unexpected way. It is the combination of "happy" and "surprise" here that is key. If you are just happy, but not surprised, then probably it means they just did something well. If you are surprised, but not happy, then while they may have tried to innovate or take initiative your lack of happiness means that they must have done something wrong (putting this into some other category that I won't talk about tracking here). When the magic combination of "happy surprise" exists, then something noteworthy has occurred and, in my estimation, is worth tracking.

While I think the "happy surprise" heuristic works, it sounds kind of funny to actually call it the happy surprise data element. I'm not sure you want your managers asking things (joking here) like "How many happy surprises did you have on that project?" Or saying things like "Wow, I got a real happy surprise today!" It's better to have something appropriately adult and important-sounding (especially since this really is an important data). Personally, therefore, I refer to these as "adds" or "pluses."

For tracking purposes, I choose to combine innovation from initiative together, they are quite similar and often overlap. Remember that a coder can show innovation and initiative on any task, assigned or unassigned, or when helping others. As with helpfulness, I believe keeping a count of the times a coder demonstrates innovation and initiative is enough for useful metrics, and there isn't anything very meaningful to gain from trying to gather greater detail about the specific types of innovation and initiative or the amount of time and effort involved. Again, keeping it simple also makes it easier to get your team to track.

Tracking initiative and innovation is important, so I recommend:

- Have team members report when a coder demonstrates significant innovation or initiative.
- Ask team leaders to keep a tally of the number of these occurrences for each coder.

Data on Software Adoption, Issues, and Competition

In addition to measuring coder skills, you need to find key measurements of how well software is received by the intended audience or by those who work with the software in various ways (external users, internal users, sales and support personnel, or all the above). You must gather data that can indicate the success of your software and the quality of people's response to your work. You will need to gather data on adoption, benefits, and problems. You can also evaluate your success relative to your known competitors.

Interest and Adoption

As a basis for a system of metrics, it is critical for you to determine whether a software product, project, or feature is received positively or negatively, and also to try to measure the magnitude of the response. The most basic indicators you can track to determine response are related to usage. While usage itself may not be an indicator of how much users like the software (since people may adopt or abandon software for many reasons of which personal preference is only one), usage trends are certainly one important measure of response. When looking at software products and how well they meet organization goals, measuring interest and adoption is arguably more important than anything else.

For response and usage, you could rely on data from sources "outside" the core software development team, such as information you get from your sales team, customer support, or product management. My recommendation, however, is that response and usage data is so critical to the software team that, as far as possible, you should be self-reliant and create your own ability to gather and measure these things. In some cases you may already have what you need in place; but in other cases, this will take some work and planning. The good news, however, is that in the age of a networked world, this is entirely possible for most software developed today.

To track interest and adoption, I suggest that you enable your software to identify and track users in evaluation (if such a stage exists) and through into adoption and regular use. This can be done, for example, by collecting data when your software is installed (for on-premise solutions) or when user accounts are created. By having different installation packages or types of user accounts, you can distinguish between evaluation users and "customers"—and from there you can track and report on usage, which can be done in terms of session durations, page accesses, transactions, or similar categories. With your software enabled in this way, for any given time period you could track the number of evaluation users, the number of customers, and the amount of user activity for each type of user (perhaps even down to specific features or portions of the software). Ideally, if you keep track when every user account is created, you can also track data on how long evaluators or customers have been using the software.

All this usage data must be centrally collected, at least in summary form. If you have a hosted software solution, then this data could just be extracted or exported on a regular basis. If you have an on-premise or distributed solution, then you could, for example, have installation and user registration data sent to a central tracking system directly through web services or indirectly through email (which could then be automatically tallied). And usage data could be sent similarly on some periodic batch basis or when users log in. For the purposes defined here, it is not necessary to send any user identifiers or any other private data, and the usage data has some legitimate support utility. Most users and most environments will allow such system-level communications as long as they are low-volume.

Decreases in the amount of software usage per user is also very significant. By tracking the numbers, you will be able to compare one time to another and observe trends. Then you can compare trends to the other metrics you have gathered for your coders and software teams to analyze if there is any cause and effect.

The final element to consider is the complete opposite of adoption, namely those customers who choose to stop using your software altogether. Some users might explicitly signal their intention by cancelling their account or uninstalling the software. Some users may simply stop logging on to the software. There are a variety of ways you could gather data on these losses. In the explicit cases, where users uninstall software or cancel accounts, you can enable your software to report these occurrences back to your central tracking system from which you can produce appropriate reports. For users who don't take explicit action but simply cease all usage, you will need to devise another approach. For on-premise solutions, you might track centrally the last time the installation reported usage, so if an installation does not get started and doesn't report back for a certain period such as 60 or 90 days, it can be flagged as inactive. In this case, if you centrally track the number of users per installation, you can determine the number of users who should be counted as inactive. For hosted solutions, you can identify users that haven't logged in for a period such as 60 or 90 days, and you could capture these counts and then flag the users as "inactive" so that you don't double count them going forward (users would of course need to have the "inactive" flag removed if they resume activity). There are a number of other approaches you could consider and implement according to your setup and the rules you define to identify "lost" or "inactive" users.

As far as possible, to keep track of interest and adoption for every software product or project, I suggest the following:

- Enable your software to track and centrally report activation for different types of users (evaluators and customers) as well as the activation date.

- Enable your software to track and centrally report summary usage by user (such as number of times logging in and duration active), with detail where possible on different product areas or features (such as number of times performing a specific type of action).

- Enable your software or data collection system to track and centrally report cancellation, deactivation, or an extended period of inactivity for users, as well as the detection date.

Notable Benefits

If, as part of a release, your goal is to make significant improvements in your software to benefit existing users as well as new users, you want to find ways to measure those key benefits in order to determine your level of success. One way you might measure success is through a reduction in bugs or support calls, which I'll discuss below. But for results that cannot be measured in that way, you need to find alternatives.

Suppose, for example, that a key goal of a release is to improve page load times in your user interface or to improve the backend transaction processing speed. Another example might be that you want to increase the scalability of your software, so it can handle an increased transaction load, or so it can store a larger number of records.

In cases like these, I suggest you instrument your software to gather and summarize statistics in a way that will allow you to track whether the software is meeting your goals and delivering the target benefits. You can do this following the same approach I outlined for gathering usage information above. First, you'll need to add monitoring to your software to measure the data you need, such as page load times, transaction times, concurrent transaction counts, or database record counts. Then you'll probably want to add some sort of batch processing that summarizes the data, maybe on a daily basis, so that you don't need to store all the detail. Finally, you'll need to have the data delivered so that you can track it. If your software is a hosted or local system, this may not be necessary, you can just retrieve the data yourself. But if your software is distributed, you can transmit the statistics electronically, using web services, email, or other means.

If you haven't done it earlier, the best time to instrument your software is when you are making the key improvements. Yes, this means some extra work, but each subsequent time becomes easier since you can reuse your instrumentation code and patterns. The value of instrumentation is well worth the incremental effort. Not only does it give you a way to analyze all your metrics in light of the reported level of success, it also gives you data that could help in considering further improvements down the road. While you may not have historical data to compare to your new statistics, you can still compare the results to your target goals and thereby measure your success. For example, if you sought to reduce page load times to under one second, you can see how you did by gathering the information on actual user experience.

For target benefits that cannot be measured by instrumentation, there's only one other way I know of to evaluate success—you have to ask. You have to figure out who the enhanced software is intended to benefit and then you need to find out from them whether or not you succeeded. This is best done, in my estimation, by asking a single simple question, such as asking users to answer yes or no on whether the software provided the intended benefit. This type of evaluation isn't possible for every bug fix or enhancement, but for work that you believe should deliver significant benefits, it's worthwhile if you can't measure through instrumentation. I don't think it's enough to assume the benefits were delivered just because the work is done.

It is beyond the scope of this book to discuss whether it's worth conducting more extensive customer surveys or user testing, and how to do that. Your organization may have the resources and time, or it may not. For organizations that do surveys or user testing, it provides a great way to evaluate the benefits of your work. Whether or not you have such capabilities, however, I believe the software team needs to be able to confirm, yes or no, whether key target benefits were delivered. If you don't have customer surveys or user testing to answer your questions, you need to find a way to ask customers yourself.

Your goal shouldn't be to evaluate whether you had the right requirements or whether you met all the customer expectations (those are important goals too, just not the goal that I'm discussing here). Your goal is to find out whether your team succeeded in delivering the benefit that the coders set out to provide. You could send a target set of users an email, for example, asking them to let you know if they tried New Feature A and if it performed its intended function. If you redesigned an interface for better usability you would want to ask users something that says exactly that, like "did the new interface deliver improved usability?" Since the answers to the question will help you measure whether or not you met your goals, you need to make sure you are asking a question that appropriately reflects your goals.

To measure the success of work designed to deliver key user benefits, I recommend:

- Instrument your software to measure, summarize, and centrally report relevant data and key statistics that will indicate if the software is meeting the target goals.
- For benefits that cannot be measured with instrumentation, identify a target subset of users and ask them a specific yes/no question to determine if they obtained the intended benefit (this data may be acquired in another way if your organization has a method to survey users or perform user testing).

User Issues

It is one thing to have users; it is another to have satisfied users. If you or your organization does customer surveys, then that is a great way to find out about user satisfaction. Another way to indirectly measure user satisfaction is by tracking customer support activity.

Production bugs, including those reported by customers, are tracked as part of quality and coder accuracy. In addition to tracking bugs, I suggest you keep track of the number of support issues that customers initiate with your support team. My theory is that the number and trend of support issues are a useful measurement to determine the relative level of user satisfaction. Generally speaking, no user who contacts the support team is ever fully satisfied, and fully satisfied users won't normally contact the support team.

A "support issue" is loosely defined as a single contact with the customer support team or as multiple contacts regarding a single issue. The contact can be in person, over the phone, over email, chat, or any other electronic communication form. It would include communications through product forums or social media such as Facebook and Twitter.

If you have a dedicated customer support team, they probably already track support issues, so hopefully you can work with them to share data. If you don't have a dedicated support team, then your software development team may be the support team, and you will need to institute some sort of basic issue tracking system if you don't already have one. You should also consider how to track any "external" support groups that you have. For example, if you have a product support web forum where users answer each others questions, you should try to track information about the issues posted there.

For every support issue, I suggest you try to identify the product area to which the issue applies and the severity or urgency of the issue from the customer's point of view. Personally, I prefer a very simple severity rating system, such as Low, Medium, and High. The severity should be based on how urgently the customer needs it resolved when they make contact. An issue could be urgent, but it might be resolved by a support person in five minutes. Again, if you have a support team or well-established support policies, you may have a formal way to rate issue severity. If not, developing a simple rule-of-thumb should work. For example, if the customer cannot complete their work or use your software, it's High severity. If the customer is highly inconvenienced but has a workaround or can live with the issue temporarily, it's Medium severity. If the customer is just annoyed and can wait indefinitely for resolution, it's Low severity. The severity rating, which is from the customer's perspective, has nothing to do with the complexity involved in solving the problem or of fixing the underlying bug if there is one.

Tracking the product area for every issue helps you identify those issues that are more likely to be in response to the work done by coders as opposed to the issues that clearly are not. If a customer calls with a billing question, for example, that may not be relevant to your software development team (unless you created the billing system). It will be necessary for you to define the product areas and to make sure that support personnel know how to categorize issues. Ideally, customer complaints about missing features or requests for product enhancements would also be put in a separate bucket. In the end, the categorization of support issues probably won't be perfect, but the imperfect data is still useful. Clusters of calls related to specific areas will be a strong indicator that customers are not satisfied.

As a way to track customer satisfaction, therefore, I suggest:

- Keep track of customer support issues categorized by areas of your software.
- Rate support issues according to the customer urgency to have the issue resolved.

Competitive Position

The final way you can measure user response, in the case of a software product, is to compare interest and adoption to your known competitors. The goal is to determine your success in attracting target users by examining your competitive position and whether you are gaining ground, losing ground, or just staying the same. If you grow your user base 100%, for example, but your competitors grow 200%, then you might look at your relative success differently. Or if you lose 10% of your customers, but your competitors lose more, then what appeared a failure might in fact be a partial success.

Competitive analysis and ranking your product or features to competitors can be challenging. It is easier if you have access to credible analyst data, such as Gartner Inc.'s research, particularly if you are working in a mature product field with well-established and well-known competitors; or if you have a product marketing or product management team tasked to track competitors as part of their regular job. But even in smaller start-ups, you can gather quite a bit of data simply by examining and tracking competitor websites and their self-reported statistics on customer acquisition or revenues (which you can translate to customer counts based on pricing information that might be obtained in various ways). Gathering this data and sharing it within the company can be useful in many ways. Usually the most difficult part is getting started, but once you begin to record the data, I believe it will prove so useful to the software team and to others that you will find yourself motivated to continue. It is fairly easy to update the data once the original methods have been established.

The first important factor that I suggest you track is functionality versus key competitors. This is a measurement of how many useful features your product has that competitors lack and how many useful features they have that you lack. The overall list of "useful" features is somewhat subjective, but once established, should be fairly consistent. Understanding how your functionality compares is important because it feeds directly into how likely your software will achieve positive user response.

The other competitive factor to track, as far as possible, is customer acquisition. If you are competing with public companies, you should be able to get good data on their rate of acquisition from their quarterly reports. Again, hopefully this is something that your marketing department is already gathering—but if not, it is something that managers could do themselves. If you are competing with private companies, especially small start-ups, this data may be much more difficult to come by, and accuracy may be highly questionable. In these cases you can use material gathered from interviews, articles, press releases, or other information on their websites about customer counts or revenues. Because this data may be so imprecise, it can be useful to keep a "confidence factor" along with competitor numbers. For example, let's say in the last quarter your product gained 500 customers; your confidence factor on this would be 100%. Your analysis of material might be that Competitor A gained 300 customers, and you might be 66% confident in that number, and Competitor B gained 50 customers, but they are smaller and you have less information, so you are only 25% confident in that estimate. Keeping confidence factors like this is very subjective, but it is a way to make sure that you don't make too much of metrics that are not as exact as others.

While it is not typically considered something that the software development team itself should measure, I highly recommend that you establish an ongoing process to gather the following competitive data, which can be useful for metrics and in a variety of other ways:

- Product features vs. competitors
- Customer acquisition rate vs. competitors

Timeout for An Example: A Tale of Two Teams

Paraphrasing Dickens, one was the best of teams, one was the worst of teams. I was part of both. Two similar-sized teams, in two generally similar situations, each tasked with developing a new product for a target niche in about one year. Both products had modest goals. One software team exceeded almost every expectation, and the other failed in almost every way. The question was, which one was which, and why.

One team appeared built for success. Seven coders, every one of them with excellent training and experience, three of them graduates from renowned computer science programs. They were considered the cream of the engineering department, brought together to build an exciting new product. Most of the team had worked together for multiple years, some were personal friends, and the team often did things together outside of work. The company was in one of the hotbeds of US software development, and there were excellent design resources, testers, and an extremely nice working environment—pretty much anything the coders needed, they got. The schedule for initial release of the product was reasonable and flexible.

The other team was a mish-mash, thrown together more by circumstance than plan. Six coders, all with good experience, one of them a graduate of a renowned computer science program, the others with solid although unspectacular backgrounds. None of them had ever worked together before, and their personalities were very different. They never became friends, they only got together outside work when forced by their manager, and even then, it was uncomfortable. Like the first team, however, the company was in one of the hotbeds of US software development, and the coders had everything they needed. The product schedule, too, was very reasonable.

By now you've probably guessed that it was the first team, the one that appeared built for success, that was the failure, and the second team was the great success. In this case, I can say confidently that one team succeeded and one team failed. The team that succeeded delivered its product ahead of the planned schedule, and the product went on to win multiple awards, exceeded adoption goals despite limited marketing, and had very few technical problems. Managers within the company hadn't known what to expect from the team, which only magnified the success in their eyes. The team that failed never shipped a real product, only a prototype, even though the project took twice as long as originally planned for a shipping product (because the team decided to redesign the internal architecture halfway through the project). Despite marketing hype, the prototype was so poorly received and had so many problems that further work on the project was cancelled. Considering that so much was expected of this team, you could say that the failure was even worse.

As a member of both teams, I can also say that I much more enjoyed the time I was working on the team that failed. Everyone was friendly, enjoyable, and very smart. I looked forward to working with them every day, and I've since maintained contact with many members of that team. Working with the other team was not nearly as pleasant. Because we were so different, we worked more in isolation—and when we did interact, it wasn't nearly as stimulating. There was tension in the workplace, and a few team members did not see eye-to-eye. They were at opposite ends of the political spectrum, which sometimes came up at work, and their philosophical differences extended to software design.

But for some reason the team that I enjoyed never gelled, and we were all extremely disappointed with our results. None of us would have argued that the project should continue, although it was a good idea and could have been a good product if well-executed. In contrast, the less enjoyable team did come together, despite our obvious differences, to produce software that, while it wasn't legendary (it is long out of circulation now), did very well in its niche at that time—and which I'm still proud of to this day.

So why did the team that should have succeeded fail, and the team that was a big question mark succeed?

Both of these projects were many years ago, but to the best of my recollection I've reconstructed a set of key data that is representative of the teams and the coders involved (since this is a reconstruction, all the obvious caveats apply). The data is shown in Tables 3-1 and 3-2. The first project (the one that failed) took ten months, and the second project took thirteen months, so factor that in when looking at the data. Because only one of the products was actually released, I am focusing here on pre-release coder skill data, and not post-release data such as user adoption, production bugs, support issues, or competitive ranking.

Table 3-1. The team that was expected to do great things but failed to deliver a product

	Number of Tasks	Avg. Task Complexity	% Areas Worked On	Helpfulness	Pluses
Coder A	112	3.62	16%	3	0
Coder B	91	3.24	22%	5	1
Coder C	104	3.77	8%	6	1
Coder D	129	2.89	14%	11	0
Coder E	84	3.82	8%	2	0
Coder F	107	3.14	12%	18	0
Coder G	88	3.65	18%	12	1

Table 3-2. The team that exceeded expectations and delivered a great product

	Number of Tasks	Avg. Task Complexity	% Areas Worked On	Helpfulness	Pluses
Coder U	118	3.44	55%	5	4
Coder V	98	3.32	45%	8	5
Coder W	181	1.81	66%	18	2
Coder X	167	1.55	70%	15	7
Coder Y	145	2.26	58%	9	1
Coder Z	179	1.66	72%	12	3

Three things stand out to me among the data for the two teams. One is that, on the team that succeeded, more of the complex tasks were concentrated among a few coders, and the other coders had a greater number of less complex tasks. On the team that failed, basically everyone had a similar workload, and there was a high average rate of complexity across the board.

The second thing that I notice is that, on the team that succeeded, a high percentage of the team worked on a large number of product areas, whereas on the team that failed almost everyone worked on a small percentage of areas.

The third thing is that the team that succeeded had multiple pluses from multiple coders. The team that failed had far fewer "pluses," which means that team had much less innovation or initiative, what I called "happy surprises" earlier in this chapter.

What can you learn from this? I have a theory about the differences between these two teams, and why one succeeded and one failed, and I think the data is consistent with my theory.

I believe that the first team, the one that failed, was too comfortable, too friendly, and too confident. Everyone wanted to have interesting, complex work to do, and everyone wanted to oblige each other. The result was that the less interesting, smaller tasks, the ones that would actually help finish a product, never really got done. And since all the complexity was spread around, it became more difficult to make sure the design was cohesive and to successfully bring it together into a real product. This distributed balance of complexity was actually a large reason why major parts of the system had to be redesigned mid-project, because the coders were not communicating well enough and realized that their original work was not properly aligned. Finally, because this team was so comfortable and so confident, I believe they became subtly complacent, which is why there was very little initiative or innovation taking place. Everyone was working hard, but nothing that happened was surprising, exciting, or new.

The second team, the one that succeeded, on the other hand, benefited from the fact that a few coders took charge of the central design and the more complex tasks, while the rest of the team was responsible for the smaller tasks. This resulted in almost everyone working across lots of product areas, which helped ensure a more cohesive design. Because the team was not particularly friendly, no one was too concerned with hurting someone else's feelings by taking a more interesting task or making sure someone handled a less glamorous task. And because coders knew they were being questioned and were not sure of their standing, they sought ways to impress and exceed expectations, which resulted in more initiative and innovations.

If I'm right, then the lessons of this single case study are that software teams are more likely to succeed if they have:

- Centralization of higher complexity tasks among a few coders
- A number of coders working across many product areas
- Coders who feel challenged and want to prove themselves

You are free, of course, to draw your own conclusions and form your own theories. That's part of the fun. Having data and metrics lets you analyze results and formulate theories, and then you can test those theories over time.

PART II

Metrics

This section provides details on a complete set of codermetrics with formulas and examples.

CHAPTER 4

Skill Metrics

A lot of times, a player has a lot of versatility. That's really what their strength is and what their role is.

—Bill Belichick, NFL Coach, 5-time Super Bowl winner, 3-time Coach of the Year

This chapter introduces a set of metrics on coder skills that I've found interesting and useful. When you look at these metrics for a set of coders taken over periods of time, you begin to see patterns about the individuals and the team makeup. Identifying those patterns can help you understand how the team is functioning, where the team is strong, and where it might be weak. Comparing one team to another, and in context with other metrics introduced in the following chapters, you can learn even more.

It's a good idea to encourage the coders, not just team leaders and managers, to look at metrics, and to measure areas that might actually change their behavior as well as reveal it. My choice of metrics, therefore, is deliberate in trying to highlight those skills that I think are worthwhile to have coders think about and focus on. People pay more attention to things that are measured. If you tell a team that you're going to keep track of how many times they assist others, for example, they will probably pay more attention to when they are helping others, and take more notice when they don't. It can spur discussion around the measured area, and increase thinking about how to improve.

Input Data

Listed in Table 4-1 are the input data elements that will be used in the Skill Metrics. These data elements were discussed in more detail in the previous chapter. It is assumed that you will measure each of these in some regular time interval. For example you might measure and record this data weekly, or if you have two-week development iterations, you might measure biweekly.

Table 4-1. Input data for Skill Metrics

Element Name	Description
Tasks	Assigned tasks completed by each coder
Complexity	Complexity rating of each assigned task
Incompletes	Assigned tasks that coder failed to complete
Product Issues	Production bugs by product area
Severity	Severity rating of each bug, possibly boosted for regression bugs
Population Affected	Percent of customers (estimated or known) affected by each bug
Areas Worked	Number of product areas worked on by each coder
Issues Fixed	Production issues fixed by each coder (as part of assigned tasks)
Interrupts	Number of times coder is significantly "interrupted" on assigned activities to respond to requests
Helps	Number of times coder proactively helps others in significant ways
Pluses	Number of times coder demonstrated significant initiative or innovation

Offensive Metrics

In line with the other sports analogies that I've used, the Skill Metrics include categories for Offense and Defense. Offensive Metrics are those where a coder is helping to move the software, the team, or the organization forward towards the target goals. This is analogous to a player on a sports team trying to move the ball forward or otherwise help the team score.

Points

Purpose

Measure the overall productivity of each coder on assigned tasks.

Formula

Points = Sum (Complexity for all completed tasks)

Example

Coder A completes the following assigned tasks in two development iterations:

Iteration 1: Task 1 with Complexity 3
Iteration 1: Task 2 with Complexity 2
Iteration 1: Task 3 with Complexity 4
Iteration 2: Task 4 with Complexity 1
Iteration 2: Task 5 with Complexity 4
Iteration 2: Task 6 with Complexity 2
Iteration 2: Task 7 with Complexity 1

For Iterations 1 and 2, calculate Points as the sum of the Complexity for all completed tasks:

Points Iteration 1 = (3 + 2 + 4) = 9
Points Iteration 2 = (1 + 4 + 2 + 1) = 8

Having calculated the points per iteration, you can then calculate Total Points, or Average Points per Iteration:

Total Points = 9 + 8 = 17
Average Points = (9 + 8) / 2 = 8.5

Notes

This is the basic metric for the amount of work coders are doing on assigned tasks. Each task is weighted by complexity, according to whatever consistent complexity-rating scale you choose (such as a simple scale of 1 to 4). The sum of complexity provides the number of "Points" that corresponds to the relative amount of work done. This, of course, says nothing about the accuracy or quality of the work (which will be indicated by other metrics).

I suggest measuring points per development iteration (such as per sprint if you are using Agile methodology) or per a regular amount of time. Measured periods should probably be at least a week but usually not more than a month. You may choose, however, whatever iteration length best suits your team and the environment.

Using the average per iteration is useful to provide a clearer comparison between coders, especially over long-running projects. For example, see Table 4-2. If a project takes 20 iterations, looking at Total Points across the project might make it seem that there is a bigger difference in coder productivity than actually exists. Looking at the average helps normalize data from longer projects and from projects of different lengths (provided the length of iterations you measure remains the same).

Table 4-2. Data from a project with 20 iterations shows how Total Points and Avg. Points provide different perspectives on coder productivity

	Total Points	Avg. Points (per iteration)
Coder A	290	14.5
Coder B	322	16.1
Coder C	264	13.2

You may also want to pay attention to the maximum Points per iteration, the minimum, and specific trends.

Utility

Purpose

Measure how many assigned tasks each coder completes.

Formula

Utility = Number of tasks completed

Example

Coder A completes the following tasks in two development iterations:

Iteration 1: Task 1 with Complexity 3
Iteration 1: Task 2 with Complexity 2
Iteration 1: Task 3 with Complexity 4
Iteration 2: Task 4 with Complexity 1
Iteration 2: Task 5 with Complexity 4
Iteration 2: Task 6 with Complexity 2
Iteration 2: Task 7 with Complexity 1

For Iterations 1 and 2, calculate Utility as the number of completed tasks:

Utility Iteration 1 = 3
Utility Iteration 2 = 4

Having calculated the Utility per iteration, you can then calculate Total Utility or Average Utility per Iteration:

Total Utility = 3 + 4 = 7
Average Utility = (3 + 4) / 2 = 3.5

Notes

Along with Points, Utility is the other basic metric for the amount of work coders are doing on assigned tasks. Whereas Points is based on the complexity rating of each task, Utility is a pure count of the number of tasks completed. As shown in Table 4-3, coders may have lower Point totals but higher Utility. Such coders may be equally or more productive than coders with higher Point totals. Higher Utility numbers may indicate that they are assigned different types of tasks and are productive in different ways. It will be useful to look at Points and Utility in combination with other metrics, in order to get a more complete picture of each coder's contributions.

Table 4-3. Coder productivity shown by the complexity of tasks (Points) and by the number of tasks (Utility)

	Total Points (20 Iterations)	Avg. Points Per Iteration	Total Utility (20 Iterations)	Avg. Utility Per Iteration
Coder A	290	14.5	114	5.7
Coder B	322	16.1	98	4.9
Coder C	264	13.2	132	6.6

In addition to Total Utility and Average Utility, you may want to look at maximum and minimum values per iteration, and trends.

Power

Purpose

Measure the average complexity of the tasks that a coder completes.

Formula

Power = Points / Utility

Example

Coder A completes the following tasks in two development iterations:

Iteration 1: Task 1 with Complexity 3
Iteration 1: Task 2 with Complexity 2
Iteration 1: Task 3 with Complexity 4
Iteration 2: Task 4 with Complexity 1
Iteration 2: Task 5 with Complexity 4
Iteration 2: Task 6 with Complexity 2
Iteration 2: Task 7 with Complexity 1

First obtain the coder's Total Points as the sum of Complexity for all completed tasks:

Total Points = (3 + 2 + 4 + 1 + 4 + 2 + 1) = 17

To obtain the coder's Power Rating, divide the Total Points by the number of tasks:

Total Power = 17 / 7 = 2.43

You can also examine the Power rating within individual iterations and across iterations:

Power Iteration 1 = (3 + 2 + 4) / 3 = 3
Power Iteration 2 = (1 + 4 + 2 + 1) / 4 = 2
Average Power per Iteration = 2.5

Notes

The Power rating will fall within the range of your complexity rating. So if you rate task complexity on a scale of 1 to 4, then the highest possible Power rating is 4 and the lowest is 1.

A higher Power rating means that a coder has completed a higher *percentage* of complex tasks than others. This does not necessarily mean that the coder completed a higher *number* of complex tasks. For example, see Table 4-4. Coders who complete the most high complexity tasks may end up with lower Power ratings if they also complete more low complexity tasks than other coders.

Table 4-4. Coders who complete more tasks with high complexity may end up with lower Power ratings if they also have more tasks complete

	# High Complexity Tasks	# Low Complexity Tasks	Total Points	Total Utility	Total Power
Coder A	6	2	26	8	3.25
Coder B	2	6	14	8	1.75
Coder C	2	1	9	3	3.00
Coder D	1	2	6	3	2.00

It's useful to look at Points, Utility, and Power together. Power is a useful measure of comparison between coders who have somewhat similar Points or Utility, and as a way to understand the types of tasks that an individual coder is handling. Comparing the Power rating of a coder who averages much lower Points to another who averages higher Points is not an apples-to-apples comparison. In Table 4-4, for example, the Power comparisons between Coder A and Coder B, or between Coder C and Coder D, are certainly relevant since they have the same Utility. It is harder to make a comparison between Coder A and Coder C, or between Coder B and Coder D. Even though their Power ratings are similar, they are based on quite different Utility and Point totals for this limited example.

As with Points, it may be useful to look at the Power ratings per iteration, as well as the maximum, minimum, and trends.

Assists

Purpose

Measure the amount of coder interruptions and how much a coder helps others.

Formula

Assists = Sum (Interrupts) + Sum (Helps)

Example
Over the course of two development iterations, Coder A is noted as having received the following number of unexpected interruptions (Interrupts) and is noted to have proactively assisted others (Helps) the following number of times:

Iteration 1: 4 Interrupts, 2 Helps
Iteration 2: 1 Interrupt, 2 Helps

The Assists can then be calculated per iteration, and you can determine Total and Average:

Assists Iteration 1 = (4 + 2) = 6
Assists Iteration 2 = (1 + 2) = 3
Total Assists = (6 + 3) = 9
Average Assists = (6 + 3) / 2 = 4.5

Notes

The Assists metric shows you a different side of the contributions that a coder makes to the team and to the organization. It can be a very useful metric to help analyze the makeup and the work patterns of software development teams.

For example, look at Tables 4-5 and 4-6. These are metrics for two four-person teams taken from two small projects, both measured in monthly development iterations, with averages calculated per iteration. In this case you have the metrics for the individual coders on each team and then a comparison of the team summaries. Team summaries are calculated by adding the individual coder totals.

Table 4-5. Basic monthly Offensive Metrics for a team of coders on one small project

	Avg. Points	Avg. Utility	Avg. Assists
Coder A	48.4	15.6	5.1
Coder B	45.2	17.4	7.3
Coder C	39.3	15.7	6.2
Coder D	40.2	18.3	8.1
Team Totals	173.1	67	26.8

Table 4-6. Basic monthly Offensive Metrics for a team of coders on another small project

	Avg. Points	Avg. Utility	Avg. Assists
Coder W	46.7	20.3	9.1
Coder X	47.1	15.2	8.3
Coder Y	40.5	18.4	15.4
Coder Z	42.9	14.8	13.6
Team Totals	177.2	68.7	46.5

Putting the basic Offensive Metrics together, you can begin to see meaningful patterns emerge for individual coders and teams. A chart comparing the monthly averages for the team is shown in Figure 4-1. Now if I told you that the second team was quite successful, and the first team wasn't, does a specific metric stand out as perhaps indicating a key difference in the makeup and work habits of the team? In this case, the balance of Assists is clearly different, and I believe it gets at why one team was more successful.

As with other metrics, it can be useful to measure Assists per iteration and then to examine the highs, lows, and trends.

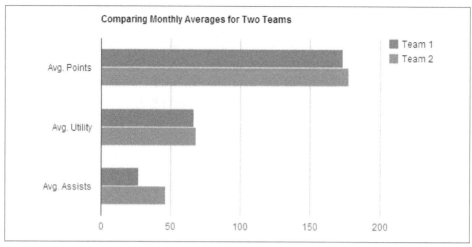

Figure 4-1. Comparing the basic offensive monthly averages for the two teams

Temperature

Purpose

> Measure how "hot" or "cold" a coder is at any given time.

Formula

> Starting Temperature = 72 at start of period measured (see Notes)
> Current Points = Points in the most recently completed measured interval
> Previous Points = Points in the prior measured interval
> Heat Index = (Current Points / Previous Points)
> Temperature = (Previous Temperature × Heat Index)

Example

Coder A completes the following tasks in two development iterations:

> Iteration 1: Task 1 with Complexity 3
> Iteration 1: Task 2 with Complexity 2
> Iteration 1: Task 3 with Complexity 4
> Iteration 2: Task 4 with Complexity 1
> Iteration 2: Task 5 with Complexity 4
> Iteration 2: Task 6 with Complexity 2
> Iteration 2: Task 7 with Complexity 1

First calculate the Points for each iteration:

> Points Iteration 1 = (3 + 2 + 4) = 9
> Points Iteration 2 = (1 + 4 + 2 + 1) = 8

The Temperature cannot be calculated until at least two iterations are complete. After the second iteration, calculate the Heat Index, then use that to calculate the new Temperature based on the initial value of 72:

> Starting Temperature (the Temperature at end of Iteration 1) = 72
> Heat Index after Iteration 2 = (8 / 9) = .89
> Temperature after Iteration 2 = (72 × .89) = 64.1

Notes
This metric highlights whether a coder is "hot" or "cold" related to the recent trend of productivity. If a coder's temperature gets higher, then her productivity has increased, and if it is down then it has decreased. The metric can be applied to teams as well by taking the Average Temperature of individual team members. You can measure Temperature at the same frequency as you measure Points, Utility, or Assists. I recommend you measure this at most weekly and at least monthly. If you are working in two- or three-week development sprints, those are excellent frequencies for measurement.

The actual numeric value of this metric is not so important, what is important is the trend line for individual coders and the software development team. The idea of calling this metric Temperature and starting with the value 72 is borrowed from the baseball statistician Bill James, who uses such metrics for hitters and teams. The number 72 is familiar as a common room temperature, and helps to keep the numbers in a range that can equate in our minds to temperature. This way, if a coder hits a Temperature of 90 or more, it is easy to remember that it means he is "hot" as a result of an increasingly productive trend. If a coder hits a Temperature of 45 or less, then it means he is "cold" as a result of lowered productivity. You can choose a different starting temperature if you prefer.

Temperature is not a way to compare overall productivity (which is better done with Points) but is useful to identify productivity trends. A coder with a higher Temperature, for example, may actually have fewer Points per iteration than a coder with a lower Temperature. The higher Temperature indicates that the coder is on a more positive trend of productivity, not that the coder is doing more work than another coder.

This metric is useful to spot improvements or declines in productivity during a project. It might reveal that certain coders are more or less productive on specific assignments. It might also indicate that certain coders have improved their productivity. When a junior coder becomes more proficient in a new area, for example, you might expect to see her Temperature increase.

Basing the Temperature on the number of Points means, of course, that Temperature moves up and down as the number of Points moves. Having this special metric serves to focus your attention and make it easier to spot the current and recent trends. For example, compare the data in Table 4-7 to the data in Table 4-8 (calculations have been rounded to one place after the decimal). The data in Table 4-8 shows the Temperatures calculated from the Points in Table 4-7. But with Temperature, it is much easier to spot the current trends.

Table 4-7. Points for coders and team through a series of iterations

	Iteration 1 Points	Iteration 2 Points	Iteration 3 Points	Iteration 4 Points	Iteration 5 Points
Coder A	22	24	26	22	18
Coder B	19	23	16	18	19
Coder C	15	16	23	20	22
Team Avg.	18.7	21	21.7	20	21

Table 4-8. Temperature for the same coders and team through the iterations

	Starting Temperature	Iteration 2 Temperature	Iteration 3 Temperature	Iteration 4 Temperature	Iteration 5 Temperature	Average Temperature
Coder A	72	79.2	87.1	74	60.7	74.6
Coder B	72	86.4	60.5	66.6	73.3	71.8
Coder C	72	79.2	110.9	99.8	109.8	94.3
Team Avg.	72	81.6	86.2	80.1	81.3	80.2

Because Temperature is designed to help you spot trends, it can be useful to chart the data. Figure 4-2 shows an example using a line chart for the data in Table 4-8. This provides an easy way to visualize the trend for each coder.

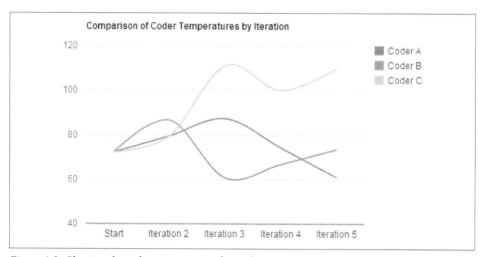

Figure 4-2. Charting the coder temperatures for each iteration

While I have used Points as the basis for Temperature, you could also consider deriving Temperature from other basic metrics, such as Utility.

O-Impact

Purpose

Provide a single "Offensive Impact" number that summarizes the contributions of a coder in moving projects along.

Formula

O-Impact = Points + Utility + Assists

Example

Coder A completes the following assigned tasks in two development iterations:

Iteration 1: Task 1 with Complexity 3
Iteration 1: Task 2 with Complexity 2
Iteration 1: Task 3 with Complexity 4
Iteration 2: Task 4 with Complexity 1
Iteration 2: Task 5 with Complexity 4
Iteration 2: Task 6 with Complexity 2
Iteration 2: Task 7 with Complexity 1

Coder A is also noted for the following number of Interrupts and Helps during two iterations:

Iteration 1: 4 Interrupts, 2 Helps
Iteration 2: 1 Interrupt, 2 Helps

The coder's O-Impact for each iteration is calculated in the following way:

Points Iteration 1 = (3 + 2 + 4) = 9
Utility Iteration 1 = 3
Assists Iteration 1 = (4 + 2) = 6
O-Impact Iteration 1 = (9 + 3 + 6) = 18
Points Iteration 2 = (1 + 4 + 2 + 1) = 8
Utility Iteration 2 = 4
Assists Iteration 2 = (1 + 2) = 3
O-Impact Iteration 2 = (8 + 4 + 3) = 15

Using the calculated O-Impact per iteration, you can calculate the coder's Total or Average:

Total O-Impact = (18 + 15) = 33
Average O-Impact = (18 + 15) / 2 = 16.5

Notes

Sometimes, when looking for trends and patterns, it is easier to look at summary metrics, even if these are merely combinations of other more detailed metrics. In baseball, there are statistics for all the different types of hits, and then there are statistics like Total Bases that summarize different types of hits together. Having such metrics allows you to quickly compare individuals and teams and to spot the correlation of values to outcomes. In the cases where patterns or interesting values are detected, you can delve into the more detailed metrics.

The theory behind O-Impact (which is shorthand for "Offensive Impact") is that Points, Utility, and Assists represent the fundamental "Offensive" contributions that coders make to software development teams, but that none of these three metrics is clearly more valuable than another. By combining them into a single metric, you come up with a value that "equalizes" the strengths that various coders might have and that gives you a way to analyze the overall Offensive productivity of coders and software teams. Table 4-9 illustrates this principle. The three coders depicted in the table each has a different strength. Calculating the O-Impact, you gain a new perspective on how these coders compare and, perhaps even more importantly, a summary metric capturing the basic Offensive productivity of the team. These numbers can be correlated to the team's results to determine how overall Offensive production correlates to success or failure.

Table 4-9. Offensive Metrics for one iteration shows how O-Impact allows comparison of overall Offensive productivity regardless of specific areas of strength

	Points	Utility	Assists	O-Impact
Coder A	14	4	2	20
Coder B	16	6	1	23
Coder C	9	7	6	22
Team Avg.	13	5.7	3	21.7

Other summary metrics (like adding different groups of Offensive Metrics) could certainly be formed and might also prove useful. For example, it might be interesting to add Power and Assists to create another derived metric. Many other more complex combinations of Skill Metrics might also be found, although it's beyond the scope of this book to explore all these possibilities more fully. Here I am focused on presenting a set of metrics that I have found most interesting or useful and also on providing concepts that will let you explore further on your own.

Defensive Metrics

Defensive Metrics cover the "non-offense" areas, where a coder's skills and actions prevent future problems or helps the team keep from losing ground in relation to the team goals. These are analogous to defensive-related metrics in sports. In baseball, these would be pitching and fielding statistics; or in football, statistics like tackles and interceptions.

Saves

Purpose

Measure how often a coder helps fix urgent production issues.

Formula

Saves = Number of Product Issues with the highest Severity that a coder helps fix

Example

The following production issues are found and are rated on a severity scale from 1 to 4:

Issue 1 with Severity 2
Issue 2 with Severity 3
Issue 3 with Severity 4
Issue 4 with Severity 1
Issue 5 with Severity 4
Issue 6 with Severity 3

For the purpose of calculating Saves, the relevant production issues are those with the highest severity. In this example, that would be Issues 3 and 5 from the list above. For these issues, Coder A is assigned the following tasks that are completed over two development iterations:

Iteration 1: Task 1 with Complexity 3 (related to Issue 3)
Iteration 1: Task 2 with Complexity 2 (related to Issue 3)
Iteration 2: Task 3 with Complexity 2 (related to Issue 3)
Iteration 2: Task 4 with Complexity 4 (related to Issue 5)
Iteration 2: Task 5 with Complexity 1 (related to Issue 5)

To calculate Saves per iteration, you sum the number of the highest severity issues that the coder helped fix, tallying each when the final task related to a production issue is completed:

Saves Iteration 1 = 0 (none of the issues is fully resolved)
Saves Iteration 2 = 2 (all tasks for issues 3 and 5 complete)

Then you can use the iteration Saves to calculate Total or Average for all iterations:

Total Saves = (0 + 2) = 2
Average Saves = (0 + 2) / 2 = 1

Notes

In calculating Saves, the size of the population affected and the complexity of the tasks that a coder completes to fix the issue are both ignored. If an issue has the highest severity for a customer, even if it is just one customer affected and even if it is very easy for the coder to fix, the coder gets credit for the Save. The idea is to put a number on the number of times that a coder is called on to help in a "crunch," assuming that the most critical production issues also have the most urgency and pressure to fix. If multiple coders work to fix an issue, they should both be credited with the Save.

For mature software, hopefully a software team does not have a frequent flow of high severity production issues. Assuming the counts are not high, this means that the number of Saves will also not be high. This metric, therefore, is probably best tracked cumulatively over the course of entire projects or longer durations, such as monthly, quarterly, semi-annually, or annually. Table 4-10 provides an example of looking at data quarterly.

Table 4-10. Saves can be analyzed in longer durations, such as quarterly

	Jan-Mar Saves	Apr-Jun Saves	Jul-Sep Saves	Oct-Dec Saves	Total Saves
Coder A	2	1	3	1	7
Coder B	0	1	1	1	3
Coder C	1	0	0	0	1
Coder D	0	0	0	0	0
Total	3	2	4	2	11

The cumulative number of Saves for a team is a metric that you can compare and trend across projects and across software development teams. You might also decide, based on how you rate the severity of production issues, to include more than just the highest severity issues in the metric calculation. Or you might decide to have a separate metric that tracks coder's work on important but somewhat less critical issues.

Tackles

Purpose

Measure how many potential issues or opportunities a coder handles proactively.

Formula

Tackles = Number of Pluses where coder demonstrates initiative or innovation

Example

Coder A is noted as having contributed the following "pluses," demonstrating significant initiative or innovation, over the course of four development iterations:

Iteration 1: 1 Plus (developed a reusable migration script when solving a specific customer production issue)
Iteration 2: No Pluses
Iteration 3: No Pluses
Iteration 4: 1 Plus (came up with a new stored procedure that improved performance on a key transaction by 100%)

You can then calculate Tackles per iteration as follows:

Tackles Iteration 1 = 1
Tackles Iteration 2 = 0
Tackles Iteration 3 = 0
Tackles Iteration 4 = 1

Finally you can calculate the Total and the Average across iterations:

Total Tackles = (1 + 0 + 0 + 1) = 2
Average Tackles = (1 + 0 + 0 + 1) / 4 = .5

Notes

In a well-functioning software development team, especially on a mature software project, Tackles may not occur at an extremely high frequency, but they will probably occur at a frequency greater than Saves. Also, unlike the work on Product Issues, the work that results in Tackles is often related directly to new development efforts in ongoing projects. For this reason, it is useful to track Tackles within each development iteration, as shown in Table 4-11. Reporting at this granularity also helps highlight for everyone the value of initiative and innovation and encourages coders to think about how they can accumulate more Tackles themselves.

Table 4-11. Tackles shown by iteration highlight the amount of innovation and initiative per coder and per team

	Iteration 1 Tackles	Iteration 2 Tackles	Iteration 3 Tackles	Iteration 4 Tackles	Avg. Tackles
Coder A	1	0	0	1	.5
Coder B	0	1	2	1	1
Coder C	1	0	1	1	.75
Coder D	0	0	1	2	.75
Total	2	2	4	5	3

Comparing trends and totals of Tackles across projects and teams provides a way to analyze the ratio of proactive accomplishments and the innovation and initiative of team members. Spotting high and low values that occur among teams or at specific times might also be of interest, and might warrant further investigation to see if there are specific circumstances or other causes that enable or inhibit this type of work.

Range

Purpose

> Measure how many areas of software a coder works on.

Formula

> Range = Number of Areas Worked by a coder

Example

Coder A completes the following assigned tasks in two development iterations:

> Iteration 1: Task 1 working on Product Area A
> Iteration 1: Task 2 working on Product Areas A, B
> Iteration 1: Task 3 working on Product Area C
> Iteration 2: Task 4 working on Product Area B
> Iteration 2: Task 5 working on Product Areas B, D
> Iteration 2: Task 6 working on Product Area B
> Iteration 2: Task 7 working on Product Area D

By counting the Areas Worked, you can calculate Range per iteration in the following way:

Range Iteration 1 = Count (Area A, Area B, Area C) = 3
Range Iteration 2 = Count (Area B, Area D) = 2

The overall Average Range for a coder is calculated the same as other metric averages, namely by taking the average of the per iteration values:

Average Range = (3 + 2) / 2 = 2.5

The Total Range, however, is not calculated merely by adding the per iteration values. In this case, the accurate result comes by taking a final count of the total number of Areas Worked:

Total Range = Count (Area A, Area B, Area C, Area D) = 4

Notes

Most coders work for extended periods on specific areas of a software product. Some coders are required to have greater versatility and work in more areas. The Range metric provides insight regarding a coder's versatility and breadth, and lets you analyze how a wide or narrow band of work areas might correlate to results.

When looking at a coder's range over the course of a specific project, it can be useful to record both the Range within a specific development iteration, and the Total Range across the entire project to date. For example, see Table 4-12. Looking at the Range within an iteration shows you one aspect of the variety of work the coder is involved with, and the Total Range shows you another aspect. Note the difference in Table 4-12 between Coders B and C. Both have the same Range in each iteration, but Coder B has a significantly larger Total Range.

Table 4-12. Looking at Range per iteration and Total Range reveals different information

	Iteration 1 Areas	Iteration 1 Range	Iteration 2 Areas	Iteration 2 Range	Total Range
Coder A	A, B	2	A, B	2	2
Coder B	A, B, C, D	4	D, E, F	3	6
Coder C	B, C, D, E	4	C, D, E	3	4
Coder D	F, G, H	3	G, H	2	3

Most coders will likely have a well-defined and fairly consistent Total Range. It is worth noting coders who have an unusually large Range, to determine what if any effect that has on individual and team results.

D-Impact

Purpose

Provide a single "Defensive Impact" number that summarizes the contributions of a coder in helping to avoid large problems.

Formula

D-Impact = (Saves + Tackles) × Range

Example

Coder A completes the following assigned tasks in two development iterations:

Iteration 1: Task 1 working on Product Area A
Iteration 1: Task 2 working on Product Areas A, B
Iteration 1: Task 3 working on Product Area C, also credited with Save
Iteration 2: Task 4 working on Product Area B
Iteration 2: Task 5 working on Product Areas B, D
Iteration 2: Task 6 working on Product Area B, also credited with Plus
Iteration 2: Task 7 working on Product Area D

Among those Tasks, Task 3 fixes a production issue with the highest severity.

Also, while working on Task 6, the coder is credited with a Plus for taking initiative to create a scheduled clean-up routine that will avoid overconsumption of disk space in the future.

Using this information, you can calculate the coder's D-Impact for each iteration and the Average across iterations in the following way:

Saves Iteration 1 = 1
Tackles Iteration 1 = 0
Range Iteration 1 = Count (Area A, Area B, Area C) = 3
D-Impact Iteration 1 = $(1 + 0) \times 3 = 3$
Saves Iteration 2 = 0
Tackles Iteration 2 = 1
Range Iteration 2 = Count (Area B, Area D) = 2
D-Impact Iteration 2 = $(0 + 1) \times 2 = 2$
Average D-Impact per iteration = $(3 + 2) / 2 = 2.5$

To calculate the Total D-Impact, you will need to determine the Total Range, which as discussed before, is not merely the sum of Range values per iteration. The following shows the method to calculate the Total:

Total Saves = 1
Total Tackles = 1
Total Range = Count (Area A, Area B, Area C, Area D) = 4
Total D-Impact = $(1 + 1) \times 4 = 8$

Notes

As with O-Impact, the D-Impact metric (shorthand for Defensive Impact) provides a single summary value useful for spotting trends or key correlations. Table 4-13 shows how D-Impact combines the other Defensive Metrics and allows another way to compare coder contributions and the strengths or weaknesses of software development teams.

Table 4-13. *Defensive Metrics for a project shows how D-Impact allows comparison of overall Defensive contributions and strength*

	Saves	Tackles	Range	D-Impact
Coder A	4	1	2	10
Coder B	3	1	3	12
Coder C	0	0	6	0
Coder D	2	2	4	16
Team Avg.	2.3	1	3.8	9.5

You might have one question: why use Range as a multiplier, rather than just add the Range value to Saves and Tackles? In Table 4-13, for example, Coder C is shown as having a D-Impact of zero even though the coder has a larger Range than any of the other coders. The reason I calculate D-Impact in this way is that Saves and Tackles are the fundamental defensive metrics, and without any Saves and Tackles, a coder has no measurable Defensive Impact. In a case where a coder had zero Saves and zero Tackles, if you just add Range, then D-Impact will just be equal to Range, which really isn't useful (since you already have the Range metric by itself). The way the formula is constructed, D-Impact provides a summary of Saves and Tackles, but coders with more Range are given further credit as having more D-Impact. You could experiment with variations on this, but I find this calculation does show that Range has meaningful value, and it highlights and summarizes a coder's defensive contributions in an interesting way.

Precision Metrics

The final group of Skill Metrics are the Precision Metrics, which help you analyze the precision and accuracy of each coder's work. This includes metrics that capture coder "mistakes" or "failures," where inaccurate, imprecise, or incomplete work was done. For metrics that measure these kind of mistakes, the lower the value the better.

Turnovers

Purpose

Measure the complexity of assigned tasks that a coder fails to complete.

Formula

Turnovers = Sum (Complexity for all completed Tasks)

Example
Coder A fails to complete the following tasks in three development iterations:

Iteration 1: Task 1 with Complexity 3
Iteration 2: Task 2 with Complexity 4
Iteration 3: Task 3 with Complexity 3

Calculate the Total and Average Turnovers as follows:

Total Turnovers = (3 + 4 + 3) = 10
Average Turnovers = (3 + 4 + 3) / 3 = 3.3

Notes

The Turnovers metric is equivalent to "Points for Incomplete Tasks." This, along with Errors, is one of the basic metrics covering coder "mistakes." Turnovers are weighted by the Complexity of each incomplete Task, assuming that it is a "bigger" mistake to leave a more complex task incomplete.

For most developers, the number of Turnovers will be small, approaching, or at, zero. It's just the nature of how we manage software projects and software development teams that most developers will not give up on a task before it's complete, and most managers will not reassign tasks. Tasks where a coder receives help do not count as Turnovers. Tasks that are reassigned from one coder to another for scheduling efficiency, simply because the original coder was too busy, also don't count. Turnovers refer specifically to tasks that a coder began and was expected to finish but couldn't due to technical struggles or other encountered problems.

In certain cases, such as when dealing with very junior coders or interns, or when a coder is assigned to a new technology area, Turnovers may be more frequent. But in those cases it may turn out that a higher frequency of incomplete tasks was expected, and therefore has little effect on the overall success of the software team.

Aside from those specific situations, any other Turnovers may be significant, and multiple Turnovers certainly could be highly significant for the effect on project success or failure. Because Turnovers are generally infrequent in software development, this metric is useful to analyze cumulatively over entire projects. Table 4-14 shows how the cumulative data might look for one software team.

Table 4-14. Turnovers are typically infrequent and therefore are useful to track on a project basis

	Project 1 Turnovers	Project 2 Turnovers	Project 3 Turnovers	Total Turnovers
Coder A	7	3	12	22
Coder B	0	2	9	11
Coder C	3	0	4	7
Coder D	0	0	0	0
Total	10	5	25	40

While the metric might normally be analyzed in a cumulative fashion, this is a metric to pay attention to, and you should still track and calculate Turnovers at the same frequency as other metrics. Although Turnovers don't occur often, they are significant when they do occur. Part of the benefit of such metrics are to call attention to these small but significant team issues, which can be instructive for individuals and the team.

Errors

Purpose

Measure the magnitude of production issues found related to areas that a coder is responsible for.

Formula

Errors = Sum (Severity for each Product Issues × Population Affected)

Example

Coder A has the following production issues found in the coder's area of responsibility during two development iterations:

Iteration 1: Issue with Severity 2 affects 100% of users
Iteration 1: Issue with Severity 2 affects 50% of users
Iteration 2: Issue with Severity 3 affects 100% of users
Iteration 2: Issue with Severity 4 affects 100% of users
Iteration 2: Issue with Severity 3 affects 33% of users

You can calculate the Errors per iteration in the following way:

Errors Iteration 1 = (2 × 1.0) + (2 × 0.5) = 3
Errors Iteration 2 = (3 × 1.0) + (4 × 1.0) + (3 × 0.33) = 8

Then you can determine the Total and Average Errors:

Total Errors = (3 + 8) = 11
Average Errors = (3 + 8) / 2 = 5.5

Notes

Turnovers and Errors are the two basic metrics for coder mistakes. Errors are weighted by the severity of each issue and the percent of the customer population affected. The more severe the issue, and the more customers affected, the larger the assigned Error value.

You might wonder whether it is fair to weight Errors by the percent of the user population affected. Is a severe bug that affects all customers a bigger Error than a severe bug that only affects a few customers? In both cases, the coder made a mistake. And maybe the size of population affected is only greater based on the area of code where the coder was assigned to work. Personally, I feel that a production bug that affects everyone is more severe than one that only affects a few people, and that it is fair or meaningful to measure a coder's precision based on the overall severity of the production issues the coder is responsible for. Most bugs will likely affect the entire user population anyway, but measuring or estimating the population affected really is no different than measuring or estimating the severity of the issue. You could just as well ask why is a severe issue weighted more heavily than a trivial issue, aren't they both mistakes, and why not just count the number of mistakes to calculate Errors? Again, I would say that a coder whose work results in a crash bug has been less precise than one whose work results in a cosmetic mistake, so you should rate their Errors accordingly.

Production issues, especially for software with a sizable user base, may be found frequently. Unlike the less frequent Turnovers, therefore, it is advisable to analyze Errors in a more granular fashion, such as weekly, biweekly, or monthly. See Table 4-15.

Table 4-15. Monthly Errors for a project team measured in the months following a software release

	Month 1 Errors	Month 2 Errors	Month 3 Errors	Month 4 Errors	Total Errors
Coder A	12	28	18	13	71
Coder B	4	9	9	7	29
Coder C	21	31	15	3	70
Coder D	14	17	12	6	49
Total	51	85	54	29	219

Both team totals and individual coder totals may be relevant for analysis. A useful way to analyze data for comparative totals, trends, and distributions is with charts, such as the example shown in Figure 4-3.

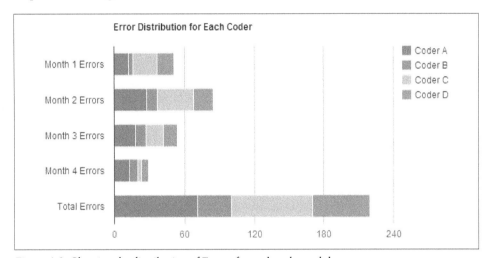

Figure 4-3. Charting the distribution of Errors for each coder and the team

Trends, peaks, and valleys in the number of Errors for each coder and each product area can be significant. Production issues might be coming from work done in prior releases and may factor into post-release analysis of coder contributions and team success.

Plus-Minus

Purpose

Measure the amount of positive contributions versus negative issues for each coder.

Formula

Plus-Minus = Points - Turnovers - Errors

Example
Coder A completes the following tasks in two development iterations:

Iteration 1: Task 1 with Complexity 3
Iteration 1: Task 2 with Complexity 2
Iteration 1: Task 3 with Complexity 4
Iteration 2: Task 4 with Complexity 1
Iteration 2: Task 5 with Complexity 4
Iteration 2: Task 6 with Complexity 2
Iteration 2: Task 7 with Complexity 1

Coder A fails to complete the following task in the second development iteration, so another coder needs to take over this task:

Iteration 2: Task 8 with Complexity 3

Coder A has the following production Issues found in the coder's area of responsibility during the two development iterations:

Iteration 1: Issue with Severity 2 affects 100% of users
Iteration 1: Issue with Severity 2 affects 50% of users
Iteration 2: Issue with Severity 3 affects 100% of users
Iteration 2: Issue with Severity 4 affects 100% of users
Iteration 2: Issue with Severity 3 affects 50% of users

To calculate the Plus-Minus for each iteration, perform the following calculations:

Points Iteration 1 = (3 + 2 + 4) = 9
Turnovers Iteration 1 = 0
Errors Iteration 1 = ((2 × 1.0) + (2 × 0.5)) = 3
Plus-Minus Iteration 1 = (9 - 0 - 3) = 6
Points Iteration 2 = (1 + 4 + 2 + 1) = 8
Turnovers Iteration 2 = 3
Errors Iteration 2 = ((3 × 1.0) + (4 × 1.0) + (3 × 0.5)) = 8.5
Plus-Minus Iteration 2 = (8 - 3 - 8.5) = -3.5

After calculating the Plus-Minus for each iteration, you can define the Total or Average:

Total Plus-Minus = (8 + (-3.5)) = 4.5
Average Plus-Minus = (8 + (-3.5)) / 2 = 2.3

Notes

The Plus-Minus weighs the "positive" contributions that a coder makes versus the "negative" issues that arise from her work. The formula presented here focuses on the completion of assigned tasks as the positive, and incomplete tasks and production issues as the negative. Many other variations of Plus-Minus could be created: for example, you could weigh Utility (tasks completed) versus the count of production issues.

The basic concept of Plus-Minus is that a "plus" number indicates that positive contributions outweigh the negative, and a "minus" number (less than zero) means that the negative issues outweigh the positive. The bigger the number, in this case, the better, and the smaller, the worse.

The formula here uses the complexity of tasks, and the severity of production issues. This will work best to produce the expected positive and negative numbers if you use the same scale for both. By this, I mean that if you rate the complexity of tasks on a scale of 1 to 4, with 4 being the highest, the formula will work best if you also rate severity of issues on a scale of 1 to 4 with 4 being the highest. In this case, you are more likely to get a negative number if the production issues outweigh the tasks completed. However, the formula can still be generally useful if you use different scales, as long as the scale for both uses higher numbers for "more complex" or "more severe." If a production issue with severity 1 is considered more severe than an issue with severity 3, then this formula will not work (and I suggest you reverse those ratings when calculating for use in metrics).

I include Plus-Minus in the Offensive Metrics, although it relies on a mix of other Offensive and Defensive Metrics. Because it includes the use of production issues, which may be discovered over a long period of time, Plus-Minus can be interesting to calculate over longer periods and in a cumulative fashion. It provides a way to determine a "balanced" view of a coder's "Offensive" contribution to the overall team success. Table 4-16 shows an example of Plus-Minus for a specific project. Note that the rating changes over time even though the project is complete as more production Issues are discovered. In this case, the picture of which coder was most productive on the project actually changes over time when looking at the Plus-Minus metric.

Table 4-16. Plus-Minus measured for a project changes over time, even after project complete

	Total Points	Total Turnovers	Errors After 3 Months	Plus-Minus After 3 Months	Errors After 6 Months	Plus-Minus After 6 Months
Coder A	290	7	37	246	81	202
Coder B	322	0	42	280	104	218
Coder C	277	3	18	256	47	227

When examined over a longer period of time, or for an entire project, clearly any negative number for Plus-Minus would be cause for major concern.

It may also be instructive to look at Plus-Minus in shorter iterations, such as monthly, as shown in Table 4-17. In this case you can examine the Plus-Minus rating in a specific month rather than the cumulative total. If a coder sees that their Plus-Minus rating in any specific month is low, then that might be cause for examination. The monthly Plus-Minus for the team can also be useful as an indicator of progress and may be a metric that correlates strongly with other indicators of success.

Table 4-17. Plus-Minus measured monthly for coders and the software development team

	Month 1 Plus-Minus	Month 2 Plus-Minus	Month 3 Plus-Minus	Month 4 Plus-Minus	Avg. Plus-Minus
Coder A	14	31	40	27	28
Coder B	32	19	34	24	27.3
Coder C	28	41	11	25	21
Team Avg.	24.7	30.3	28.3	25.3	27.2

The trend and size of Plus-Minus are both meaningful for software teams and individual coders. When analyzing multiple dimensions, in addition to looking at the metric values, sums, and averages, it can be useful to lay the data out in charts. If you store your data in spreadsheets, this is easily done. Figure 4-4 shows an example chart for the Plus-Minus data in Table 4-17. You can see how this makes it easier to spot the trends and changes in totals.

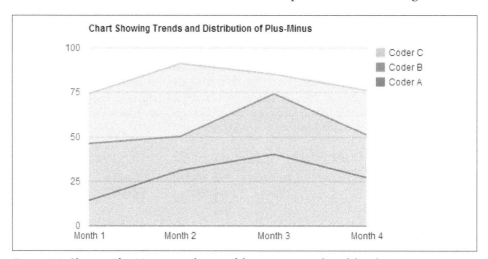

Figure 4-4. Charting Plus-Minus provides a useful way to see trends and distributions

Skill Metric Scorecards

One simple way to calculate and track metrics is to use spreadsheets. I have found Google Docs to be a great way to enter data, automatically calculate the latest metrics, and then share them online with the team. The charting features of Google Docs spreadsheets make it easy to present data visually when appropriate, too.

Keeping a single spreadsheet per project, per project team, you can enter data after each development iteration. See Figure 4-5, which shows a skills "scorecard" for an individual coder. In this example, you enter data rows for tasks or production issues, and as you enter data, the current to-date metrics are calculated at the top. You can enter the data one task or issue at a time, or you can summarize multiple sets of data into a single row (although this particular format has some limitations around entering summary data). The calculations at top are based on the data entered below. In this case the metrics are all calculated as Totals, but you could easily create versions that calculate Averages, Minimums, Maximums, or other desired values.

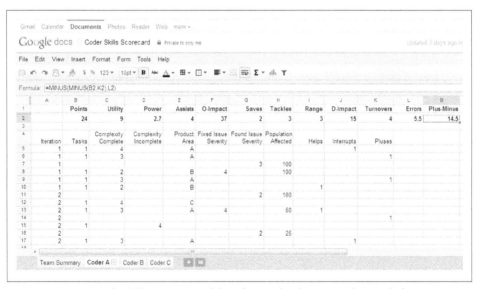

Figure 4-5. An example Skill Metrics spreadsheet for a coder showing to-date totals for metrics on a specific project

You can have a worksheet for every coder, and then a summary page to view the current metrics for all the coders. It may also be useful to include a chart on the summary page, to highlight key metrics and how the coders on the team compare. Figure 4-6 shows an example summary sheet with chart.

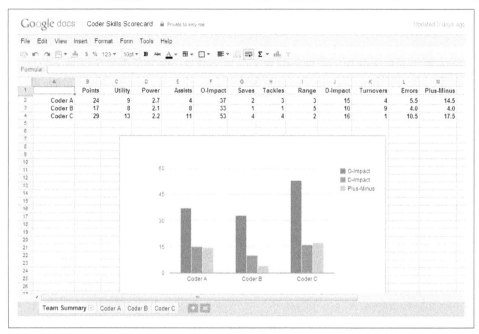

Figure 4-6. An example Skill Metrics summary sheet for a team of coders on a project showing to-date totals and a chart with key metrics

For certain metrics, either because calculation requires data in a different format or because you would like separate charting or trending, you may decide to have a separate spreadsheet. Figure 4-7 shows a tracking sheet to calculate the Temperature metric for a coder. You enter the Points per iteration, and the sheet shows the Temperature after every iteration. The summary sheet shown in Figure 4-8 lists the Temperature after each iteration for all the coders on the team, and the chart shows the trend line for each coder.

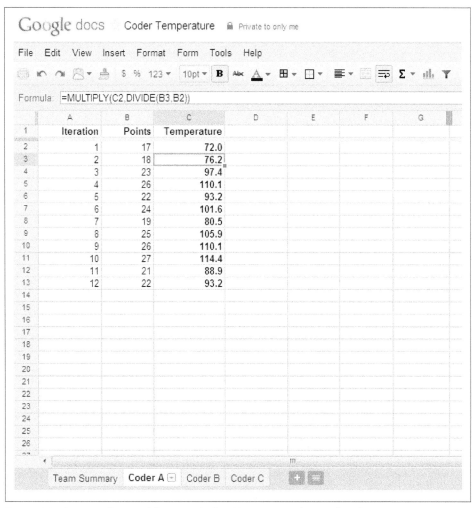

Figure 4-7. An example spreadsheet to calculate Temperature for a coder after every iteration

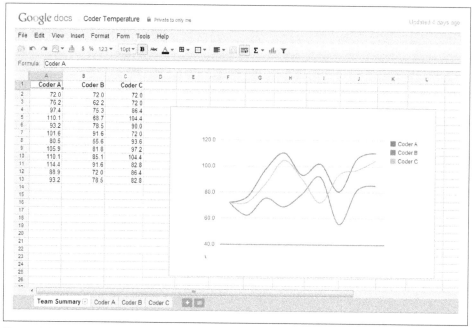

Figure 4-8. A summary sheet charting Temperature after every iteration for a small software team

Observations on Coder Types

As a wrap-up to this chapter, I'd like to offer some observations on how Skill Metrics might apply for different types of coders. Not to stereotype or draw too broad of strokes, but at certain stages of development, coders are more likely to demonstrate certain strengths and weaknesses. You may choose to watch certain metrics more closely depending on the experience level and obligations of certain coders.

Architects

Coders designated as "architects" are usually the more experienced members of the team. Their assignments may differ from other coders, with a higher percentage of complex tasks, including design tasks. They may also be expected to spend more time guiding and assisting other team members, to ensure that the software is well-designed and high-quality.

The following Skill Metrics can be particularly relevant for architects:

Power

It is likely that architects will have a higher Power rating than many other coders, since they will probably have a higher percentage of more complex tasks. It would not be surprising for an architect to average lower Utility, since having a high number of complex tasks typically means fewer tasks as well.

Assists

Architects are often sought out for help by other members of the team, and should also be proactively guiding, mentoring, or otherwise helping team members, so you would expect architects to have a higher number of Assists than most coders.

Range

An architect will likely need to be involved with many areas of the software. The architect's Range, therefore, will typically be above average for the team.

Tackles

Good architects will proactively anticipate issues and help solve key problems, so you should expect them to have an above-average number of Tackles over the course of a project.

Senior Coders

Senior coders are more experienced technically, therefore you will typically expect more productivity, higher quality, and in some cases more leadership. In some cases they may be specialized, in some cases they may be generalists, but either way they should be among the stronger and more consistent contributors on the team.

The following Skill Metrics can provide key insights for the contributions of senior coders:

Points

In general, you should expect senior coders to have higher average Points than other members of the team, either due to handling more complex tasks or simply completing more tasks.

O-Impact

The overall Offensive Impact of senior coders will also likely be above-average, as measured through the combination of Points, Utility, and Assists.

D-Impact

> While it may not be a stated key responsibility for all your senior coders, many times the senior coders are those that field the most critical issues or provide added benefit through initiative and innovation. Overall, Defensive Impact will provide you insight as to how much the senior coders contribute in these dimensions, and you would expect some if not all your senior coders to measure well for D-Impact.

Temperature

> Consistency of performance is something that you will typically expect from senior coders, and the Temperature metric will provide you a way to analyze that. If a coder is performing consistently, the Temperature will never get too low. Also, some senior coders may get "hot," with periods of especially high productivity. Watching the Temperature metric, you may be able to spot those periods and take advantage of them (management adjustments based on metrics will be discussed more in later chapters).

Junior Coders

Junior coders may provide all kinds of contributions and display many types of skills, based on their education, background, personal tendencies, and capabilities. Unlike architects and senior coders, who are by definition more senior members of the team who probably have more well-established patterns (at least for teams that have been together for some time), junior coders are more unknown quantities. You may have an idea what a junior coder will do, where their strengths and weaknesses lay, but you can't be sure.

For this reason, all Skill Metrics bear watching for junior coders and also for any interns you might have on a software development team. Metrics can be an excellent way to spot tendencies, strengths, and areas for improvement.

Among the metrics, however, a small set may be especially useful and bear close monitoring for junior coders:

Utility

> In many cases junior coders will not be assigned the most complex tasks, and so Utility becomes the key metric to track and compare productivity.

Tackles

> You won't necessarily expect junior coders to demonstrate innovation or initiative, or proactively take on new areas and unassigned tasks—but when they do, it will be worth noting. Most junior coders will record few (if any) Tackles, making those that do have Tackles more impressive.

Turnovers

Clearly, with junior coders you want to spot times and areas where they might be struggling. Turnovers can be a key metric to help in this regard. Junior coders with a higher number of Turnovers, or a spike in Turnovers, might need more assistance. Alternatively, a lower number of Turnovers is a positive sign.

Plus-Minus

While this can be a useful metric for everyone on the software development team, for junior coders it bears close watching. You want to see how much the "positive" contribution of tasks completed outweighs the "negative" outcomes, such as production issues or incomplete tasks. Comparing junior coders to other members of the team (and to each other) with this metric, you can get a summary view of their overall contribution. Also it will be useful to watch the trend over time. Architects and senior coders may have a more consistent Plus-Minus, but with junior coders there will likely be variance. Ideally, you will see steady progression until a general plateau is reached, but spotting lack of progress can also be useful in helping identify where assistance is most needed.

CHAPTER 5

Response Metrics

The numbers either refute my thinking or support my thinking, and when there's any
question, I trust the numbers. The numbers don't lie.

> —Daryl Morey, general manager of the Houston Rockets, 2006–present

This chapter covers metrics that help you analyze the response, both positive and negative, for the software released by development teams. These metrics provide the basis
to determine whether the software team is meeting team and organizational goals, and
is thereby "winning" or "losing." Included also are metrics that involve comparing
results to key competitors.

Overall, these metrics are designed to be as straightforward and simple as possible.
They are meant to be achievable, meaning that you can get the data and calculate them.
And they are meant to be understandable, meaning that software team members can
appreciate them and the relevance to their own work.

The Response Metrics show you how well and in what ways each project succeeded or
failed. When examined side-by-side with a team's Skill Metrics, you will be able to
analyze which skills or combination of skills correlate with positive or negative results.
If you are not already collecting the data for Response Metrics, it may seem more challenging than the work required to gather data for Skill Metrics. But the payoff comes
in your ability to begin to see the patterns of success over time. Therefore, I strongly
urge you to gather data and keep Response Metrics for your team.

Input Data

Table 5-1 shows the input data elements that will be used in the Response Metrics.
These data elements were discussed in Chapter 3. It is assumed that you will measure
each of these in some regular time interval, although not as frequently at the data used
for Skill Metrics. For example, you might measure and record this data monthly or
quarterly.

Some of these data elements may seem challenging for you to gather if you don't already do so. As discussed in previous chapters, however, there are a variety of ways you can put this in your own hands, mostly by implementing the data gathering directly in your software. If you haven't already done this, of course, it will take time, but it's my belief that the extra effort will be worth it. This data will be highly useful in helping you improve your software development teams, and once you've established a way to gather the data for these metrics, it will be relatively easy to continue and even enhance the data gathering on an ongoing basis.

Table 5-1. Input data for Response Metrics

Element Name	Description
User Activations	New user activations (not including trial or demo users), tracked either through software installation, user registration, licensing, or other means
User Deactivations	Users (not trial or demo users) who explicitly deactivate or cancel accounts or who stop using software, tracked either through cancellations, software uninstall, detection of non-usage, or other means
Trials Completed	Trial or demo users or accounts that are completed, whatever the outcome, tracked either through software uninstall, cancellation, or other means
Successful Trials	Trial or demo users or accounts who become active, tracked either through software registration, user registration, or other means
User Accesses	Use of specific product functions or features
User Benefits	Features or software changes that have direct user benefit as determined through software instrumentation, user surveys, or other means
Population Benefited	Percent of user population that receives each User Benefit
User Issues	Customer support issues categorized by product area
Urgency	The customer-assigned urgency of every User Issue
New Users vs. Competitors	Rating newly activated users for software product vs. key competitors
Features vs. Competitors	Rating features of software product vs. key competitors

Win Metrics

Win Metrics measure the success of specific software releases. The actual level of success can be determined by comparing the value of Win metrics among projects, to established goals, or to competitors.

Wins

Purpose

> Measure the number of active users added.

Formula

> Wins = Sum (User Activations)

Example

A new software release is issued at the end of June. The following new user activations are recorded for the three months following release:

> Month of July: 225 new user activations
> Month of August: 270 new user activations
> Month of September: 350 new user activations

The number of Wins for the software release can then be calculated as follows:

> Wins in July = 225
> Wins in August = 270
> Wins in September = 350
> Total Wins at end of August = (225 + 270) = 495
> Total Wins at end of September = (225 + 270 + 350) = 845

You can also evaluate the Average number of Wins:

> Average Wins per month at end of August = (225 + 270) / 2 = 247.5
> Average Wins per month at end of September = (225 + 270 + 350) / 3 = 281.7

Notes

There are a variety of ways you might calculate Wins. The most important point, however, is that you should have a Win metric. It is surprising how many software teams do not keep track of some fundamental measure of success, such as the number of customers or users. If you don't like the specific formula presented here, I still suggest you choose and establish a metric to use as your basic measure of progress and achievement.

Why not just call it the "New Users" metric, rather than calling it Wins? As with other metrics presented in this book, I like to use conceptual names for metrics, which I think makes them more memorable, easier to discuss, and also helps everyone understand the purpose and not just the contents of the metric.

The Wins formula that I use here focuses specifically on new user activations, not on the total number of users. Both, of course, are relevant to the overall success of a software product, but the theory is that new user activations is a better measure of recent success and recent software changes.

No doubt that many things go into gaining new users, and many are beyond the control of a software development team. The amount of money spent on marketing and the effectiveness of marketing and sales teams are obvious examples. To the best of your ability, you might factor external elements into your analysis of the Win values. For example, if your company doubles its marketing spend and the resulting number of new users doubles, then everyone will understand that doubling the number of Wins was good but not all the credit goes to the software development team. Partial credit, however, certainly does, so the number is still relevant. It has been my experience that over time, dramatic changes in marketing and sales are infrequent, so the value and trends of Wins is a highly meaningful measure of progress for the software team.

Table 5-2 shows the Wins by month for three separate software products from a single organization. By themselves, the raw number of Wins are difficult to analyze, so they are augmented with comparison to goals and trends. For example, just knowing that Product 1 had 585 Wins in January doesn't tell you whether that number is good or bad. By comparing the monthly numbers and analyzing the trends, and comparing those numbers to target goals, you can see how well each product is succeeding and how their success compares across product lines. Although it has the lowest Total Win numbers, Product 2 is highly successful based on comparison to goals and the month-to-month trend, while Product 3 (which has the highest numbers) may in fact be seen as unsuccessful based on the goals.

Table 5-2. Two-month Wins analysis for three non-competitive software products

	Jan Wins	Jan % Goal	Feb Wins	Feb % Goal	Jan-Feb Trend
Product 1	585	94%	542	87%	down 17%
Product 2	28	93%	67	134%	up 140%
Product 3	2,080	69%	1,445	48%	down 30%

For this reason, you want to calculate and track Wins, but you'll then want to analyze the Averages, Trends, and comparison to goals, to put them in context for each individual situation.

Wins can be measured for features as well as products, which is appropriate if those features are licensed or registered separately, meaning that only users who really want that feature get it and use it. In this case you will need to gather the registration, licensing, or activation data for the specific feature and that will allow you to calculate Wins by feature.

Win Rate

Purpose

Determine the average amount of time it takes to get a win.

Formula

Win Rate = (Time Elapsed / Wins)

Example

A new software release is issued at the end of June. The following new user activations (Wins) are recorded for the three months following release:

Month of July: 225 new user activations
Month of August: 270 new user activations
Month of September: 350 new user activations

Assume that you want to calculate Win Rate in term of hours and minutes, which means that you want to determine how many hours and minutes on average it takes to get each Win. The calculation can be performed as follows (results are rounded):

Win Rate in July (month with 31 days) = (31 × 24) / 225 = 3 hours 20 minutes
Win Rate in August (month with 31 days) = (31 × 24) / 270 = 2 hours 45 minutes
Win Rate in September (month with 30 days) = (30 × 24) / 350 = 2 hours 6 minutes
Average Win Rate (all months) = ((31 + 31 + 30) × 24) / (225 + 270 + 350) = 2 hours 36 minutes

You can calculate different time increments with simple conversions:

Win Rate of 3 hours = Win Rate of .125 days

Notes

Win Rate simply provides a different way to describe and analyze Wins, showing you on average how long it takes to get each Win (new user activation). Technically you could refer to this as the "mean time between Wins."

Wins and Win Rate convey the same information in different forms, and you may find one version or the other is more useful in certain contexts and analysis. Personally I like the Win Rate metric because I often find it's more memorable and impactful for the software team to think about the fact that the software is adding a new user every 3 hours and 20 minutes (the Win Rate) than to say the software added 225 new users in the month. I also find Win Rate to be an interesting way to compare results across releases and software projects.

Depending on how many Wins a software project is accumulating, it may make sense to calculate Win Rate in terms of days or hours or minutes. For software that accumulates Wins extremely rapidly you might even want to look at Win Rate in terms of seconds. My general suggestion is that if your values are larger than three digits or less than one then you should convert to another time interval. For example, I believe it's more useful to say that the Win Rate is 3 hours 12 minutes rather than to say it is 192 minutes (a value with three digits), and it's also more useful than saying it is .133 days (a value less than one).

The lower the Win Rate, meaning the faster that Wins are accumulated, the better. Software with a Win Rate of 30 minutes is doing "better" than software with a Win Rate of 45 minutes. As with all other Win Metrics, however, the actual evaluation of whether results are "good" or "bad" must involve comparison to past history, to goals, and to competitors. Table 5-3 shows an example of tracking Win Rate and differentials for the same products across two months, as shown in Table 5-2. Note one very interesting difference that highlights the usefulness of Win Rate. In Table 5-2, for Product 1 there are less Wins in February than in January, and when looking at the month-to-month trend, the result shows that February was down 17% from January. When looking at Win Rate, however, because February has 3 fewer days than January, the metric actually shows that February was a small improvement over January in terms of the average time for each Win.

Table 5-3. Two-month Win Rate analysis for three non-competitive software products

	Jan Win Rate	Feb Win Rate	Jan-Feb Differential
Product 1	1 hr 16 mins	1 hr 13 mins	improved 3 mins
Product 2	26 hr 34 mins	10 hr 2 mins	improved 16 hrs 32 mins
Product 3	22 secs	28 secs	declined 6 secs

As with Wins, you can also calculate Win Rate for specific features if you are able to capture activation information for those features.

Win Percentage

Purpose

Measure the percentage of trials that successfully convert to active users.

Formula

Win Percentage = (Successful Trials / Trials Completed) × 100

Example

A new software release is issued at the end of June. The following trial data is recorded for the three months following the product release:

Month of July: 81 Trials Complete, 67 Successful Trials
Month of August: 107 Trials Complete, 88 Successful Trials
Month of September: 142 Trials Complete, 119 Successful Trials

The monthly Win Percentages for the product release can then be calculated as follows:

Win Percentage in July = (67 / 81) × 100 = 83%
Win Percentage in August = (82 / 107) × 100 = 77%
Win Percentage in September = (124 / 142) × 100 = 87%

The Total and Average Win Percentage will basically be the same, although they could be slightly off based on rounding. They can be calculated in either of the following ways:

Total Win Percentage = ((67 + 82 + 124) / (81 + 107 + 142)) × 100 = 83%
Average Win Percentage = (83 + 77 + 87) / 3 = 82%
Win Percentage in September = (124 / 142) × 100 = 87%

Notes

The value of the Win Percentage metric is to provide you an indicator of how well the software succeeds with the target users. Obviously if your software does not offer trials or demos, then the formula presented here will not work for you. In that case you might consider whether there is another way to determine Win Percentage. For example, if the first 30 or 60 days of use of your software typically translates to an initial trial (even if customers are paying for usage during this period), then you might keep track of the percentage of customers who continue usage after that period ends.

As with the Wins metric, since Win Percentage is based on the number of successful trials, it is very dependent on many factors not directly attributable to the software or the software development team. Price, sales execution, and quality of customer support are clear examples. This needs to be factored in to the analysis and use of this metric. It's assumed, however, that in general people who become "trial users" are for the most part well-qualified, since they probably wouldn't begin a trial without a real interest and some capability to purchase. If your data includes trial users who register but then never actually use the software, you might want to exclude them from the count of trial users, since this may be a strong indicator that they were never actually well-qualified, nor did they give your software a fair trial.

Also note that you can either track Win Percentage based on a per-user or per-account basis. The result should amount to the same thing, so choose the approach which makes it easiest for you to gather the necessary data.

Because there are multiple factors that influence the conversion of trial users to active customers, while the Win Percentage itself may be informative to the software team and indicative of the relative improvement in each release, the trend may be even more informative, especially when comparing one release or one product to another. For example, Table 5-4 shows the Win Percentages for multiple releases of two software products. Examining the data, it would be hard to say whether the results on the first release of each product were good or bad (although with contextual information from your organization, you might be able to make such judgments). But what is clear is that the Win Percentage of Product 1 improved after the second release, while Product 2 remained basically the same after its second release. These results are likely at least in part attributable to the work of the software team on those specific releases.

Table 5-4. Analyzing Win Percentage for multiple product releases

	1st Qtr Win %	2nd Qtr Win %	Avg. Win %
Product 1, Release 1	57%	54%	55.5%
Product 1, Release 2	68%	72%	70%
Product 2, Release 1	62%	66%	64%
Product 2, Release 2	63%	69%	66%

Examining Win Percentage per release and the trends across releases will help you identify noticeable shifts in user response. Using charts can help identify the trends, as shown in Figure 5-1.

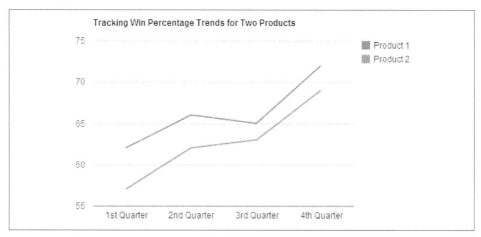

Figure 5-1. Charting Win Percentage can help make the trends more visible

Boost

Purpose

   Measure the amount of additional user benefits delivered.

Formula

   Boost = Sum (Population Benefited for each User Benefit)

Example

A new software release is issued at the end of June. In the three months following the release, the following data is gathered regarding user benefits contained in the release:

- Key transaction performance improvement, validated by embedded performance measurements, Population Benefited is 100%
- Key new reports, validated by usage data, Population Benefited is 75%
- Usability improvements in most used product area, validated by customer survey, Population Benefited is 100%
- New integration utility, validated by usage data, Population Benefited is 10%

The Boost for the release is calculated by adding the Population Benefited amounts for the four measured user benefits as follows:

   Boost = (1.0 + .75 + 1.0 + .10) = 2.85

Notes

The concept is to measure the relative user benefit of each software release and, thereby, the "boost" to the software's "win capabilities" delivered by each release. User benefits would be key enhancements such as measurable performance improvements on key transactions, major usability improvements, or key new features. The higher the Boost for a software release, the better.

In general, I suggest that user benefits should be measured and validated, but where that's not possible you may still choose to assign value to delivered benefits. One question is where to draw the line, which benefits to include? Clearly a bug fix, for example, has a benefit to at least some users. This is another reason to only include measurable benefits under the Boost. Only more significant improvements or changes will be worth the effort to measure and validate, and in general I suggest you focus on the "significant" benefits in each release. But your main goal should be to try to maintain consistency in the type of improvements you measure and include from release to release and across projects, since this metric is a relative measure that allows you to compare projects and releases.

Taken together, the three Win Metrics provide a picture of the measurable and assumed positive user response to each software release. Boost is useful in highlighting the positive benefits delivered by the software team that may not show up in new customer acquisition, for example, because they are benefits to existing users.

Examine the data in Table 5-5 covering the Win Metrics for a product across five software releases. What you'll notice is that some releases had improved Win Rate and Win Percentages, while others had higher Boost. This is exactly what you might see if, for example, you are staggering feature and maintenance releases. The releases with major feature improvements will have the greatest possibility to affect Win values, while releases with the most quality improvements will likely have the greatest benefit to existing users and, therefore, the higher Boost. A release with a higher Boost might not be expected to yield as great an improvement in Wins or Win Percentage, and the inverse might also be true.

Table 5-5. Win Metrics for a software product across five releases

	Win Rate	Win %	Boost
Release 1 (feature release)	2 hrs 32 mins	54%	8.5
Release 2 (feature release)	2 hrs 25 mins	65%	6.0
Release 3 (maintenance release)	2 hrs 26 mins	64%	16.75
Release 4 (feature release)	2 hrs 18 mins	77%	5.25
Release 5 (maintenance release)	2 hrs 18 mins	78%	21.0

Analyzing the actual "success" of any project or release involves comparing the results to the goals of each. In Table 5-5, Releases 3 and 5 were maintenance releases, so they were successful despite the fact that the Win Rate and Win Percentage stayed basically the same.

Loss Metrics

Loss Metrics are the indicators of negative user response or user-related problems. For each software release, the Loss Metrics are the counterbalance to the Win Metrics. As with the Win Metrics, you may well have defined goals that you can measure the Loss Metrics against to determine whether you have succeeded by maintaining losses below target thresholds.

Losses

Purpose

Measure the number of active users lost.

Formula

Losses = Sum (User Deactivations)

Example
A new software release is issued at the end of June. The following user deactivations or cancellations are recorded for the three months following release:

Month of July: 18 deactivations or cancellations
Month of August: 13 deactivations or cancellations
Month of September: 24 deactivations or cancellations

The number of Losses for the software release can then be calculated as follows:

Losses in July = 18
Losses in August = 13
Losses in September = 24
Total Losses at end of August = (18 + 13) = 31
Total Losses at end of September = (18 + 13 + 24) = 55

You can also evaluate the Average number of Losses:

Average Losses per month at end of August = (18 + 13) / 2 = 15.5
Average Losses per month at end of September = (18 + 13 + 24) / 3 = 18.3

Notes

The Losses metric is the counterbalance to the Wins metric. The lower the number of Losses, of course, the better. As with Wins, there are a variety of ways you might calculate Losses. Also as with Wins, however, the most important point is that you should define a formula to track Losses. Just as software teams should have a fundamental measure of success, you should also have a fundamental measure of failure. My belief is that the most straightforward and meaningful way to do this is by counting users lost.

The Losses formula that I use here, therefore, focuses specifically on user deactivations. As discussed earlier, this can be determined in a variety of ways, including account cancellation, software uninstall, or suspension of use.

Of course there are many factors that can result in the loss of users, much of which is beyond the control of a software development team. Pricing, competition, customer economics, and changing user needs are all examples. As far as possible, you might factor these into your analysis of Losses. For example, if there is a crisis in the national economy, you know that this might result in much higher Losses, so the higher Losses might not be a strong indicator of any "failures" of the software or the software development team.

Table 5-6 shows the Losses by month for three software products from one company. As with Wins, by themselves the raw number of Losses are difficult to analyze. Just knowing that Product 1 had 23 Losses in January doesn't tell you whether that number is good or bad. By comparing the monthly numbers and analyzing the trends, you can see if the Losses reveal cause for concern and how the numbers might correlate to changes or issues in the software.

Table 5-6. Three-month Loss analysis for three non-competitive software products

	Jan Losses	Feb Losses	Jan-Feb Trend	Mar Losses	Feb-Mar Trend
Product 1	23	22	down 5%	22	even
Product 2	28	24	down 17%	19	down 26%
Product 3	14	17	up 18%	25	up 32%

In addition to analyzing the Averages and Trends of Losses, it will be useful to put them in context with the off-setting number of Wins during each period.

If appropriate and you are able to gather the data indicating the deactivation or suspended use of individual features, Losses can also be measured for features as well as products.

Loss Rate

Purpose

Determine the average amount of time it takes to accumulate each loss.

Formula

Loss Rate = (Time Elapsed / Losses)

Example

A new software release is issued at the end of June. The following user deactivations or cancellations (Losses) are recorded for the three months following release:

Month of July: 18 deactivations or cancellations
Month of August: 13 deactivations or cancellations
Month of September: 24 deactivations or cancellations

Assume that you want to calculate Loss Rate in term of hours and minutes, which means that you want to determine how many days and hours on average between each Loss. The calculation can be performed as follows (results are rounded):

Loss Rate in July (month with 31 days) = 31 / 18 = 1 day 17 hours
Loss Rate in August (month with 31 days) = 31 / 13 = 2 days 9 hours
Loss Rate in September (month with 30 days) = 30 / 24 = 1 day 6 hours
Average Loss Rate (all months) = (31 + 31 + 30) / (18 + 13 + 24) = 1 day 16 hours

You can calculate different time increments with simple conversions:

Loss Rate of 18 hours = Loss Rate of .75 days

Notes

Loss Rate is the parallel metric for Win Rate, providing another way to measure and analyze Losses by calculating on average how long it takes to accumulate each Loss (user deactivation, cancellation, suspension of use, or the like). Loss Rate is equivalent to the "mean time between Losses."

As with Win Rate, I like the Loss Rate metric because I believe that people have a stronger appreciation for the time between each lost user than the number of lost users themselves. For example, discussing the fact that a software product is losing a user every 8 hours is more tangible for most people than saying that the product is losing 100 users every month. Using the time element also provides an interesting way to compare the results across releases and different software projects.

Depending on how frequently the software is accumulating Losses, it may make sense to calculate Loss Rate in terms of days or hours or minutes. For software that accumulates Losses very rapidly, you might even need to calculate Loss Rate in seconds. As with Win Rate, I suggest you should try to keep the Loss time values less than three digits and greater than one or switch to another time interval. For example, if you calculate Loss Rate as 118 hours (a value with three digits) I'd suggest it would be better to translate it to 4 days 22 hours, but if you calculate a Loss Rate as .8 days (a value less than one) it would be better to translate it to 19 hours 12 minutes.

Loss Rate is a "negative" metric, so the higher the Loss Rate, the better—that means that there are fewer overall Losses. Software with a Loss Rate of 18 hours is doing "better" than software with a Loss Rate of 12 hours. As with many other Response Metrics, however, the actual evaluation of whether results are "good" or "bad" must involve comparison to past history and goals (and maybe to competitors). Table 5-7 shows an example of tracking Loss Rate for the same products across the same three months as shown in Table 5-6. Note one interesting difference that highlights the usefulness of Loss Time. In Table 5-6, for Product 1 there are less Losses in February than in January, and when looking at the month-to-month trend, the result shows that in February, the Losses were down 5% from January. So that appears to be an improvement. When looking at Loss Rate, however, because February has three fewer days than January, the metric actually shows that in February the Loss Rate was actually one hour less than January—meaning that the product was accumulating Losses at a slightly faster rate, which is worse.

Table 5-7. Three-month Loss Rate analysis for three non-competitive software products

	Jan Loss Rate	Feb Loss Rate	Mar Loss Rate
Product 1	1 day 8 hrs	1 day 7 hrs	1 day 10 hrs
Product 2	1 day 3 hrs	1 day 4 hrs	1 day 15 hrs
Product 3	2 days 5 hrs	1 day 16 hrs	1 day 6 hrs

As with Wins, Win Rate, and Losses, you can also calculate Loss Rate for specific features if you are able to capture deactivation information for those features.

Penalties

Purpose

Measure the overall urgency of customer support issues.

Formula

Penalties = Sum (Urgency for each User Issue)

Example

During a two-week timeframe for one software release, the following user issues are reported to the customer support team either over the phone or through email, and are rated on a scale for urgency from 1 (least urgent) to 4 (most urgent):

Week 1: Issue 1 with Urgency 2
Week 1: Issue 2 with Urgency 3
Week 1: Issue 3 with Urgency 1
Week 1: Issue 4 with Urgency 1
Week 2: Issue 5 with Urgency 4
Week 2: Issue 6 with Urgency 2
Week 2: Issue 7 with Urgency 2
Week 2: Issue 8 with Urgency 3

To calculate Penalties, add the urgency for all reported user issues as follows:

Penalties during Week 1 = (2 + 3 + 1 + 1) = 7
Penalties during Week 2 = (4 + 2 + 2 + 3) = 11

The Total and Average Penalties can then be calculated simply:

Total Penalties for 2-week period = (7 + 11) = 18
Average Penalties per week = (7 + 11) / 2 = 9

Notes

When customers contact your support team with problems, it's a sign of some level of trouble that might result in negative user response. Among the Loss Metrics, therefore, I include the Penalties metric that measures these reported problems. This is similar to Penalties incurred by players in some sports such as football and soccer. Penalties don't necessarily result in losses—but accumulating *many* penalties could result in losses, and they may be an indicator of player mistakes that require more attention or a plan to improve.

Urgency is rated from the perspective of the user, and the more severe the urgency, the higher the weighting in this metric. You might wonder whether lower urgency issues should be counted at all, and you might be right. If, for example, your support team takes a call from a customer asking where they can find documentation or training, and that gets logged as an issue, should that be counted within Penalties? Or if a customer calls to ask questions about an invoice or a bill, should that be counted? Neither situation might have anything to do with the work done by the software team (although they might and it depends), so counting them as Penalties against the software team might seem wrong.

The easiest thing to do, of course, in terms of making the tracking and calculation simple, is to include all customer support issues without discrimination. This is the approach I usually take. My argument for this simplistic approach is that the percentage of issues related to assisting customers with simple things or with issues that are not really related to the results and contributions of the software development team will be fairly constant, and therefore you know that a certain percentage of Penalties are related to those sorts of things and are therefore OK. When these are included, you focus more on the trends than the raw number of Penalties. But if you are able to factor out specific types of customer issues, you may want to do that to increase the accuracy and value of the metric. You could filter out user issues by type, or you might choose to not include any user issues with the lowest urgency in the calculation. I believe this can work well either way.

Once you've decided how to calculate Penalties, it makes sense to track it in regular intervals following each release. Table 5-8 shows an example, tracking Penalties accrued in one month, three months, and six months following three subsequent software releases. In this case, the number of Penalties accrued is going down gradually across releases, a sign of improvement.

Table 5-8. Tracking Penalties across three subsequent software releases

	Penalties After 1 mo.	Penalties After 3 mos.	Penalties After 6 mos.	Avg. Penalties Per Month
Release 1	87	264	489	81.5
Release 2	78	258	457	76.2
Release 3	62	237	435	72.5

To more easily identify trends and make comparisons, consider laying the data out in charts. The bar charts in Figure 5-2 provide an alternate presentation of the data in Table 5-8 that makes the differences easy to see.

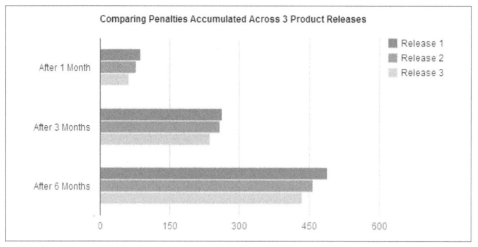

Figure 5-2. Chart comparing the Penalties accrued per month on each product release

If you are able to categorize user issues by product area, then you can also produce reports and analysis of Penalties by product area. Some user issues might be easy to categorize and others might not. Even in this case, it can be useful to understand the Penalties for each product area as far as possible. This will give you more insight into the patterns or issues that might exist related to the work done on specific features and the contributions of specific team members.

Penalties Per Win (PPW)

Purpose

> Measure the overall urgency of customer support issues relative to the number of new users.

Formula

> Penalties Per Win = Penalties / Wins

Example
During a two-week timeframe for one software release, the following user issues are reported to the customer support team either over the phone or through email, and are rated on a scale for urgency from 1 (least urgent) to 4 (most urgent):

Week 1: Issue 1 with Urgency 2
Week 1: Issue 2 with Urgency 3
Week 1: Issue 3 with Urgency 1

Week 1: Issue 4 with Urgency 1
Week 2: Issue 5 with Urgency 4
Week 2: Issue 6 with Urgency 2
Week 2: Issue 7 with Urgency 2
Week 2: Issue 8 with Urgency 3

During the same two-week period, the software release records the following new user activations:

Week 1: 18 new user activations
Week 2: 22 new user activations

You can calculate the PPW per week and overall as follows:

PPW during Week 1 = (2 + 3 + 1 + 1) / 18 = .4
PPW during Week 2 = (4 + 2 + 2 + 3) / 22 = .5

The Total PPW is not calculated by adding the weekly totals; instead it should be calculated across the entire period as follows (in this example it would be the same as taking the Average across the two weeks):

Total PPW = (2 + 3 + 1 + 1 + 4 + 2 + 2 + 3) / (18 + 22) = 18 / 40 = .45

Notes

Penalties Per Win is a normalized view of Penalties, since a software release that is accumulating users more quickly might also accumulate a proportional amount of user issues. If, for example, one software product adds one hundred users a month (100 Wins) and another adds ten (10 Wins), it would not be unexpected for the first product to have more calls into customer support, simply as a factor of the number of users. PPW provides a better way to compare results over time and across software projects, where the rate of user adoption differs.

The higher the PPW, the "worse" the results. A high PPW either indicates a large number of user issues, or a higher ratio of user issues with higher urgency, or both. Anything approaching 1.0 for PPW is probably cause for concern, in that it might indicate that you are generating more issues than new users, which is typically not a sustainable situation for most organizations. A higher PPW could well result in greater Losses, a lower Win Percentage, and the like. You should, however, be able to determine what is a "normal" and "acceptable" baseline for your software projects, and from there, the most useful analysis will be to observe changes and trends.

It can be useful to look at PPW along with other Win and Loss Metrics. For example, see Table 5-9, showing Win Rate, Loss Rate, and PPW for three software products, two releases each. While certainly there are many other factors to analyze, this snapshot of data indicates that releases with higher PPW are likely to have higher (slower) Win Rates and lower (faster) Loss Rates. In this case, Products 1 and 2 made progress from Release 1 to Release 2, but Product 3 actually regressed. The fact that PPW is significantly higher for Product 3 in Release 2 might indicate that the worse Win Rate and Loss Rate are directly tied to quality problems (as highlighted by the Penalties Per Win value) in the release.

Table 5-9. Analyzing key Win and Loss Metrics for multiple releases of three software products

	Win Rate	Loss Rate	PPW
Product 1, Release 1	2 hrs 32 mins	1 day 8 hrs	0.24
Product 1, Release 2	2 hrs 5 mins	2 day 13 hrs	0.18
Product 2, Release 1	6 hrs 8 mins	5 days 6 hrs	0.66
Product 2, Release 2	5 hrs 52 mins	4 days 12 hrs	0.43
Product 3, Release 1	2 days 7 hrs	12 days 1 hr	0.84
Product 3, Release 2	2 days 14 hrs	10 days 18 hrs	2.03

Momentum Metrics

The final group of Response Metrics are the Momentum Metrics, which identify the "momentum" indicated by user response or rankings versus competitors. The metrics in this section provide key summaries that can be used to rank results across releases and, in context, across projects. Comparing the values of the Momentum Metrics over time, you can summarize whether a software product is gaining or losing ground—and how quickly.

Gain

Purpose

Measure the number of Wins minus the missed opportunities and Losses.

Formula

Gain = Wins - ((Trials Completed – Successful Trials) + Losses)

Example

A new software release is issued at the end of June. The following new user activations are recorded for the three months following release:

Month of July: 225 new user activations
Month of August: 270 new user activations
Month of September: 350 new user activations

The Total Wins for the software release during this period can then be calculated as follows:

Wins in July = 225
Wins in August = 270
Wins in September = 350
Total Wins = (225 + 270 + 350) = 845

The following trial data is recorded for the three months following the product release:

Month of July: 81 Trials Complete, 67 Successful Trials
Month of August: 107 Trials Complete, 88 Successful Trials
Month of September: 142 Trials Complete, 119 Successful Trials

The Total number of Unsuccessful Trials during this period can then be calculated as follows:

Unsuccessful Trials in July = 81 − 67 = 14
Unsuccessful Trials in August = 107 − 88 = 29
Unsuccessful Trials in September = 142 − 119 = 23

The following user deactivations or cancellations are recorded for the three months following release:

Month of July: 18 deactivations or cancellations
Month of August: 13 deactivations or cancellations
Month of September: 24 deactivations or cancellations

The number of Total Losses for the software release during this period can then be calculated as follows:

Losses in July = 18
Losses in August = 13
Losses in September = 24
Total Losses = (18 + 13 + 24) = 55

Using the above data, the Gain per month can be calculated as:

Gain for July = 225 - (14 + 18) = 193
Gain for August = 270 / (29 + 13) = 228
Gain for September = 350 / (23 + 24) = 303

The Total Gain can then also be determined:

Total Gain = 193 + 228 + 303 = 724

Notes

Gain is a way to determine how well a software release is doing in gaining new users while taking into account how many users were lost and how many potential users were lost. Clearly, the higher the Gain, the better.

By taking into account the lost opportunities in unsuccessful trials, Gain is more than a calculation of "net users gained"—it can be thought of as the net of team wins versus losses, since a lost opportunity is in some sense as much a loss as a lost user. Including this is, of course, based on your ability to get data on the number of software trials that were unsuccessful. To ignore this data element, however, would be to ignore a potentially telling indicator of the improvements made by software teams in each software release.

For example, see the results in Table 5-10. Between Releases 1, 2, and 3, there is a significant improvement in the Gain in each release. Between Releases 1 and 2, the improvement is mainly due to the increased number of Avg. Wins, although it was also affected by the slight improvement in Avg. Unsuccessful Trials and reduced Losses. The even bigger jump in the Gain between Releases 2 and 3, however, was accomplished even though the Avg. Wins per month went down (slightly), because there was a large decrease in the number of unsuccessful trials. Gain puts weight into each of the key basic measures of success, namely attracting new users, converting interested users, and avoiding the loss of existing users.

Table 5-10. Analyzing the averages per month on key metrics across four software releases

	Avg. Wins	Avg. Unsuccessful Trials	Avg. Losses	Avg. Gain
Release 1	28	12	6	10
Release 2	36	11	4	21
Release 3	35	4	3	28
Release 4	38	5	3	30

As with many other Response Metrics, the Gain for any software release is dependent on many factors that are outside the control of the software development team. But also as with the other metrics, I believe you can factor those elements into your analysis and still get great value in looking at the results, watching the trends, and relating those to the metrics gathered for the software team in an attempt to better identify and understand the patterns of success.

Besides external factors such as marketing, competition, and sales execution, Gain will be affected by the maturity of a software product and the size and familiarity of its target users. A new software product will likely have a very different Gain than a well-established product, for example, and highly innovative software will have different results than software that competes in a well-defined space. As a means to compare across products and projects, therefore, Gain as well as other metrics must be understood in context of the specific software projects and goals.

See Table 5-11 for an example. In some cases, it can be as meaningful to look at the trends and percentage change of Gain over multiple releases as to look at the raw numbers, but even the trends will be relative to the specific software. In the example, Product 1 and Product 3 are showing positive trends, and Product 2 has what appears to be a decent Gain but is showing a negative overall trend. To analyze further, you need more context. If you know that Product 1 is very new and Product 3 is very mature, then that might explain why Product 1 is showing a much faster Gain progression. Whether a new product like Product 1 will ever achieve the Gain of another product like Product 3 will be highly dependent on the type of software and the market opportunity (as well as all the other usual external factors such as sales execution). In the end, Gain must be analyzed in context and how "good" or "bad" the specific values are is dependent on the context, the history, and the defined goals.

Table 5-11. Analyzing Gain and Trends across products requires context

	Gain	Gain Trend
Product 1, Release 2	330	+ 65%
Product 1, Release 3	500	+ 52%
Product 2, Release 2	480	- 7%
Product 2, Release 3	430	- 12%
Product 3, Release 2	710	+ 18%
Product 3, Release 3	820	+ 16%

All that said, if you are looking for one summary metric to analyze the overall success of a software release, and the trends over time, I believe Gain is probably the best. I would still recommend examining the individual Win and Loss metrics, which provide key details and can help reveal key patterns for specific software projects and product development teams, but Gain can be very useful as a summary both for analysis and for targeted improvement of software teams.

Gain Rate

Purpose

Determine the average amount of time it takes to accumulate each Gain.

Formula

Gain Rate = (Time Elapsed / Gain)

Example

A new software release is issued at the end of June. The following new user activations (Wins) are recorded for the three months following release:

Month of July: 225 new user activations
Month of August: 270 new user activations
Month of September: 350 new user activations

The following trial data is recorded for the three months following the product release:

Month of July: 81 Trials Complete, 67 Successful Trials
Month of August: 107 Trials Complete, 88 Successful Trials
Month of September: 142 Trials Complete, 119 Successful Trials

The Total number of Unsuccessful Trials during this period can then be calculated as follows:

Unsuccessful Trials in July = 81 – 67 = 14
Unsuccessful Trials in August = 107 – 88 = 29
Unsuccessful Trials in September = 142 – 119 = 23

The following user deactivations or cancellations (Losses) are recorded for the three months following release:

Month of July: 18 deactivations or cancellations
Month of August: 13 deactivations or cancellations
Month of September: 24 deactivations or cancellations

Using the above data, the Gain per month can be calculated as:

Gain for July = 225 - (14 + 18) = 193
Gain for August = 270 / (29 + 13) = 228
Gain for September = 350 / (23 + 24) = 303

From which the following are the Gain Rate calculations per month and the Average:

Gain Rate in July (month with 31 days) = (31 × 24) / 193 = 3 hours 51 minutes
Gain Rate in August (month with 31 days) = (31 × 24) / 228 = 3 hours 15 minutes
Gain Rate in September (month with 30 days) = (30 × 24) / 303 = 2 hours 22 minutes
Average Gain Rate (all months) = ((31 × 24) + (31 × 24) + (30 × 24)) / (193 + 228 + 303) = 3 hours 3 minutes

Notes

I call this metric Gain Rate because it represents how quickly the Gains are being accumulated. I think of this like the time difference between competitors in a bike, running, or horse race. Clearly, the longer the Gain Rate, the safer the "leader" is. In this case, the race is to gain more users and to lower the number of losses and failed trials. The lower the Gain Rate, the faster you are gaining and making progress. If the Gain Rate grows, then you are losing ground.

As with the other metrics in this chapter, comparing Gain Rate across projects and products is fraught with complexity and you must consider the context. But in tracking a single product or project over time, over many releases, Gain Rate is an effective metric to identify momentum and your rate of progress. See Table 5-12 for an example, looking at the Gain Rate over the course of five releases provides a quick summary of how the changes in Wins, Losses, and trial results are affecting overall results. In this case, the Gain Rate improved in every release except between Release 3 and Release 4. The Gain Rate improved partially because Wins increased, and even more because Losses and unsuccessful trials decreased. The Gain Rate got worse after Release 4 because the Losses went up, meaning that after the release, there were users deactivating more frequently. By looking at Gain Rate first, you can quickly identify which releases are following positive or negative patterns, and from there you can study the other metrics in more detail to gain greater understanding. Here, Gain Rate is a quick way to identify that Release 4 had unusually negative results, From there, you would clearly want to examine other metrics to try to determine the difference between Release 4 and the other releases.

Table 5-12. Gain Rate provides a useful summary of the changes in Wins, Losses, and trial results across multiple releases (all releases measured over 120 days)

	Wins	Unsuccessful Trials	Losses	Gain Rate	Change from Prior Release
Release 1	935	71	85	3 hours 42 minutes	---
Release 2	1,110	64	77	3 hours 0 minutes	- 42 minutes
Release 3	1,245	60	75	2 hours 36 minutes	- 24 minutes
Release 4	1,255	67	118	2 hours 42 minutes	+ 6 minutes
Release 5	1,295	62	71	2 hours 29 minutes	- 13 minutes

Acceleration

Purpose

Measure the ratio of user benefits delivered to urgent user issues created.

Formula

Acceleration = (Boost / Number of User Issues with the highest Urgency) × 100

Example

A new software release is issued at the end of June. In the three months following the release, the following data is gathered regarding user benefits contained in the release:

- Key transaction performance improvement, validated by embedded performance measurements, Population Benefited is 100%
- Key new reports, validated by usage data, Population Benefited is 75%
- Usability improvements in most used product area, validated by customer survey, Population Benefited is 100%
- New integration utility, validated by usage data, Population Benefited is 10%

The Boost for the release is calculated as follows:

Boost = (1.0 + .75 + 1.0 + .10) = 2.85

Also in the three months following the release, the customer support team records 22 User Issues with the highest customer Urgency rating of 4.

With this data, Acceleration during this timeframe can be calculated in this way:

Acceleration = (2.85 / 22) × 100 = 13

Notes

While Gain gives you a view of how a software release is doing in gaining more users, and Gain Rate gives you a view of the rate and momentum of growing the user base, the Acceleration metric gives you a summary of the gains made for existing users. I call this metric Acceleration because when the "boost" of user benefits exceeds the "drag" of severe issues, then the positive response of existing users is greatly "accelerated." If the drag exceeds the boost, then it is only marginally "accelerated."

One little interesting tweak in this formula is that I like to take the ratio of Boost to Urgent User Issues and then multiply by 100. Why by 100? You don't have to: clearly, it just moves the decimal point. My reason for using it is to adjust the result to reflect a percentage of the customer base, which while not exactly accurate, is a reasonably fair general approximation. My theory is that, in some sense, Boost is a metric that if multiplied by 100 would represent the percentage of customers receiving user benefits. So, for example, a Boost of 2.0 is roughly equivalent to saying that 200% of the user base received a Boost, meaning that every customer received an average boost of 2 key benefits. The formula for Acceleration also is based on the idea that every Urgent User Issue diminishes those key benefits proportionally. While with Boost I prefer to use the factor rather than the percentage (so 2.0 rather than 200), with Acceleration I prefer to use the larger "percentage" number. So that's why I multiply by 100. But this is partially a matter of taste and experience. You might choose to multiply by an even larger number.

Software that is "accelerating" quickly is software that has higher positive values of the Acceleration metric. This means that the software is delivering more key user benefits and having few urgent customer issues. Table 5-13 shows an example of Acceleration across a series of software releases. Unlike many other metrics, the trend of Acceleration is not as important as the measurement for a given timeframe or a specific software release. For example, in Table 5-13, the fact that Release 4 has a lower Acceleration than Release 3 doesn't mean that things got "worse" or that the software team failed in any way. Release 4 still has a positive Acceleration, and comparing this value with historical results and expected goals is more important in this case than trending the values from release to release. In fact, rather than looking at trends across releases, it could be more interesting to look cumulatively. For Releases 3 and 4 in Table 5-13, for example, the cumulative Acceleration is 149.

Table 5-13. Acceleration provides a summary analysis based on Boost (key benefits) weighted against Urgent User Issues

	Boost	Urgent User Issues	Acceleration (this Release)	Cumulative Acceleration (all Releases)
Release 1	8.5	18	47	47
Release 2	6.0	23	26	73
Release 3	16.75	16	105	178
Release 4	5.25	12	44	222
Release 5	21.0	13	162	384

You can have fun and call attention to the Acceleration metric and its meaning by charting the metric in creative ways and posting the charts on the wall or on an office big screen. Figure 5-3 shows an example using race cars. In this case, charting the cumulative Acceleration after each release illustrates to the software development team the positive progress.

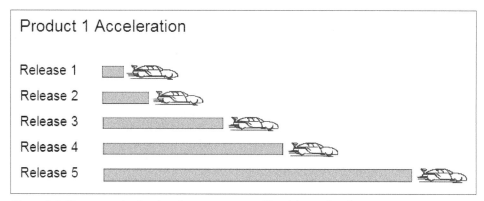

Figure 5-3. *You can make Acceleration more memorable with creative charts*

Win Ranking

Purpose

    Establish ranking versus key competitors based on number of new user activations.

Formula

    Win Ranking = Numeric position based on New Users vs. Competitors

Example

In the first three quarters of the year your software product records the following new user activations:

    Product 1 Quarter 1: 748 new user activations
    Product 1 Quarter 2: 861 new user activations
    Product 1 Quarter 3: 922 new user activations

During the same three quarters, you gather information about two key competitors and record the following estimated new user activations for each:

    Competitor 1 Quarter 1: estimated 500 new user activations
    Competitor 1 Quarter 2: estimated 750 new user activations
    Competitor 1 Quarter 3: estimated 1000 new user activations

    Competitor 2 Quarter 1: estimated 200 new user activations
    Competitor 2 Quarter 2: estimated 240 new user activations
    Competitor 2 Quarter 3: estimated 300 new user activations

Based on this, you can establish the following quarterly rankings:

    Quarter 1 Rankings: (1) Product 1; (2) Competitor 1; (3) Competitor 2
    Quarter 2 Rankings: (1) Product 1; (2) Competitor 1; (3) Competitor 2
    Quarter 3 Rankings: (1) Competitor 1; (2) Product 1; (3) Competitor 2

Specifically for Product 1, then, the Win Ranking by quarter is:

Win Ranking Quarter 1 = 1st
Win Ranking Quarter 2 = 1st
Win Ranking Quarter 3 = 2nd

Notes

This is a straightforward metric that simply involves measuring the new user activations (Wins) for a software product against those known or estimated for key competitors, thereby establishing a simple ranking. While there is not much to this metric, I include it because I think it is important and useful, as an overall measure of user response, to know where your software stands in relation to key competitors.

Obviously, if your software doesn't have any competitors, such as in the case of software developed for internal use, this metric will not apply.

Similar metrics could be developed for the total number of known users or for other Response Metrics, such as Losses. All of this requires that you are able to gather or estimate user activity for your key competitors, which was discussed more in previous chapters. The formula presented here for Win Ranking focuses on new user activations, under the theory that tracking how many new users are added in a given timeframe is most directly relevant to the recent work done by the software development team. Another potentially meaningful way to analyze the same data would be to look at the number of new user activations as a percentage of the total number of existing users.

Table 5-14 shows various numbers that might exist and that you can analyze. Personally, I believe the number of new user activations is the most relevant direct comparison and the best for competitive ranking, since percentage added is still highly dependent on the total size of the historical customer base. In Table 5-14, for example, if you were to rank by the percentage gain then Competitor 2 would rank first, although it added far fewer new users. If you were to rank by total users, then Competitor 1 would rank first, and that ranking wouldn't change for quite some time, even though Product 1 clearly outgained that competitor in the measured quarter. The most relevant value, therefore, for a ranking to measure recent user response is the number of new users.

Table 5-14. Comparing existing and new users for a product and key competitors during a specific quarter

	Total Users	New Users	% Added	Win Ranking
Product 1	8,500	800	9%	1
Competitor 1	24,500	500	2%	2
Competitor 2	2,500	300	12%	3

If you get data and metrics like this from other groups inside your organization like the product marketing team; or from outside groups like industry analysts, that's fine. The important point is to have at least one metric that shows you and your software development team how you rank versus competitors in attracting new users, to help you determine how the work your team is doing translates to user response.

Capability Ranking

Purpose

Establish ranking versus key competitors based on breadth and depth of software features.

Formula

Capability Ranking = Numeric position based on Features vs. Competitors

Example

After a new software release, assume that you compare your software product to those of two key competitors, rating each on 32 separate features with each feature rated on the following scale:

0: Does not have the feature
1: Minimal capabilities for the feature
2: Moderate capabilities for the feature
3: Maximum capabilities for the feature

The following are the ratings you come up with for the 32 features for each:

Product 1: 8 features rated 0 (no capability)
Product 1: 4 features rated 1 (minimal capability)
Product 1: 12 features rated 2 (moderate capability)
Product 1: 8 features rated 3 (maximum capability)

Competitor 1: 4 features rated 0 (no capability)
Competitor 1: 11 features rated 1 (minimal capability)
Competitor 1: 6 features rated 2 (moderate capability)
Competitor 1: 11 features rated 3 (maximum capability)

Competitor 2: 9 features rated 0 (no capability)
Competitor 2: 15 features rated 1 (minimal capability)
Competitor 2: 4 features rated 2 (moderate capability)
Competitor 2: 4 features rated 3 (maximum capability)

Based on this data, you can calculate the capability for the product and competitors as follows:

Product 1 Feature Capability = $(8 \times 0) + (4 \times 1) + (12 \times 2) + (8 \times 3) = 52$
Competitor 1 Feature Capability = $(4 \times 0) + (11 \times 1) + (6 \times 2) + (11 \times 3) = 56$
Competitor 2 Feature Capability = $(9 \times 0) + (15 \times 1) + (4 \times 2) + (4 \times 3) = 35$

From there, the Capability Rankings are determined simply:

Capability Rankings: (1) Competitor 1; (2) Product 1; (3) Competitor 2
Product 1 Capability Ranking = 2nd

Notes

If you have a mature product marketing team, it is likely you can get enough data for this metric from them. The above example just provides one way that features can be rated and compared. There are of course many others. You could simply count features, or you could rate features on many other scales.

While the data for this metric is somewhat different, I include this as one of the Response Metrics because any improvement that the software development team achieves in capability versus key competitors is likely to result in at least some positive user response. You need to look at this aspect of accomplishment as well as the more basic accomplishments such as Wins (new user activations), to get a complete picture of the success and progress of each software development team.

The Capability Ranking also provides insight that might indicate where other factors have diminished other metrics. For example, Table 5-15 shows summary metrics for four products. What's most telling in these values is that Product 3 ranks fourth among key competitors in terms of Wins, but ranks first in terms of Capability. While there would certainly be much to be learned from examining the other metrics for these products, the Win Ranking and the Capability Ranking, along with what appears to be a solid Gain, would tell you that the software team working on Product 3 has likely done a solid job, and the lower Win Ranking may be due to outside factors, such as less marketing, poorer sales execution, or other issues.

Table 5-15. Capability Ranking can provide a balanced view when success and improvement doesn't show in other metrics

	Gain	Win Ranking	Capability Ranking
Product 1	7.3	3	4
Product 2	10.25	1	2
Product 3	5.5	4	1
Product 4	4.9	2	3

Response Metric Scorecards

As with Skill Metrics, a simple way to track metrics is to create a spreadsheet where you enter the data elements and the metrics are then calculated. You might have separate spreadsheets for each product, perhaps summarizing results over chosen timeframes like by month or by quarter—or you might have one spreadsheet that tracks multiple projects over a given timeframe.

As mentioned in the previous chapter, I find Google Docs very suitable to the purpose of inputting the data, calculating the Response Metrics, dynamically creating charts, and sharing the results securely with members of the software development team. I typically keep a separate spreadsheet for each quarter (each three month period), and I track all the software projects in the single spreadsheet. Every project has a separate "scorecard," which is a separate sheet where the data for that project is entered. I summarize the data for user activations and deactivations in one part of the sheet, and separate areas are used for tracking data on the trials, the key benefits, and the user issues. Figure 5-4 shows a sample project response scorecard for three months, with the Response Metrics calculated at the top.

	A	B	C	D	E	F	G	H	I	J	K	L
1		Wins	Win Time (hours)	Win %	Boost	Losses	Loss Time (hours)	Penalties	PPW	Win Ratio	Lead Time (hours)	Acceleration
2		167	13	75	2.25	18	121	292	1.75	4.07	108	14
3												
4	Days Elapsed	User Activations	User Deactivations		Trials Completed	Successful Trials		Key Benefit	% Population Benefited		User Issues	Urgency
5	30	48	7		24	18		1	100		78	1
6	31	56	5		32	25		2	75		42	2
7	30	63	6		36	26		3	50		22	3
8											16	4

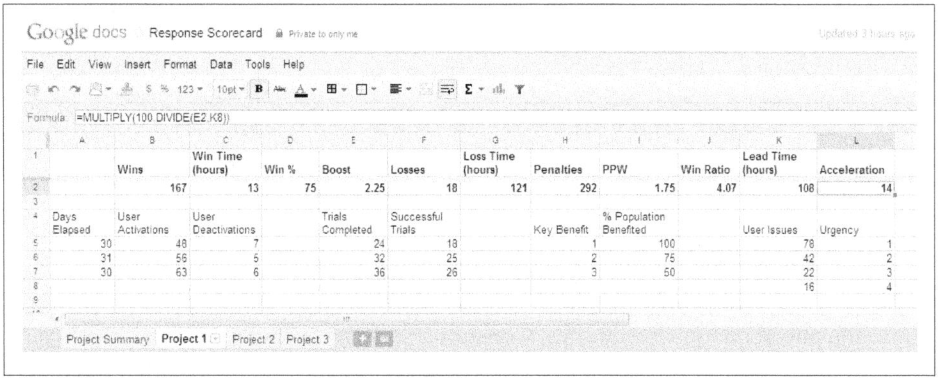

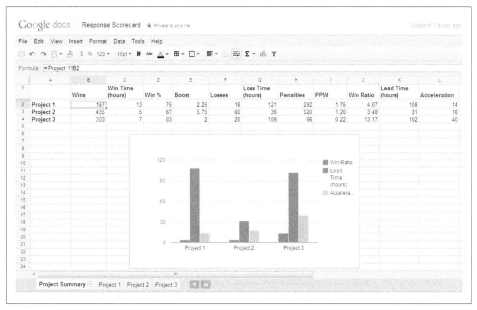

Figure 5-4. A sample Response Metrics spreadsheet for a project during a three-month period

The metrics for multiple projects can then be summarized on a single sheet, and key chosen metrics can be charted. Figure 5-5 shows how a sample project summary sheet might look.

	A	B	C	D	E	F	G	H	I	J	K	L
1		Wins	Win Time (hours)	Win %	Boost	Losses	Loss Time (hours)	Penalties	PPW	Win Ratio	Lead Time (hours)	Acceleration
2	Project 1	167	13	75	2.25	18	121	292	1.75	4.07	108	14
3	Project 2	435	5	67	5.75	60	36	520	1.20	3.48	31	16
4	Project 3	303	7	83	2	20	109	66	0.22	13.17	102	40

Figure 5-5. A sample project summary sheet from a Response Metrics spreadsheet includes summary metrics for each project and a chart of key Momentum Metrics

Observations on Project Types

As a wrap-up to this chapter, the following are some observations on which Response Metrics might deserve special focus for different types of software projects. Different project types will have different dynamics and expectations, such as the size of the target user base, the level of competition, and the amount and type of customer support that can be expected or tolerated. In general, any of the Response Metrics could be relevant and useful to help any type of software team gain insight and understanding of user response. But certain metrics may prove more significant according to the type of software you are working on and delivering.

Consumer Software

Consumer software is downloaded to consumer devices, either desktop, laptop, tablet, or mobile phone computing devices. Consumer software is targeted at individual buyers, although it can be for personal or business use. The software, like all others, may have a price or it may be free. Consumer software includes traditional packages such as local document editors, personal information management products, games, and all manner of applications in between—including those delivered today for smart phones. By definition, each version of the software is run by one user at a time, although the software might enable multiple users to communicate concurrently when running the software.

The following Response Metrics can be particularly useful for a software development team working on consumer software projects:

Wins

> The main goal for most consumer software is to gain new users, so monitoring the number of Wins is clearly important. The trend and average bear watching, and keeping the software development team aware of the cumulative Wins for any software release will help the team stay focused on the top-line goal.

Penalties

> Since consumer software typically targets a large audience, maintaining a manageable number of customer support issues, or reducing the number of customer support issues, can be critical to building a successful product and a successful business. Focusing on the values and trends of the Penalties metric will therefore be important for most consumer software products.

Capability Ranking

> The competition among many types of consumer software products will be driven by feature and capability comparisons, since there are usually only small price differences, especially in mature markets. Having a higher Capability Ranking can therefore be a leading indicator of positive user response, and raising the Capability Ranking can represent important progress and success for the software development team.

Enterprise Software

Enterprise software is designed for business use and is typically differentiated from consumer software in that it requires specialized enterprise-class servers or is designed to be run on a server and accessed by multiple users. This category refers specifically to on-premise or managed enterprise software, meaning that it is software that someone installs either locally or in a managed hosting environment.

The following Response Metrics can provide key insights for software teams working on enterprise software projects:

Win Percentage

> Many customers test an enterprise software package before committing to on-going use. Sometimes these are competitive trials, sometimes they are just demonstrations or trial periods for users to determine whether the software meets their needs. For enterprise software, therefore, success in trials is very important, and the Win Percentage of trials that convert to customers is one of the most important indicators of positive user response for a particular software release. Gauging the results of this metric is a good indicator to the team on the overall user response.

Penalties Per Win (PPW)

> Many enterprise software products do not achieve or target the same size user base as consumer products or cloud services. The business model for enterprise software is often based on a relatively smaller number of new customers, but a more sizable amount of revenue per user. In such a model, it is very important that the software does not require extensive customer support, and improvement in the amount of support required per customer is especially important because it improves the overall profitability per user. By focusing on PPW, the software team can gain a picture on how well the project is doing in this regard and can identify when the team's work yields progress.

Win Ranking

> Since enterprise software is typically targeted at a somewhat constrained population of total potential customers or users, every Win achieved is significant and the Win Ranking against competitors is both a snapshot of current position and a leading indicator of future success. Enterprise software users and buyers are often conservative in their choices, for obvious reasons, so they are as influenced by what others have bought as well as by other factors. If a software product was clearly a leader in the past, it stands a better chance of remaining a leader going forward. Tracking the Win Ranking is, therefore, especially important to the enterprise software development team.

Developer and IT Tools

Developer and IT Tools is a broad category in which I'm referring to software targeted at developers and IT professionals. Depending on the size, breadth, and complexity of the software, it might share many characteristics with consumer products or enterprise software products, and clearly some of the notable metrics discussed in those sections might also apply. I am focusing here on Developer and IT Tools delivered as packaged software, as opposed to those that might be delivered as cloud services.

Among the metrics in this chapter, the following may be particularly useful for software teams that deliver Developer and IT Tools:

Win Rate

> Developer and IT Tools, when successful, often grow their user base through word-of-mouth. While tracking just Wins will show gains, using Win Rate as a key metric will help the team see how the pace of adoption is increasing (or decreasing). Positive user response will most likely be demonstrated in improved Win Rate, although the improvements may show up gradually.

Losses

> As with all software projects, losing users is clearly something to be watched, especially if it can be directly correlated to changes made or problems introduced by the software development team. In the case of Developer and IT Tools, it will be especially helpful if you can track normal usage and gain insight when usage declines. While users may not have explicitly cancelled or sent some other clear indicator that they no longer intend to use the software, the fact that they are no longer actively using the product can be an early signal that the users are "lost." The users of Developer and IT Tools are technically adept, so they often migrate quickly to products that they find new and better, and clearly it is one of the goals of the software development team to protect against such Losses.

Boost

Due to the high potential for fast churn (users switching from your product to other "better" tools), it's especially important to keep introducing key improvements and benefits for existing users. Delivering such improvements will protect against Losses and increase positive user response that should also lead to more Wins and better Win Rate. The Boost metric can be an excellent focal point for the software development team to track how well it is doing in delivering key user benefits.

Cloud Services

An increasing number of software developers and development teams are now working on projects delivered as cloud services. This includes all kinds of applications, including entertainment, e-commerce, personal interest, and front- and back-office business systems. Some are offered free of charge, sometimes without any activation or registration at all, while some involve registration and subscription fees.

The following metrics are worth noting for teams working on cloud services and cloud applications:

Gain

Most cloud services are targeted at large audiences, and for many types of applications, there may be a great deal of turnover and volatility in the amount of usage. Gain is an excellent summary metric for high-volume, high-volatility applications, essentially measuring the number of new users to lost users and failed opportunities. Tracking this metric and the trend will help the software team track the top-line progress and determine how work done is translating to positive results.

Gain Rate

Again, since cloud services generally target a large number of users, the rate of gaining users versus losing users and failed opportunities is a very good measurement to determine success. The shorter the Gain Rate, the better the rate of growth. By following the Gain Rate, the software development team can better identify how well the application is progressing, including how well existing users are staying engaged and being retained.

Acceleration

Retaining existing users is an important factor for cloud services and cloud applications, where users often have low barriers to choose other options. Since many cloud services are offered at low or no fees, there are often few if any financial barriers to keep users from migrating away. Therefore, the software development team will often be called upon to continue delivering new and key benefits for existing users, while ensuring that there are not major problems impacting the users. Watching the Acceleration metric is an excellent way for the software team to keep its eye specifically on how well it is doing in moving the software forward for existing users.

CHAPTER 6

Value Metrics

I don't pay attention to measuring sticks until we get to the end.

—Bill Polian, NFL General Manager, 6-time NFL Executive of the Year

The final set of metrics described in this book are the Value Metrics. These rely on the metrics presented in the previous chapters. I call them Value Metrics because they are meant to help identify the specific type of value that each coder brings to the team. Using the Skill Metrics and the Response Metrics, this section defines measurements that highlight how the skills add up to specific strengths, and how you can measure coder contributions in terms of team achievements. In most cases, these metrics are mainly useful after software projects are done and the software is released—and in some cases, many months after release so that complete data is accumulated.

It's important to note upfront that there are many different types of Value that a coder can have for a team and an organization. One type of Value is not necessarily better than another. What's important is to begin to determine the mix of Skills and Values that you see on successful software development teams, to help you identify the complementary Skills and Values that might be added to teams for better results. The Value Metrics are meant to provide you a high-level view of individuals on a team, so that you can better assess the mix of skills and contributions and more easily identify the patterns of success or the key weaknesses on existing teams. Various examples of how metrics can be used in practice and analysis will be presented in the following chapters.

As with the information presented previously, I am trying to provide a useful set of metrics, but I am also trying to give categories and examples so that you might also develop your own metrics. There are *many* variations of metrics that could be devised like the ones in this chapter. What you find here can be useful and applied immediately, and will also teach you an approach that you can adjust to fit your situation.

Input Data

The input data for Value Metrics is the output of Skill Metrics and Response Metrics. Table 6-1 lists the specific metrics that are used for Value Metrics. For details on these metrics, including the data required for each and the formula to calculate them, please refer to the appropriate chapter and section.

Table 6-1. Input data for Value Metrics

Metric	Chapter	Description
Utility	Skill Metrics	Measures how many assigned tasks each coder completes
Power	Skill Metrics	Measures the average complexity of the tasks that a coder completes
Temperature	Skill Metrics	Measures how "hot" or "cold" a coder is at any given time
O-Impact	Skill Metrics	"Offensive Impact" that summarizes the contributions of a coder in moving projects along
Saves	Skill Metrics	Measures how often a coder helps fix urgent production issues
Tackles	Skill Metrics	Measures how many potential issues or opportunities a coder handles proactively
Range	Skill Metrics	Measures how many areas of software a coder works on
D-Impact	Skill Metrics	"Defensive Impact" that summarizes the contributions of a coder in helping to avoid large problems
Turnovers	Skill Metrics	Measures the magnitude of assigned tasks that a coder fails to complete
Errors	Skill Metrics	Measures the magnitude of production issues found related to areas that a coder is responsible for
Wins	Response Metrics	Measures the number of active users added
Losses	Response Metrics	Measures the number of active users lost
Acceleration	Response Metrics	Measures the ratio of user benefits delivered to urgent user issues created

Contribution Metrics

The Contribution Metrics define summary measurements that indicate to what degree coders are responsible for team results. Like any other summary, the downside of these metrics is that they might obscure meaningful details. The upside of summary metrics, on the other hand, is that they can help you spot patterns that might not be as apparent when looking at all the details.

Obviously, not everyone will have the same level of contribution. A successful team will have coders at many different levels (and an unsuccessful team will, too). I believe it's useful, however, for everyone to understand the level of contribution they've made, and how their own activity translates directly to team results. These metrics help show that. They don't tell you whether the team actually did well or poorly, but they do highlight the relative strengths of the team members.

Influence

Purpose

Measure the percentage of positive contributions by each coder relative to others on the team.

Formula

Influence = Individual (O-Impact + D-Impact) / Team (O-Impact + D-Impact)

Example

The individual coders on a software team have the following Offensive and Defensive Impact totals during work on a software release:

Coder A: O-Impact 20, D-Impact 10
Coder B: O-Impact 23, D-Impact 12
Coder C: O-Impact 22, D-Impact 0
Coder D: O-Impact 33, D-Impact 16

The sum total of the O-Impact and D-Impact for the team is then:

Team (O-Impact + D-Impact) = (20 + 23 + 22 + 33) + (10 + 12 + 0 + 16) = 136

The Influence for each individual coder can then be calculated as follows:

Influence Coder A = (20 + 10) / 136 = .22
Influence Coder B = (23 + 12) / 136 = .26
Influence Coder C = (22 + 0) / 136 = .16
Influence Coder D = (33 + 16) / 136 = .36

Notes

I call this the Influence metric because, by adding up Offensive and Defensive Impact, it summarizes the level of impact, or influence, that each individual coder has on the results achieved by the software team. The higher the number, the better.

The way the metric is calculated, the sum of all team member's Influence values will add up to 1.0. There's no inherent meaning in a particular Influence value, but they are meaningful in relative measurement to each other. In other words, if a coder has an Influence of .24, that alone doesn't tell you much, but it does mean that the coder has twice the Influence as another coder who has a value of .12.

You will see later that I use this as a factor to calculate further metrics, and ensuring that this value is less than one fits that usage. But another way to calculate this specific metric would be to multiply by 100 and refer to it as a percentage. In the example above, Coder A has an Influence of .22, but you could also multiply by 100 and say that Coder A has an Influence of 22%.

Influence can be calculated as a summary at the end of a project or software release, or it can be tracked at regular intervals during a project. You can calculate it after every development iteration or at the end of each month.

Another interesting way to look at Influence is to analyze how far each coder is above or below the mean average. For example, see Table 6-2. Highlighting the percentage above or below the average makes it easy to see which coders had the greatest Influence on the team's results, and how the coders compare to each other.

Table 6-2. To analyze Influence, you can compare individual values to the mean average

	Jan Influence	Jan +/- Avg.	Feb Influence	Feb +/- Avg.
Coder A	.21	- 12.5%	.25	0
Coder B	.24	- 4%	.28	+ 12%
Coder C	.19	- 24%	.16	- 36%
Coder D	.36	+ 44%	.31	+ 24%

An effective way to visualize Influence and other Value Metrics is with pie charts. See Figure 6-1 for an example.

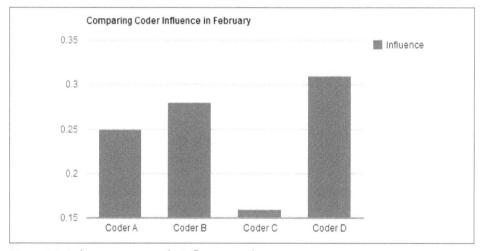

Figure 6-1. A chart comparing coder Influence in February

Again, Influence alone is not the sole indicator of value to a team. A coder with low Influence may still be valuable. They may be a junior member of the team, so they are not expected to have as much impact as a more senior member. Or they may provide other types of value to the team, such as helping others get items done, covering many areas, or handling hard problems. Some of these will be highlighted by metrics later in this chapter.

Efficiency

Purpose

Measure the percentage accuracy of each coder relative to others on the team.

Formula

$$\text{Efficiency} = 1.0 - (\text{Individual (Turnovers + Errors)} / \text{Team (Turnovers + Errors)})$$

Example

The individual coders on a software team have the following total Turnovers and Errors during work on a software release:

Coder A: Turnovers 22, Errors 71
Coder B: Turnovers 11, Errors 29
Coder C: Turnovers 7, Errors 70
Coder D: Turnovers 0, Errors 49

The sum total of the Turnovers and Errors for the team is then:

Team (Turnovers + Errors) = (22 + 11 + 7 + 0) + (71 + 29 + 70 + 49) = 259

The Efficiency for each individual coder can then be calculated as follows:

Efficiency Coder A = 1.0 - ((22 + 71) / 259) = .64
Efficiency Coder B = 1.0 - ((11 + 29) / 259) = .85
Efficiency Coder C = 1.0 - ((7 + 70) / 259) = .70
Efficiency Coder D = 1.0 - ((0 + 49) / 259) = .81

Notes

Like Influence, the Efficiency metric provides a relative ranking of how efficient each coder is in the work they've done, in the sense that the work they've done had less errors and fewer incomplete tasks. The formula calculates the fractional percentage of Errors plus Turnovers that each coder has relative to the team, then subtracts from 1.0 to represent the "positive" aspect, so that coders with higher values are the ones with greater efficiency. You could also have a slightly different metric, in which you did not subtract the calculation from 1.0, and you might call that metric something like "Inefficiency" or "Handicap." This would produce the exact opposite relative ranking, so coders with a higher Efficiency would have a lower Inefficiency / Handicap. Personally, when faced with choices like this on calculating a "positive" versus "negative" metric, I choose the positive. I think it's easier to talk with each other about how every person is doing in terms of Efficiency, as opposed to how they are doing in terms of Inefficiency. And, in the long term, I think people do better when they are focused on achieving the positive rather than avoiding the negative.

You will see below that Efficiency is used to calculate other metrics. Efficiency is designed to have a value below 1.0 so that it can serve as a weighting factor in calculating other metrics such as Win Shares and Loss Shares. If you subtract the value of Efficiency itself from 1.0, as is done in Loss Shares, you get a value that you might call "Inefficiency."

As with Influence, Efficiency can be useful as a total taken for an entire project or software release, or it can be measured at regular intervals during a project. The numbers by themselves are not meaningful, but they help you spot which coders are more efficient than others. A coder with a .80 Efficiency is more efficient than a coder with a .60 Efficiency, and is twice as efficient as a coder with a .40 Efficiency.

Since Efficiency produces a relative ranking, it can be helpful to establish another rating element when analyzing the raw values. For example, you could use percentile, or a simple ranking number for each coder's Efficiency. Personally, as with Influence, I like to measure how far each coder's Efficiency is above or below the mean average. This is a little trickier than with Influence, because in this case not all the coder Efficiency values will add up to 1.0—they will instead add up to Count(Coders) - 1.0. If you have four coders, their Efficiency values will add up to 3.0, and the average Efficiency would be .75. Either using that method, or just by calculating the average from your Efficiency values, you can determine the percentage that each coder's Efficiency deviates from the average. This becomes a quick way for you to assess relative strengths. See Table 6-3 for an example.

Table 6-3. To analyze Efficiency, you can compare individual values to the mean average

	Jan Efficiency	Jan +/- Avg.	Feb Efficiency	Feb +/- Avg.
Coder A	.65	- 13%	.68	- 9%
Coder B	.84	+ 13%	.86	+ 15%
Coder C	.62	- 17%	.70	- 7%
Coder D	.89	+ 19%	.76	+ 1%

While I call this metric Efficiency, it is a particular type of Efficiency. It is essentially showing you what percentage of a team's errors belong to each individual. More complicated metrics could take into account the ratio of work done (Points) to the number of errors, and possibly take into account other metrics, too. As a starting point, I believe simpler is better. I find it is very useful for coders to know how they compare with peers on fairly straightforward measurements such as this one. Not every coder will be expected to produce the same Efficiency. Based on experience and skill level, it is understood that there are bound to be differences—but every coder can strive for more Efficiency.

Advance Shares

Purpose

> Assign a relative level of credit to each coder for user advances.

Formula

> Advance Shares = Acceleration × Influence

Example

The individual coders on a software team have the following Influence for a software release:

> Coder A: Influence .22
> Coder B: Influence .26
> Coder C: Influence .16
> Coder D: Influence .36

Based on the measured Boost and the number of User Issues with the highest Urgency, the software release is calculated to have an Acceleration of 13.

The Advance Shares for each individual coder can then be calculated as follows:

Advance Shares Coder A = 13 × .22 = 2.9
Advance Shares Coder B = 13 × .26 = 3.4
Advance Shares Coder C = 13 × .16 = 2.1
Advance Shares Coder D = 13 × .36 = 4.7

Notes

"Share" measurements show how much each team member contributed, relative to the others. Based on each coder's relative contributions, they are given a number of "shares." You can think of it like shares of stock in a company. In this case, the shares are taken from the total value of the Acceleration metric for a software release, which represents the key advances delivered for existing customers. The amount of Acceleration is divided among coders based on their individual Influence. So this metric tells you the relative amount of existing user benefits that is attributable to each coder based on their overall influence on a release.

Granted, just because Coder A has a strong influence on a software release, it doesn't mean that the coder was directly responsible for the key user benefits. Coder B, who perhaps has a lower overall Influence, might actually be the one who did the work that resulted in greater benefits for existing users and, therefore, the higher Acceleration value. You could, if you wanted, come up with a different formula for Advance Shares that measures the direct impact coders had on the specific benefits delivered. However, personally, I think that software development is a team undertaking, and it is difficult to separate the direct and indirect impact each person has on the results. For example, while Coder B may have done the work on the feature that resulted in Acceleration, perhaps Coder A handled more complex tasks that were higher priority, thus allowing Coder B to work on the key benefits. Or perhaps Coder A worked on infrastructure that Coder B was able to leverage. These kind of indirect influences and impact are hard to track.

In the end, my philosophy is that individuals on the team should share equally in the positive and negative results, relative to their own related contributions and work results within the team. Put another way, that means that coders who make a greater amount of measurable positive contributions get more credit for the team's positive accomplishments, and coders who have a greater amount of negative issues take more responsibility for the team's negative outcomes. This is a philosophical standpoint, and if you don't agree with it, you could certainly adjust the metrics to reflect different values based on more direct involvement.

Advance Shares allows coders to see the Acceleration metric in a more personal way, and it allows them to see how their own Influence translated to advances for existing users. As you track Acceleration, you can track the Advance Shares for each coder. Table 6-4 shows an example. This approach helps coders see the value they've provided, and prompts them to consider whether they could make stronger individual contributions in the future.

Table 6-4. Advance Shares helps make Acceleration more personal and puts Influence into context

	Release 1 Influence	Release 1 Adv. Shares (Acceleration=47)	Release 2 Influence	Release 2 Adv. Shares (Acceleration=26)
Coder A	.22	10.4	.17	4.4
Coder B	.26	12.2	.31	8.1
Coder C	.16	7.5	.24	6.2
Coder D	.36	16.9	.28	7.3

The total number of Advance Shares, when added up for all coders, will equal the team's overall Acceleration value. As with other contribution metrics, however, for analytic purposes the main meaning comes from the relative comparison of one value to another, one coder to another. Looking at the average or cumulative Advance Shares over time might be informative, but the main use is to look at this number for each coder by release.

Win Shares

Purpose

> Assign a relative level of credit to each coder for new users.

Formula

> Win Shares = Wins × Influence × Efficiency

Example

The individual coders on a software team have the following Influence for a software release:

> Coder A: Influence .22, Efficiency .64
> Coder B: Influence .26, Efficiency .85
> Coder C: Influence .16, Efficiency .70
> Coder D: Influence .36, Efficiency .81

During the period measured, the software release accumulates 845 Wins.

The Win Shares for each individual coder can then be calculated as follows:

> Win Shares Coder A = 845 × .22 × .64 = 119.0
> Win Shares Coder B = 845 × .26 × .85 = 186.8
> Win Shares Coder C = 845 × .16 × .70 = 94.6
> Win Shares Coder D = 845 × .36 × .81 = 246.4

Notes

The Win Shares metric identifies a relative share for each coder based on the number of Wins accumulated for a software release and their individual Influence and Efficiency. Coders with a larger Influence and a higher Efficiency are attributed a higher number of Win Shares, and the number of Win Shares is exactly proportional to their Influence and Efficiency. Again, as with Advance Shares, this metric takes the perspective that direct and indirect influences should be taken into account when attributing the number of relative shares for each coder.

The usefulness of this metric is to make the number of Wins more personal and to put the Influence and Efficiency ratings in context of real results. Like all other Value Metrics, it provides a relative measure, in this case based on the combination of Influence and Efficiency, which is a powerful aggregate. Wins are a proxy for a specific type of team success, and Win Shares summarize the credit each coder deserves for Wins.

As Wins are accumulated and tracked at regular intervals, you could also calculate Win Shares. For example, it could be useful to evaluate coder Win Shares every month. The Influence for the software release for each coder will already be established, since it is based on the work done and the metrics tracked prior to the release. But the Efficiency for each coder may change as new production issues are found over time. Table 6-5 shows an example. Again, calculating and publishing Win Shares monthly makes the results more personal and highlights the effects of each person's contributions.

Table 6-5. Win Shares can be tracked at regular intervals to make the number of Wins more personal and to put Influence and Efficiency into context

	Influence at end of Release	Efficiency at end of Jan	Jan Win Shares (Wins=225)	Efficiency at end of Feb	Feb Win Shares (Wins=270)
Coder A	.22	.65	146.3	.68	183.6
Coder B	.26	.84	189.0	.86	232.0
Coder C	.16	.62	139.5	.70	189.0
Coder D	.36	.89	200.3	.76	205.2

You may also choose to calculate the average and cumulative Win Shares for each coder over multiple projects or releases. Given that the context of each project and release can be quite different, however, I think the main usefulness of this metric is to help coders appreciate the value of their individual contributions within a release, and to help you analyze the strengths and weaknesses of the team in a specific timeframe. Trending or totalling this metric over many releases over a long period of time, therefore, may not be extremely useful.

Loss Shares

Purpose

Assign a relative level of responsibility to each coder for lost users.

Formula

Loss Shares = Losses × (1.0 - Efficiency)

Example

The individual coders on a software team have the following Efficiency for a software release:

Coder A: Efficiency .64
Coder B: Efficiency .85
Coder C: Efficiency .70
Coder D: Efficiency .81

During the period measured, the software release has 55 Wins.

The Loss Shares for each individual coder can then be calculated as follows:

Loss Shares Coder A = 55 × (1.0 - .64) = 19.8
Loss Shares Coder B = 55 × (1.0 - .85) = 8.3
Loss Shares Coder C = 55 × (1.0 - .70) = 16.5
Loss Shares Coder D = 55 × (1.0 - .81) = 10.5

Notes

Loss Shares identifies a relative share of Losses attributed to each coder based on their Efficiency. Coders with a lower Efficiency, and therefore a higher inefficiency, are assigned a higher number of Loss Shares. The number of Loss Shares attributed to each coder is relative to their Efficiency. A coder with a .80 Efficiency will have exactly half the Loss Shares as a coder with a .40 Efficiency.

As with Advance Shares and Win Shares, this formula does not base Loss Shares on specific involvement or direct cause and effect. In most cases, you will not be able to pin the loss of a user to something specific done by individual coders. The philosophy of this metric is that the entire software team shares in the responsibility of each user loss, and coders who have produced a larger amount of issues or negatively affected the team's progress with a greater amount of inefficiency, therefore, deserve a higher responsibility for user losses.

This may not seem precise or exactly fair to some. A coder who is responsible for a particularly bad error might actually have greater responsibility for a specific set of Losses than other coders, and this metric won't identify that. But the goal of Loss Shares, as well as Advance Shares and Win Shares, is not to be exactly precise. The goal is to draw a reasonable parallel between a coder's contributions and activities and meaningful team outcomes and results. In this case the metric connects Efficiency to Losses. While it may not be exactly precise, at the very least it has the benefit of helping coders realize that their personal Efficiency is an important factor in avoiding Losses. It also makes the number of Losses more personal.

If you are tracking Losses at regular intervals, I suggest you also calculate Loss Shares at the same time. You might record and publish Loss Shares monthly or quarterly. The Efficiency for each coder will change as new production issues are found over time, so the proportional amount of Loss Shares may rise or fall as the Efficiency ratings change. Table 6-6 shows an example of Loss Shares calculated monthly.

Table 6-6. Loss Shares can be tracked at regular intervals to make the number of Losses more personal and to put individual Efficiency into context

	Efficiency at end of Jan	Jan Loss Shares (Losses=23)	Efficiency at end of Feb	Feb Loss Shares (Losses=18)
Coder A	.65	8.0	.68	5.8
Coder B	.84	3.7	.86	2.5
Coder C	.62	8.7	.70	5.7
Coder D	.89	2.5	.76	4.3

As with Win Shares, the Loss Shares metric is designed to be analyzed at a specific point in time, particularly to help coders correlate their personal contributions to team results. It is not clear that there is great value in trending, averaging, or summing a coder's Loss Shares over time, since this probably can be done more effectively using the underlying Skill Metrics for each coder.

Rating Metrics

The Rating Metrics listed in this section provide summary ratings for individual coders in important dimensions. These metrics can help you determine the specific types of value that each coder provides on the team, and when analyzed in context of results, these metrics can help you identify the overall strengths and weaknesses of the team. If you have a set of coders who rate strongly on a small set of Rating Metrics, and you do not have any coders who rate well on other Rating Metrics, then you may decide that you should strengthen the team in those areas, perhaps by increased focus, mentoring, or personnel changes.

It would be natural to have coders higher on some Rating Metrics and lower on others, and part of the purpose of these metrics is to categorize different types of strengths. This is done by summarizing specific Skills Metrics to create "composite" metrics. Many other Rating Metrics could be devised; these below are ones I have found particularly interesting or useful.

Teamwork

Purpose

> Establish a relative rating for team-oriented contributions.

Formula

> Teamwork = Assists + Saves + Range - Turnovers

Example

The individual coders on a software team are measured to have the following Skill Metric values for a software release:

> Coder A: Assists 62, Saves 7, Range 2, Turnovers 22
> Coder B: Assists 48, Saves 3, Range 6, Turnovers 11
> Coder C: Assists 91, Saves 0, Range 4, Turnovers 7
> Coder D: Assists 70, Saves 1, Range 3, Turnovers 0

The Teamwork metric for each coder can then be calculated as follows:

> Teamwork Coder A = 62 + 7 + 2 - 22 = 49
> Teamwork Coder B = 48 + 3 + 6 - 11 = 46
> Teamwork Coder C = 91 + 0 + 4 - 7 = 8
> Teamwork Coder D = 70 + 1 + 3 - 0 = 74

Notes

Summarizing the Skill Metrics that correlate with a variety of ways that coders help and support teammates, the Teamwork metric provides a relative value to identify coders who are strongest in this regard. Coders with a high Teamwork rating can be said to exhibit a higher level of teamwork in the kinds of contributions they make.

Having a low Teamwork rating does not mean a coder is a bad teammate, or even that the coder is lacking in teamwork in any way. That coder may have had other responsibilities that fall outside the elements this metric measures. A coder might take note if they have a lower Teamwork rating than others, but it doesn't necessarily mean they did anything wrong. In this sense, I suggest you look at this metric (and all other Rating Metrics) as especially useful for identifying coder strengths but not necessarily an accurate indicator of coder weaknesses.

The Teamwork formula adds three key "team-oriented" Skill Metrics which are Assists, Saves, and Range. Assists and Saves represent positive contributions that are specifically team-oriented, and having a greater Range is also assumed to represent a special value to the team. Then the formula subtracts Turnovers, because a Turnover is assumed to have a negative impact on the team. The higher the Teamwork number, the stronger a coder is in regard to the measured positives versus the negatives. The ranking of individual coders in this regard may be noteworthy, but the actual difference between the values is probably not significant. By nature of the formula and the underlying metrics, I don't think you can say that a coder who has a Teamwork rating of 80 is "twice as good in Teamwork" as a coder with a Teamwork rating of 40. All you can say in this case is that the first coder was particularly strong in Teamwork. Also, if coders are fairly close in Teamwork ratings, such as in the case where one coder is calculated as Teamwork 46 and one as Teamwork 49, it is not clear that there is any meaningful difference. In this case, you would likely just say that the two coders exhibited a similar or equivalent level of Teamwork.

Over time you may begin to notice specific patterns in this metric and the values in your organization. For example, you may begin to notice that coders who are strong in Teamwork have monthly values for this metric in the twenties, whereas for most coders the normal range is in the teens (or even less than ten). As you observe these trends and learn about the "baseline" (normal) values for each coder and each team, you may be able to gain further or faster insights from specific values.

Teamwork can be analyzed on a project by project basis, and it can also be usefully analyzed at regular intervals during a project. Determining the average over time, for individuals or for teams, can help you spot the normal baselines, and calculating the cumulative Teamwork over longer periods can help ensure that no single time period is weighted too heavily. Both techniques can be useful for identifying meaningful trends and for identifying the coders who are particularly strong in this regard. Table 6-7 shows an example measuring Teamwork over a period of time.

Table 6-7. Teamwork tracked for a software team over a series of months

	Month 1 Teamwork	Month 2 Teamwork	Month 3 Teamwork	Month 4 Teamwork	Total Teamwork	Avg. Teamwork
Coder A	8	4	12	9	33	8.25
Coder B	5	6	3	8	22	5.5
Coder C	14	10	11	13	48	12
Coder D	11	7	13	15	46	11.5
Total	38	27	39	45	149	--
Average	9.5	6.75	9.75	11.25	37.25	--

The Teamwork rating might be higher at specific times for the entire team or for portions of the team. It might rise and fall depending on the phases of a project or the type of development work being done. For example, during a design phase or a bug-fixing phase, it's possible that the number of Assists and Saves might rise and, therefore, Teamwork values might rise. Once again, looking at averages and totals can help identify overall shifts, and you can factor that into your analysis. Analyzing the data in charts, as shown in Figure 6-2, can be helpful to spot trends and distributions.

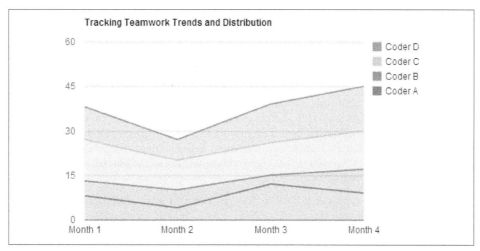

Figure 6-2. Charting the Teamwork totals over a series of months

Fielding

Purpose

Establish a relative rating for the range and breadth of work successfully handled.

Formula

Fielding = (Utility + Range) - (Turnovers + Errors)

Example

The individual coders on a software team are measured to have the following Skill Metric values for a software release, calculated through four months following the release:

> Coder A: Utility 114, Range 2, Turnovers 22, Errors 71
> Coder B: Utility 98, Range 6, Turnovers 11, Errors 29
> Coder C: Utility 132, Range 4, Turnovers 7, Errors 70
> Coder D: Utility 106, Range 3, Turnovers 0, Errors 49

The Fielding metric for each coder can then be calculated as follows:

> Fielding Coder A = (114 + 2) - (22 + 71) = 23
> Fielding Coder B = (98 + 6) - (11+ 29) = 64
> Fielding Coder C = (132 + 4) - (7 + 70) = 59
> Fielding Coder D = (106 + 3) - (0 + 49) = 60

Notes

The Fielding metric is so named for the idea of "fielding" from baseball, which refers to players on the field catching the ball. Conceptually this metric represents how much activity a "player" is involved in, and how proficient she is in handling the activity. In this case, the Utility and Range Skill Metrics are the indicators of how much "stuff" each coder handled, and that is offset by the number of Turnovers and Errors, which are the counter-indicative magnitude of mistakes made.

A coder with a high Fielding rating is someone who successfully handles a number of items while keeping the number of mistakes relatively low. As with other Rating Metrics, you need to be careful about drawing too many conclusions or in assuming anything is wrong for coders who have low Fielding ratings. These coders may have been assigned a smaller number of tasks, for example. A senior coder who successfully handles a small number of complex tasks still might end up with a low Fielding rating. This may only mean that Fielding is not that coder's area of "strength," or that he did not have a chance to demonstrate utility and range because of the concentrated workload. A coder with a high Fielding rating, on the other hand, is providing a certain kind of value to the team, although it doesn't mean that she is incapable of handling more complex tasks.

As with other Rating Metrics, it is hard to draw conclusions from or make sense of specific numeric values without previous context. What does a Fielding rating of 80 mean? Nothing by itself. But a coder with a Fielding rating of 80 is stronger and adding more value in this respect than a coder with a Fielding rating of 40. Small differences, plus or minus ten percent for example, are not really meaningful for this or other Rating Metrics, so you are looking for the larger differences and the coders with Fielding values that stand out.

Fielding is best examined on a project-by-project basis, since the number of Errors is best determined after a release has been issued and used for some time. You could calculate and analyze Fielding during a project, and one option would be to calculate the Fielding metric without including Errors. But I suggest using this metric by looking at Fielding a quarter or more after a project is released, and then looking at Fielding averages across multiple projects.

Table 6-8 shows an example calculating the Fielding ratings for a team of coders across three software releases. In this case, you can say that Coder D is strong and improving in Fielding, and Coder A is the weakest on the team. It can be useful to check such analysis versus your expectations for each coder, based on their experience and skills. Also, you would want to examine the success of each release to try to determine if the overall Fielding of the team correlates with the relative success of each release. In this example, Release 3 shows improved overall Fielding, so it would be interesting to know if Release 3 also showed improved results such as more Wins or fewer Losses.

Table 6-8. The Fielding metric tracked for a software team over a series of releases

	Release 1 Fielding	Release 2 Fielding	Release 3 Fielding	Avg. Fielding
Coder A	23	44	51	39.3
Coder B	64	61	57	60.6
Coder C	59	46	53	52.6
Coder D	60	73	82	71.6
Average	51.5	56.0	60.75	56.0

As with Teamwork and other Rating Metrics, the Fielding values may fluctuate with the type of work done during a release. For example, a maintenance release may result in higher Fielding ratings than a feature release. Examining the averages will help you identify the group trends, identify normal baselines, and make allowances in your analysis based on the type of work done.

The Fielding metric is designed, as are all Rating Metrics, to help you spot specific types of value that coders add to the team. This, in turn, helps you analyze the composition of teams. When you look at a team's success or failure, as measured by the various Response Metrics, you can determine whether a team with high-Fielding coders is one that is more likely to succeed.

Pop

Purpose

> Establish a relative rating for the amount of complex work, innovation, and initiative.

Formula

> Pop = Power + Tackles

Example

The individual coders on a software team are measured to have the following Skill Metric values for a software release:

> Coder A: Power 2.5, Tackles 2
> Coder B: Power 3.3, Tackles 4
> Coder C: Power 2.0, Tackles 3
> Coder D: Power 2.6, Tackles 3

The Pop metric for each coder can then be calculated as follows:

Pop Coder A = 2.5 + 2 = 4.5
Pop Coder B = 3.3 + 4 = 7.3
Pop Coder C = 2.0 + 3 = 5.3
Pop Coder D = 2.6 + 3 = 5.6

Notes

This metric is designed to help you identify the "big hitters" on the team, if there are any. I use the term "Pop" because it captures how much "burst" or "propulsion" a coder adds over time, like the "pop" of the ball off of a baseball hitter's bat when he hits a home run. Coders with a high value for Pop will have handled a significantly higher number of complex tasks or have provided more innovation and initiative—or both.

You may not have coders like this on the team. If complex work is shared equally and the amount of innovation is equally divided among coders, then many or most coders on a team will fall into a similar range. As with other Rating Metrics, coders with a Pop within ten or fifteen percent of each other are probably delivering similar value in this regard.

Having a high Pop rating is not necessarily "good" or "better" than the alternative. Coders who handle more complex tasks may just be meeting expectations, and coders handling less complex tasks are possibly just as important to the team. I find this an important metric to look at, however, because it illustrates the composition and approach of the team. Knowing whether you have coders who have significantly more Pop than other coders, then examining the results of the software team, you can begin to analyze the effect that such coders and such work distribution has on a team.

Pop can easily be measured at regular intervals during a project. However, in that case, you must take into account that some periods may be devoted to more complex tasks and will, therefore, result in a higher Pop rating. In some sense this may be "temporary" and misleading. Say, for example, all coders work on the more complex tasks at the beginning of a project. Then all the coders will have a high Pop rating in the beginning. But over the course of the project, as coders work on less complex tasks, the Pop ratings will adjust down. For this reason, I personally don't use Pop as a metric during a project—instead I just look at the underlying Power and Tackles. But I like to analyze Pop after a project is complete to see the final distribution of complexity, innovation, and initiative. I find it useful to analyze the final distribution for team chemistry and to see whether it matched my expectations going in. It is useful to look at Pop for individuals on the team, and also for the team as a whole.

Table 6-9 provides a sample analysis of Pop over multiple releases. Again, as with other Rating Metrics, overall values may fluctuate based on the work included in a release and the length of the development effort. These must be taken into account. Also, the raw numbers themselves are not meaningful—at least not until you have established enough history to identify patterns and changes. Relative to each other, however, coders with significantly higher or lower Pop are worth noting, not because they are good or bad, but because they are delivering different types of value to the team. In the example shown in Table 6-9, in Release 1 and Release 2 Coder B has significantly higher Pop than the other coders, and the overall average Pop is also somewhat higher. In Release 3, the Pop is much closer for all coders, but lower overall. It would be interesting to analyze whether this matched expectations and whether the results in Release 1 and Release 2 were noticeably different than those in Release 3.

Table 6-9. The Pop metric tracked for a software team over a series of releases

	Release 1 Pop	Release 2 Pop	Release 3 Pop	Avg. Pop
Coder A	4.5	4.1	4.2	4.3
Coder B	7.3	8.2	5.5	7.0
Coder C	5.3	4.8	5.6	5.2
Coder D	5.6	5.1	4.9	5.2
Average	5.7	5.6	5.0	5.4

The goal of these metrics is not to have you think that there are simple rules such as "a team with more Pop will be more successful." Instead, the purpose is to provide concepts and techniques that you can put to use in your own analysis, knowing that different people and different teams will work in different ways. These are methods you can use to help you analyze team performance and then, with this more detailed knowledge and insight, guide your teams to greater success.

Intensity

Purpose

Establish a relative rating for heightened productivity and dealing with demanding issues.

Formula

Intensity = Saves + Tackles + (Avg. Temperature - 72)

Example

The individual coders on a software team are measured to have the following Skill Metric values for a software release:

Coder A: Saves 7, Tackles 2, Avg. Temperature 79.6
Coder B: Saves 3, Tackles 4, Avg. Temperature 66.3
Coder C: Saves 0, Tackles 3, Avg. Temperature 84.8
Coder D: Saves 1, Tackles 3, Avg. Temperature 69.5

The Intensity metric for each coder can then be calculated as follows:

Intensity Coder A = 7 + 2 + (79.6 - 72) = 16.6
Intensity Coder B = 3 + 4 + (66.3 - 72) = 1.3
Intensity Coder C = 0 + 3 + (84.8 - 72) = 15.8
Intensity Coder D = 1 + 3 + (69.5 - 72) = 0.5

Notes

The Intensity metric is designed to help identify coders who provide high-energy value to a software team by handling pressure situations (Saves), dealing with problems proactively (Tackles), or by just finishing a lot of work (Avg. Temperature). I call this metric Intensity because all these accomplishments require a certain focus or intensity, and a coder who demonstrates significantly greater accomplishments in these areas is a coder with greater intensity.

The formula relies on determining the difference between the Average Temperature and the starting "base" temperature of 72. If you choose to use a different base temperature (which I call "room" temperature in the Skill Metric formula) then you would use that base temperature here. The idea in this metric is to determine how much a coder's average temperature is above or below the initial starting point.

A coder with a low Intensity rating is not necessarily doing a bad job. Not everyone on a team will have high Intensity. In fact, it may be that no one has significantly higher Intensity than anyone else. As with all Value Metrics, coders with different experience and skills are likely to have different ratings—that is natural and expected. What's significant is to see whether values match expectations, especially where values are significantly higher or lower than the norm. And it's significant to examine the overall composition of a team in order to analyze what levels of Intensity, or what percentage of coders with higher Intensity, lead to better results and greater success.

Similar to the Pop metric, the Intensity metric is one that you can calculate during a release, but it is one that I prefer to calculate at the end of a release. In the middle of a release, Intensity may fluctuate dramatically based on the current workload and assignments, so while a project is underway, I prefer to just look at the underlying metrics for Saves, Tackles, and Temperature. By the end of a release, the fluctuations will have evened out, at which time I like to analyze Intensity to see how it matches expectations, and as a key metric to correlate with team results. I also suggest that you analyze the average Intensity across releases, again as a key indicator that you can use to determine what factor Intensity might play in the results, positive or negative, for each software release.

Table 6-10. The Intensity metric tracked for a software team over a series of releases

	Release 1 Intensity	Release 2 Intensity	Release 3 Intensity	Avg. Intensity
Coder A	16.6	5.8	9.4	10.6
Coder B	1.3	13.4	3.0	5.9
Coder C	15.8	16.7	16.1	16.2
Coder D	0.5	4.6	0.8	2.0
Average	8.6	10.1	7.3	8.7

Table 6-10 shows an example tracking Intensity for a small team across three software releases. For many coders, such as Coder A and Coder B in this example, Intensity is likely to vary widely from release to release, partially based on assignments, but also based on the fact that this metric tends to highlight bursts of activity. For the example data shown in Table 6-10, you can note a few things. Coder C clearly has higher and more consistent Intensity than any of the other coders across the three releases, and Coder D clearly has lower Intensity. It would be interesting to see if this matches expectations based on their relative experience and skills. Also, the overall Intensity of all coders was measurably higher in Release 2. You would want to correlate these measurements with the actual results of the three releases, such as Wins or Losses or other Response Metrics, to determine if Intensity is a strong contributor to team success. You might also correlate the Intensity of individual coders with their other Value Metrics, such as Win Shares and Loss Shares, to see if Intensity might also be an important indicator of individual contribution to success.

As I've mentioned many times, you should be careful not to draw too many conclusions from a single set of data or from a single release. But as you gather more data over multiple releases, looking at this and other Value Metrics alongside the Response Metrics and supplemented by the Skill Metrics, you can begin to analyze and hopefully recognize the patterns of success.

Value Metric Scorecards

As with Skill Metrics and Response Metrics, a simple way to calculate and track Value Metrics is with a spreadsheet. A single master spreadsheet for each project could be used to track and calculate all your metrics, with the types of metrics on separate worksheets. As new data comes in, you enter it and the metrics are automatically updated. More elaborate systems, of course, could also be developed. You could design spreadsheets to pull data from files or a database, for example, or you could develop simple web applications to enter and calculate metrics using an integrated development system such as Ruby on Rails.

As mentioned before, I like to use the spreadsheet documents within Google Docs. I find that it excels in ease of use, has good charting, offers reliable storage and availability, and makes it easy to share with coders in multiple locations. Certainly other good hosted or local spreadsheet options are available. I call these metric spreadsheets "scorecards."

Figure 6-3 shows an example of a project scorecard that includes calculations for the Value Metrics. There is a worksheet for every coder, with their individual data and their Skill Metrics. Then there is a worksheet for the project with the data and the calculations for the Response Metrics. The Value Metrics worksheet shown in Figure 6-3 uses the values from the other worksheets, and then it also provides a set of charts that produce a type of "dashboard" for the key value provided by each coder on the project.

Observations on Team Stages

To conclude this chapter, the following are some observations on how specific Value Metrics might be particularly noteworthy for companies and software development teams in early, growth, or mature stages. While I believe all the Value Metrics are applicable across all the stages, based on my experience working in different stages of development these are just some thoughts about how particular coder qualities may be especially aligned with the key priorities at different stages.

Early Stage

Early stage applies to companies that are bootstrapped or investor funded, where the software development team is usually small and is tasked with creating new software. Early stage could also apply to a small development team inside a large or mature organization that is tasked with creating new software. Typically, the software would

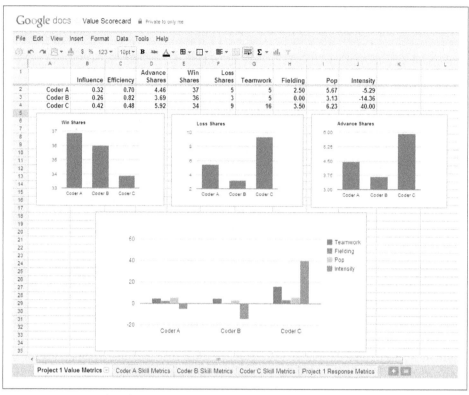

Figure 6-3. An example Value Metrics spreadsheet for one software project

still be considered "early stage" through its first year or two of development, although it is highly dependent on the type and complexity of the software and the size and experience of the team. The main goals of software development teams and organizations in the early stage are to create software that garners interest, attracts new users, and delivers new capabilities on what is usually an aggressive schedule.

The following Value Metrics are particularly relevant for early stage companies and teams:

Influence

> Small software development teams, in the early stage, usually rely on every coder making a strong contribution. If that is the philosophy on an early-stage team, you would want to make sure that there is not a big disparity in Influence. Having a large difference might indicate that the team is not as strong or balanced as desired. Many teams function very successfully with some coders who are far more influential than others, so a wide spread of Influence ratings does not necessarily mean there's a problem, but especially on early stage teams it bears watching.

Pop

Since the focus in the early stage of a software product or project is usually to deliver major new functionality and compelling features for users, there needs to be at least one coder on the team who consistently provides Pop. On many early-stage teams, you might actually expect more than half your coders to handle many complex tasks and to provide innovation, which would mean that more than half the team should have strong Pop ratings. In more mature organizations, teams might be highly successful and meet organization goals without much Pop at all. But in the early stage, it is probably mandatory.

Intensity

While we might hope that everyone works hard and with intensity all the time, on early-stage projects, it is often a requirement. The software development team is expected to meet schedules, sometimes very aggressive schedules, while still handling any side issues that might arise. While the Intensity metric may not be a perfect measure of how hard each coder is working, it is a good indicator, and on an early-stage team you would want to see positive values for Intensity, and probably you would not want to see a large discrepancy from one coder to another. Coders who are outliers on the low side, who have a much smaller Intensity rating, may be a cause for concern in an early-stage project.

Growth Stage

Once a company or software development team successfully passes through the early stage, they enter the growth stage. Initial releases of the software have been at least partially successful, an initial user base is established, and the user base is growing. Growth in some cases may be rapid, in some cases gradual, and this will often depend on the type of software, the marketplace, and the target users. But in most cases, the organizations and software development teams that have entered the growth stage have similar goals, such as continuing to attract new users while continuing to address the requirements of existing users, and continuing to work efficiently although also reducing risk. Things that might have been required or tolerated in the early stage, like taking dramatic chances with new functionality or putting up with talented but highly volatile members of the team, may no longer be advisable or tolerable.

For organizations and teams in the growth stage, these Value Metrics can be especially meaningful for the team and individuals to focus on:

Efficiency

> Once you have an existing and growing user base, you need to continue to deliver new capabilities, but you need to avoid quality regression and mistakes. Also, for most organizations in the growth stage, you are still operating under general financial constraints with limited resources, so there is not a lot of room for work that isn't accomplished in a timely manner, or work that is done badly and then needs to be redone. All this means that coders must be efficient and therefore, in the growth stage, you would seek to have most (if not all) coders on the team rate well for Efficiency. The main thing to look for, in this case, is that all or most of the coders are in a similar range. If one or a few coders have very low Efficiency, that would be a cause for concern that the team is not properly balanced, especially if the team is still somewhat small.

Win Shares

> In the growth stage, the number one goal is usually still obtaining new users. You can use Win Shares as a metric to make sure the coders stay focused on this fact and on their individual contributions to building further success. Not every coder will be as strong as the others in value and contribution of Win Shares, but highlighting this metric will prompt individuals to think about how they might improve or contribute more.

Teamwork

> As software products and teams become more mature, meaning they have been in existence longer and are experiencing growth, it typically becomes even more important for the software team members to help each other in order to sustain success. There is often just more to do, since an increased number of users translates to an increased need for support, and more opportunities drive more requirements or other activities in which the coders must pitch in. Assuming that the organization is still operating with limited resources, all of the extra work won't get done along with new software development unless there is good teamwork. If the teamwork is bad, some tasks will suffer or get missed, resulting in more stress in the workplace and possibly further deterioration from there. Bad teamwork in the growth stage can lead to coder dissatisfaction and departures. You can use the Teamwork metric to keep track of how the team and individuals are doing in this regard and to highlight to everyone the importance of these contributions at this particular stage. You would want to see at least a portion of the team exhibiting strong Teamwork, perhaps even only one person on small teams, but at least someone. If no one on the team is rating well for Teamwork, then that would likely be something that you need to address.

Mature Stage

Once a software company and software development team has passed through the early and growth stages, and acquired some level of success and consistency, it reaches the mature stage. At this point, priorities shift, and the amount of shift is dependent on the amount of success already achieved. For mature-stage projects, it can be as important to keep existing users happy as it is to attract new users. Taking large risks becomes unacceptable, and even small risks may be a problem. While efficiency, intensity, and innovation are always welcome and desirable, overall these may be de-emphasized in favor of quality, stability, and responding to existing user needs.

Among the Value Metrics, then, consider the following as particularly useful to software teams working on projects that have clearly entered a mature stage:

Advance Shares

> The larger the existing user base, the more important it becomes to keep that community happy. Delivering key benefits to users will keep them from moving on to other software and can increase profitability if users pay for new features of if the improvements help reduce support costs. Cultivating happy users, and especially many happy users, can also be a direct path to further growth through positive word-of-mouth. The Advance Shares metric can be useful to help coders identify their personal contributions to this important goal and to stay focused on the team's results. Not everyone will contribute equally, but even small contributions matter, and those whose contribution is less than might be expected may be motivated to improve upon seeing the Advance Shares rating and any discrepancies that may exist.

Loss Shares

> For successful software, avoiding the loss of existing users may be the number one goal. You want every coder on the team to identify personally with this goal, and to think about the value and contributions they make to avoid losses. The Loss Share metric highlights for everyone how individual issues may correlate to user attrition. Clearly coders with higher Loss Shares should be concerned and motivated to improve their ratings. In general, you would expect the least experienced or least skilled members of the team to have the highest Loss Shares. Junior coders with higher Loss Shares would not necessarily be cause for concern, but the metric can help make sure they realize why quality matters. Senior coders with higher Loss Shares, on the other hand, might be an indicator of some unexpected problems on the team.

Fielding

> A mature team, working on a mature software project, often has more areas to cover, more existing issues to address, and often has a longer list of less-glamorous items that must be addressed. For the reasons stated above, these tasks not only have to be completed, but they need to be completed well so

that they don't introduce other problems and negatively impact existing customers. The Fielding metric identifies coders who do a good job covering a variety of areas and tasks while maintaining a high level of quality. These types of coders are very useful to any team, but they are often a must on a mature team. Tracking this metric can help you make sure you have at least some strong Fielding coders on your mature team and can highlight to everyone the importance of these skills and the value these coders provide, since these are the types of contributions that often go overlooked.

PART III

Processes

This section presents recommendations for getting started with codermetrics and integrating them into existing processes.

CHAPTER 7

Metrics in Use

Essentially this has been a business that's been around for over a hundred years and it really hasn't changed much so any time someone's doing something differently, it's probably going to take some friction.

—Billy Beane, general manager of the Oakland Athletics, 1998–present

Software development has existed as a significant industry for less than fifty years. But that's more than long enough for organizational philosophies to take hold and become entrenched, especially given the size that the industry has grown to. Certainly, many practices have evolved and improved, and software itself has facilitated faster and wider communications that have increased the pace of its evolution. But within each organization, within every team, you develop a way of doing things, and once methods are established then change is hard. Why change, especially if things are already working well?

As I will try to explain in this chapter, I don't suggest you change what you're doing, I only suggest you incorporate metrics to inform your decisions and help you find gradual ways to improve your software teams. Metrics don't have to involve a change in process or methodology or management style. They can be woven into your existing practices with just a small amount of additional effort and time.

Not everyone, of course, will be receptive or even interested. Even for those who accept that codermetrics don't require radical change, they still might ask what the value is, and why bother? We are all too busy anyway. Codermetrics might seem like one more fancy idea for which you don't have time.

In this chapter, I will offer ideas for how to gradually introduce codermetrics in your teams, and how to integrate them into your development practices in a step-by-step approach. I will also try to explain the benefits you can expect to achieve along the way, and how you can verify those benefits to justify the (relatively small) time and effort involved. Like the metrics themselves, think of the ideas here more as templates, from which you can choose and adapt to your own situation.

Getting Started

Let's say you are interested in using codermetrics, but you have no experience and you are not sure how well they will be received or whether they will provide any benefit. You also aren't sure which metrics will work the best for you and your software development team. Or, alternatively, let's say you do have experience with codermetrics, but you have joined a new organization and you'd like to introduce metrics to the team. This section introduces a simple set of steps you can use to introduce and test metrics in either of these cases, and then can be used to expand the use of metrics over time.

Find a Sponsor

Like every project that might eventually expand to wider use in an organization, it is helpful if you identify a project sponsor, or multiple sponsors, up front. A sponsor is someone who has the authority to approve a codermetrics trial in your organization—and if that test is successful, the sponsor can then support or authorize wider use. Typically, an effective sponsor would be one of the more senior people in a software development organization.

You might be the project sponsor yourself—but if not, once you have identified a sponsor candidate you can discuss the ideas for codermetrics and the initial steps outlined in this chapter, including the plan for a focus group and an initial trial. The project sponsor may or may not actually be involved in the trial, but they should be included in the analysis after the test is conducted and will play a key role in any decisions and plans to move forward.

Create a Focus Group

As the next step, I suggest you decide who in your organization will initially be involved in choosing, gathering, and reviewing metrics. You can think of this as a focus group for the use of metrics in your team. The focus group performs a "trial" of using codermetrics, and, if the results of the focus group are positive, then you can expand the use of metrics to a larger team. If you are on a small team, or you don't think others have any interest, you could even start with a focus group of one, just yourself. If you are the leader on a small team, you might be the focus group and the project sponsor, too.

Likely candidates for a focus group are team managers or team leaders. You might also want to include one or more coders from the team. The best participants will be those who are experienced and respected by others on the team. The focus group needs to approach codermetrics with an open mind but with a critical eye. In the end, the focus group will help you decide if and how codermetrics might help within your software development organization, and if you do decide to expand metrics use beyond the focus group, then the members will become advocates to the rest of the team.

Even in a large organization, a good-sized focus group probably doesn't need more than five people. A small team is better able to communicate effectively, and a larger team might make the trial too complicated. In a very large organization, start with one focus group—then if that's successful, you can expand to multiple focus groups (and eventually, to the larger team).

Whether you are a single individual forming a "focus group of one" or you have more people involved, I suggest you publicize the experiment. You can let others know what the focus group is doing, even to the point of publishing the initial plan and the eventual findings for those who might be interested. I'm not saying you should make a big deal about this, which might raise more questions and unnecessary initial concerns, but you can just let everyone know that the focus group is going to examine whether tracking codermetrics could help improve your software teams and your software development process. There are two benefits to letting everyone know and keeping the process open. First, some of the people outside the focus group may have some useful insights or suggestions to offer during the initial trial. Second, it will lay the groundwork for discussions that will ensue if the focus group recommends expanding the use of metrics.

The members of the focus group will be the ones to choose the initial metrics and to pick the software teams or products that will be measured. The focus group then gathers the data, tracks the metrics, and reviews the results among themselves and with the project sponsors. Not everyone in the focus group has to do all these things. For example, you might have an initial meeting or series of meetings to discuss codermetrics and to choose the metrics you will start with. Then a subset of the focus group, maybe one or two members, might be responsible for gathering the data and publishing the metrics. At somewhat regular intervals, the focus group can reconvene to discuss the data gathered so far and to offer observations on the value and benefits of those metrics.

Choose Trial Metrics

Once the focus group is set, they should meet and choose metrics for the initial trial. As a first choice, I suggest you include metrics that are relevant and of interest to the entire team. These can be chosen from the Response Metrics presented in Chapter 5. It will be easiest to start your trial if the focus group chooses metrics for which the data is easily obtained. Three or four metrics are probably enough for an initial trial. Metrics to consider are:

- Wins
- Losses
- Win Rate
- Loss Rate
- Penalties
- Penalties Per Win (PPW)

The focus group should also choose a set of metrics that relate to the skills or contributions of individual coders. These can be chosen from the Skill Metrics presented in Chapter 4. Again, it will be easiest to choose metrics that don't require new processes to record and gather data. However, as long as someone in the focus group is willing and able to record the necessary data, then any metrics can be considered. A set of four or five of these metrics is probably sufficient to start. Likely candidates to choose are:

- Points
- Utility
- Saves
- Errors

I don't suggest that the focus group chooses any Value Metrics from Chapter 6 in an initial trial. These are more complex to analyze—and in most cases, more useful after the completion of a project. For an initial trial of codermetrics, it is better to choose metrics that can be useful in the middle of a development project. This will allow the focus group to review the metrics and discuss the potential value at regular intervals in the context of current work being done. Later in this chapter, I'll suggest steps to begin using Value Metrics.

In addition to identifying the trial metrics, the focus group must decide on the software team and a timeframe for the trial study. In an organization with just one software team, the first part of that decision is simple. In an organization with multiple software teams, a few criteria can be used to select a good candidate. First, it will be ideal if the focus group includes at least one coder from the studied software team, since he will help add credibility to the study and may offer unique firsthand observations and explanations as metrics are reviewed. Second, it will make the trial study most widely applicable if the studied team is considered "typical" for the organization, meaning that it is fairly similar to the "average" software team in the organization. This might mean that it is of average size, with coders who have a typical mix of skills and experience. Mainly, teams that are considered exceptional or different in any significant way are probably not the best for a trial study (although they certainly would be interesting to study and compare in more detail to others in the future). Using a "typical" team will help the focus group make a better recommendation about how potential usefulness of codermetrics found in the trial study may translate to other teams.

As far as timeframe for a trial, one month is too short and one year is probably too long. Three or four months is a good length for a codermetrics trial. If the studied software team operates in iterations of specific duration, it makes sense to define the timeframe as a specific number of iterations. For example, if the software team works in two-week Agile sprints, you might conduct the trial for eight iterations (sixteen weeks). Another very good approach would be to conduct the codermetrics trial for an entire project, which can work very well—especially if you have a project that will be about four or six months long. After the project is completed and the software released, you can extend the trial to gather data for Response Metrics.

First, it will be ideal if the focus group includes at least one coder from the studied software team.

Conduct a Trial and Review The Findings

You've found a project sponsor, set up a focus group, chose metrics, identified a software team to study, and specified a trial duration. At this point, you are ready to begin the trial.

The first step is to begin actually collecting the data and calculating the metrics. One or a few people in the focus group should be assigned to this task. This will be the hardest part of the process, and even if the metrics you are starting with are simple and the data mostly on-hand, this should not be trivialized. Chances are that some of the data will need cleaning, and the software team involved may need to be instructed to more accurately or more regularly enter data. If some data isn't available, then the assigned data gatherers will need to act as spotters or institute some other mechanism to gather the target data. You will need to define documents, such as the scorecards discussed in previous chapters, where the metrics will be stored for review. You may need to allocate as much as one to two person-weeks of time to make sure the metrics-gathering is established and decent enough "tools" are in place. In most cases, this reasonable time investment should yield reusable processes or capabilities if you choose to continue using metrics after the trial is complete.

Once the method for gathering and calculating metrics is established, you should circulate them regularly to everyone in the focus group. This might be weekly, biweekly, or monthly, either via email or published on a shared site to which the group has access. During the trial, the metrics shouldn't be sent to anyone outside the focus group. The whole point of the focus group is to learn about the process and evaluate the potential usefulness of codermetrics. It would be premature to share the metrics more widely.

You might store the metrics in one or more spreadsheets or using another simple document format. Spreadsheets will allow you to include charts which could be helpful to focus group members, so that they can more quickly analyze the metrics, make comparisons, and spot trends. Various chart types can be used. In general, you should select charts that provide a clear presentation. Examples are shown in Figures 7-1, 7-2, and 7-3.

The focus group should meet at least monthly to discuss the metrics. These meetings don't need to be very long, but everyone on the focus group should have a chance to offer their individual observations about what the metrics are showing and how the information might be new or useful. The kind of questions that might be discussed can include:

- Do the metrics reveal information that people previously didn't know or weren't sure about?
- Do the metrics corroborate or challenge existing assumptions?

- Could the metrics be used by team managers to improve their software teams? If so, how might this happen?
- Could the metrics be used by individual coders to improve their own contributions? If so, what might they learn and do?

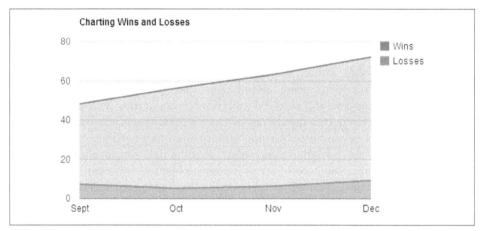

Figure 7-1. An example chart for Wins and Losses

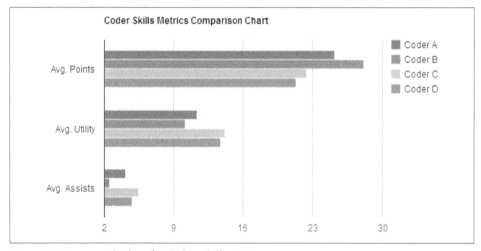

Figure 7-2. An example chart for Coders Skill Metrics

By the time the trial is complete, assuming the focus group has met multiple times in the process and discussed questions such as those above, chances are that the members of the focus group will have formed an opinion about codermetrics. You will have identified the potential benefits and the relative success or failure of the trial. At this point, the focus group should meet with the project sponsor(s), and the final findings should be discussed. Alternatively, these findings could be written into a report or

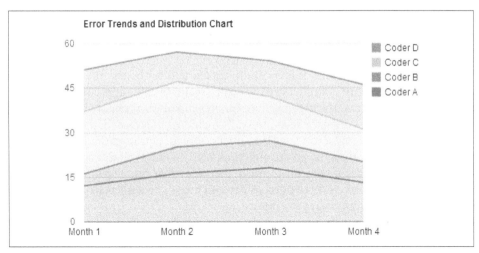

Figure 7-3. An example chart for coder Errors

presentation. In either case, the goal is to review the findings and focus group opinions with the project sponsor(s), and to make a decision on next steps.

There are three possible paths that the parties can decide to follow:

1. If the trial was deemed a success, then expand the use of codermetrics across the organization (further steps for this path are discussed below).

2. If the trial was only a partial success or was deemed inconclusive, then continue the current trial or start one or more new trials, possibly choosing new focus groups, different metrics, and different software teams to study.

3. If the trial was a failure, then conclude the trial and discontinue the exploration of codermetrics.

Whatever the outcome and the decision on next steps, the focus group should let everyone in the software development organization know about the final decision. If there was a written findings document or presentation, at this point it might make sense to also publish that document, if only for educational purposes.

Introduce Metrics to the Team

If you have completed a successful trial and decided to expand the use of codermetrics, the next step is to introduce the concepts and use of metrics throughout your software development organization. The amount of time and effort on this will be dependent on the size of your organization. You can use all or some combination of written documents, video presentations, and in-person meetings.

One or more members of the initial focus group should be involved in the introduction. Ideally, the trial project sponsor or sponsors will be involved, too. To start with, codermetrics should be introduced to the software team managers and team leaders.

Making "tools" such as metric scorecards available to team managers, and defining who and how on teams should be involved in gathering metrics, will make the process easier. All of this may have already been defined by the trial focus group.

Once the team managers and leaders are informed and on board, the concepts and plans can be shared with the coders on the team. Again, the best approach depends on the size of the teams and the organization, but in general it's probably best to discuss this in a meeting just among the team, possibly including members of the focus group. There is no reason to make too big a deal about adding metrics-gathering to existing processes. It can be thought about and presented as an evolutionary step, not a revolutionary step. It is important to make the point that metrics are not grades or judgments: they are just a way to bring clarity and focus to what has happened so that it will be easier to identify ways to improve.

The remaining sections in this chapter and the next will discuss various ways that codermetrics can be used. These don't need to be implemented all at once or quickly. Start slowly, gather metrics, share metrics with the team, and discuss the findings. Basically, turn each software team into a focus group of its own. Over time, as the benefits and possibilities become more apparent and as more data has been gathered, individual team members or team managers may decide to use codermetrics in other ways, such as to facilitate mentoring, to inform hiring, or as part of the performance review process. I'm not trying to discourage you from jumping in faster, but for most teams a gradual approach will work best, and even the strongest champions will benefit from progressively adding supporters along the way.

One question is whether codermetrics is something that should be "mandated" within an organization? Rather than something that needs to be mandated, you should think of codermetrics as a set of techniques and concepts that separate teams can implement differently, according to their own preferences and needs. It's fine and healthy if teams and leaders take different approaches, and some use metrics while others don't. This won't inhibit the potential usefulness to those who choose to use them.

Create a Metrics Storage System

As teams begin to gather codermetrics on their projects, I suggest you create a centrally accessible system where the metrics can be stored. I like Google Docs for this purpose, but other good options are Sharepoint, a Wiki, or simply a shared network drive. You can store scorecard templates in the central location, and teams can store their own revised versions or templates.

The analysis that an interested person can do with metrics is increased by the amount of metrics gathered and stored over time. Creating an online and central repository, even if the metrics are in separate documents, will allow someone to do this sort of analysis.

One question is whether you should allow everyone in the software development organization to see all the metrics. I'm in favor of this approach. I think there is more to be gained from everyone having open access to all metrics, even though that means all personal and team statistics are exposed. By seeing all metrics, people may gain a more objective view of themselves, their teams, and their peers. Also, by sharing, you may find that certain individuals take an interest and begin to point out interesting things that can be learned from the metrics, or other metrics that might be added for good purpose. The potential downside of publishing all metrics for everyone to see is that some people may be embarrassed or feel that the metrics incorrectly portray their contributions or accomplishments. While this could have a negative effect on morale, I would argue that if you are using codermetrics you want to identify issues like this anyway, and publishing the metrics will help make sure they come to light. In situations like this, perhaps the coder's concerns are unfounded and can be addressed with further education about the metrics. Or, if the concerns have merit, you will want to see whether the metrics are accurate or if better metrics can be used.

Expand the Metrics Used

After your teams get some experience gathering and reviewing codermetrics, you can begin to experiment with other metrics. Interest in additional metrics may already be spurred by observation from those in use, or by realizing that there are more questions that the team or individual members want to analyze.

Once you are have established procedures to gather data and you have a central storage system, it is easier to add metrics. As with the original metrics, you can try them out for a period of time and determine the benefits. You might follow the focus group approach, testing new metrics within one or a few teams, or teams may start trying new metrics themselves. If the results are good, you can continue and possibly expand the use, and if not, the new metrics can be abandoned or adapted further.

As you gather more Skill and Response Metrics and begin to build up a history of data in your central repository, it will be easy to try some of the Value Metrics. You may also begin to expand how and when you use metrics in your processes, perhaps following some of the suggestions later in this chapter. Expanded use in different areas, such as in performance reviews or mentoring, may naturally lead you to try new types of metrics.

Since different people may use metrics for different purposes, once you are gathering data and calculating a metric you may want to be cautious about discarding it. Just because one person (or even most people) don't find a certain metric useful doesn't mean that someone isn't finding that metric useful now or that it won't be useful in the future. Once you are gathering and storing codermetrics, there is usually little cost in keeping extra metrics around with the possibility that they might prove useful at some point. At the very least, before discarding a metric, you should canvas everyone and make sure that no one is unexpectedly using it.

Establish a Forum for Discourse

To facilitate use, education, and improvement of codermetrics, I suggest you establish an online forum, set up regular in-person meetings, or both. Some people prefer in-person meetings, while some prefer the "interaction on your own time" model that a Wiki or other discussion forum software will allow. Either way, the goal is to allow people to share observations, questions, ideas, and to generate the kind of peer-to-peer exchanges that might increase understanding, adoption, and benefits.

For in-person discussion groups, a good frequency might be every other month or once a quarter. It's good to keep such meetings casual, maybe even to have food involved. A pizza lunch gathering, for example, or an after-hours beer or ice cream bash. Having some food involved, of course, also spurs more attendance and often stimulates more participation.

These meetings should be open to whomever is interested. Everyone is invited, and attendance is optional. It is an open discussion group, with a model similar to a book club. It helps if someone acts as moderator, with a new volunteer moderating each meeting. It helps if you have a topic, too. Attendees at one meeting can nominate and decide on the topic for the next meeting. In some cases, you might ask for volunteers to spend extra time and come up with a short presentation on that topic for the next meeting, in order to kick off discussion. Example topics might be specific metrics, or a specific class of metrics, or tools to make metrics easier or more useful, or possible areas of new and untried metrics.

If you use an online forum, you might connect it to the in-person meetings by posting topics and questions or points raised in the meetings. The danger of using an online forum without in-person meetings is that it might result in a stagnant forum. However, it can work if you have devoted participants and communicators. If you choose to only have an online forum, you will want to make sure you have at least a few people in your organization who are regular contributors to help keep the forum active and spur others to get involved.

Timeout for an Example: The Seven Percent Rule

In the 1990s, when corporate downsizing was all the rage and watching the NYSE and NASDAQ stock markets became a regular pastime, many business publications mentioned the "seven percent rule." The gist of the "rule" was that a public corporation that announced large layoffs would see a quick seven percent jump in its stock price.

As James Surowiecki pointed out in a 2007 New Yorker article (*http://www.newyorker .com/talk/financial/2007/04/30/070430ta_talk_surowiecki*), the data over the last two decades doesn't support this rule. Downsizing doesn't always result in a stock price boost any more than downsizing always results in a better, more profitable business. In the end, as Surowiecki points out, the value that the employees create and the opportunities lost in layoffs sometimes outweigh the cost-cutting benefits of workforce reductions.

Whether you work in a for-profit or a not-for-profit software development organization, and whether your coders are paid or unpaid, it is always desirable to get more "value" from the existing coders. Adding new team members is great if you are able, but changing team members is usually costly. So we all look for ways to do better, both for our own satisfaction and for the success of our team and our organization.

I have a new "seven percent rule" for you to consider related to software development teams. This rule doesn't have anything to do with downsizing—instead, it has to do with increased productivity and results from existing workers. Like any other organizational "rule," of course, this is a generalization and individual results will vary. But my experience in various capacities with multiple teams leads me to believe this is true enough to put forth as a "rule." I also believe that this rule might extend beyond software development to other types of teams and organizations, but for that I have no data or proof, only a hypothesis.

Here is the rule:

> A software team that starts using codermetrics will see at least a seven percent jump in their core performance (productivity and precision).

This is a bold statement, I realize. However, it matches my experience with multiple teams in multiple organizations. Table 7-1 shows example improvement results for team members on four teams that I worked with. These measurements show the increased monthly productivity and precision within nine months after implementing the use of metrics within the team. This is based on introducing teams to core metrics such as Points, Turnovers, and Errors, and then reviewing them in regular team meetings. The Plus-Minus metric provides the overall summary to jointly rate productivity and precision, and it is where you look for that seven percent jump.

Table 7-1. Introducing metrics positively impacted a team's productivity and precision within nine months, as shown in the following example data taken from four teams

	Points Per Month % Increase	Turnovers Per Month % Reduce	Errors Per Month % Reduce	Plus-Minus Per Month % Increase
Team 1	9.2%	8.3%	22.1%	10.8%
Team 2	4.3%	12.2%	14.5%	7.1%
Team 3	7.3%	10.1%	16.3%	9.6%
Team 4	8.6%	7.7%	19.3%	11.5%

I have a theory why this happens. For most software teams today, it's not a regular part of the process for coders to review data on their productivity or precision. Yes, teams discuss tasks, bugs, and schedules; and yes, most teams set plans and review progress regularly. And yes, productivity and precision may be discussed in individual meetings or performance reviews. But the common process in most software teams today does not include a regular review of detailed data about what each coder has accomplished and where they made mistakes.

By gathering simple metrics on what coders have done and on the quality of their work—and by sharing them publicly and reviewing them regularly with the entire team—the coders get more focused on the items being measured. They don't necessarily get better at what they do, or improve their skills. But maybe they use their time more wisely, or give in to distractions less. They get more focused because they see the numbers, and they know others are seeing the numbers.

They get at least seven percent more focused. So the results get at least seven percent better.

Is it exactly seven percent? The exact number isn't the point. What I've found is that people get more focused on what is measured, and the increased focus itself will lead to a small but meaningful improvement. Seven percent is a fair estimate of the level of improvement you can expect from using metrics to measure core coder responsibilities, and my limited data is consistent with that. The other important note is that the improvement then becomes the new norm. Once the seven percent or greater gain is realized, it will at least be maintained as long as you continue using metrics.

Granted, this method is not scientific. There are many changing variables. Software gets more mature over time, and team members get more experienced. Teams may react and get more focused under a new manager. Many other factors might also come into play. However, my experience in seeing the reaction of coders to the use of metrics, and the consistency of the positive results, makes me believe that there is a true cause-and-effect between metrics and results.

This is not a benefit I originally sought or expected in using metrics. My main interest in metrics has always been helping teams identify and appreciate all the contributions and skills that are important for success—and providing me, as a manager, more information and ability to improve teams. The increased productivity and precision that seems to come from just gathering and showing metrics was an unanticipated benefit, although it's certainly a nice one.

As others begin to try codermetrics, I look forward to feedback on whether the seven percent rule holds true.

Utilizing Metrics in the Development Process

If you have successfully moved beyond the trial stage of codermetrics, there are many ways you can make further use of metrics in your software development process. This section covers some of the other ways you can use metrics.

Team Meetings

The most obvious place to start regularly using metrics is in team meetings. This is different than the idea of a "metrics discussion group" presented previously. What I suggest here is that you should incorporate the review of metrics into your already scheduled regular team meetings. In these meetings, you should review the key metrics you are gathering for each team, including Skill, Response, and Value Metrics, choosing the data appropriate to the meeting (as discussed in more detail below).

You may, of course, focus more attention and time on the metrics that you believe matter the most. Reviewing key metrics in team meetings can help drive positive behavior and reinforce a desired "culture," to the extent that elements you desire are included in your metrics. Repeatedly measuring, sharing, and discussing key metrics is more likely to result in behavioral and systemic changes than, for example, having an executive simply declare that certain behaviors should change.

I don't recommend that you review metrics with the team on a daily basis. If you are using Agile methodology and your teams conduct daily stand-ups, for example, it won't make sense to discuss or review metrics in those meetings. Review of metrics is more appropriate on a weekly, biweekly, or monthly basis.

What works well is to include the review of individual coder's metrics (Skill Metrics) in each team's regularly scheduled review and planning meetings, then to include the review of all the project success and user response metrics (Response Metrics) in a regularly scheduled organization or department meeting that includes all teams. The team meetings that include the individual coder metrics might be more frequent than the organizational meetings that include the project metrics.

If, for example, you follow an Agile methodology and you have sprint review and planning meetings for each team every two weeks or every month, I'd suggest that part of the review should include each team's gathered metrics. If you are keeping a scorecard for each sprint, then you can present a summary from this document. You can create a dashboard to highlight the core metrics that you want coders to focus on. See Figure 7-4 for an example. Simply present the scorecard to the team and leave it open for discussion on any points that stand out. You also might review how the current scorecard compares to those in the past by presenting trends and averages. If team performance has dipped noticeably in one or more areas, those would be worth highlighting in the meeting.

One concern you might have is that showing everyone the metrics for each coder could cause embarrassment or an unproductive sense of competition between teammates. Actually, some embarrassment (when warranted) might be healthy, and some sense of competition can be positive if it leads to more productivity or focus—and if it's not taken too far. To avoid unnecessary embarrassment or fostering an overly competitive environment, you mainly should avoid offering praise or blame when reviewing metrics. The metrics are simply another record of what happened, no different than reviewing tasks completed in a sprint review. There may be more details, but they should

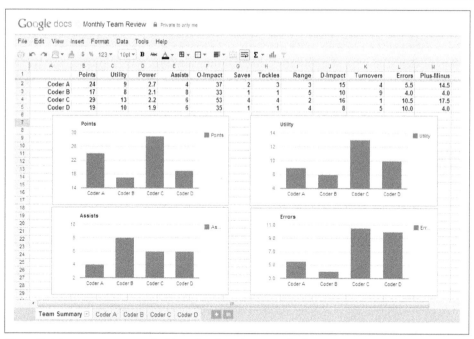

Figure 7-4. Present a summary dashboard such as this example showing codermetrics for the current project in each team meeting

be seen as "just the facts" about recent work. Citing coders for great performance or discussing where they had problems should be handled no differently than you did in past team meetings. At first, when metrics are new, it may seem unusual and coders may be a bit sensitive or feel exposed. But after a few meetings, if these are presented efficiently and objectively, this should be no more upsetting than reviewing tasks completed, open tasks, and open bug counts.

If you have monthly or quarterly department meetings, that is a good time to review the project-by-project Response Metrics. In this case, if you are keeping scorecards for each project, I'd suggest you go through them one by one, again leaving it open for discussion and observation, and again presenting comparative information for each project to that project's history using trends or averages. Where metrics are trending particularly well or poorly, those should be highlighted. In order to keep the meetings interesting and the focus fresh, you might find an interesting story that the metrics reveal and spend a few minutes presenting that in each meeting.

Provided you are keeping metrics in scorecards or other fairly simple and centrally stored documents, the amount of time to gather the metrics and put them in a presentable form for each of these meetings should be manageable. The most time should go into deciding if there are particular trends that should be highlighted, or finding an interesting story to tell. If it does take too much time and effort, you should revisit how you are gathering and storing the metrics and try to come up with improvements to make this process easier.

Including metrics in team meetings gives team members real information about what they've done, what their peers have done, and how well the team's work is being received. This data can help the team in many ways, but it's likely that sharing this information will spur discussion. Some of the discussion may involve insights on how the team might improve or feedback on how the metrics themselves might be improved. You may need to lengthen the team meetings by half an hour and the department meetings by as much as an hour to include discussion time for the metrics. The benefits here, such as increased awareness and focus and reinforcing positive behaviors, should outweigh the extra meeting time required.

Project Post-Mortems

A good time to review metrics is in project post-mortems—the meetings that occur after a project is complete, to review what worked (and what didn't) during the project and what might be improved in the future. Codermetrics, in fact, can help make such meetings more effective and factual, as opposed to relying strictly on everyone's memory and subjective analysis of events. Personal observations and opinions are certainly still valuable and should be discussed and addressed, but having a historical record of metrics provides an alternate set of information to review, and in some cases a clearer set of information.

If you are keeping a record of metrics, you can assign someone to put together a "project metrics summary" document and presentation. This is probably best done by whomever is the "lead" metrics gatherer or analyzer on the team. You will need to do some preparation to pull the data together into a suitable presentation for a project review meeting, and it will take some time. As with the team meetings discussed in the previous section, your goal here should be mostly to present the data so that the team can review, discuss, and possibly identify follow-up actions. In general, it's better to avoid presenting any conclusions or opinions from the metrics gathered. While the conclusions you've already drawn may be correct, presenting them might limit others from finding or offering other conclusions that also might be correct and useful.

The presentation might be a slideshow or similarly formatted document, and it can include all Skill, Response, and Value Metrics you are using and for which you have data at the time (you may only have early Response Metrics if the post-mortem is conducted soon after the software is released). You might present monthly breakdowns and then project totals and averages, showing the metrics for each individual as well as summarized values for the team. If you have gathered metrics for previous projects, then you might also show some comparison between the project and those that came before. Rather than just presenting the numbers, you can also use charts to highlight trends and comparisons, as shown in Figures 7-5 and 7-6.

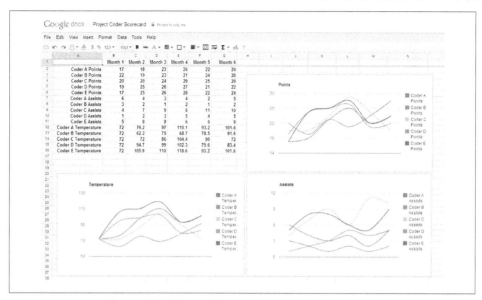

Figure 7-5. An example using line charts to highlight trends in a project review

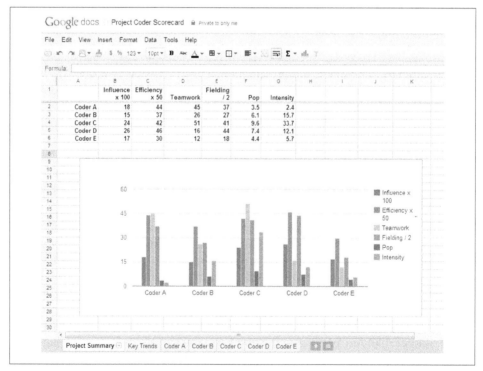

Figure 7-6. An example using bar charts to highlight coder comparisons in a project review

Reviewing metrics at the end of a project is also a good time to see if particular management or process changes were effective. For example, if you made changes in your development methodology, or if you introduced new incentives or techniques to increase productivity, you can review the metrics to see how well those changes worked. While these topics may be of particular interest to team leaders and managers, in most cases it would be beneficial to include the analysis of such changes as part of the post-mortem meeting, so that the entire team can review them. In the case where the metrics reflect that the changes had the intended results, the entire team will be able to appreciate that—and if the metrics reflect otherwise, the entire team will understand why further changes may be required.

If you start using codermetrics and you don't already conduct project post-mortems, then I highly recommend you start (if you prefer to call them "project reviews," that's totally understood; the oft-used "post-mortem" is definitely a morbid term). In general, reviews at the end of a project are a great chance for teams to learn, reflect, internalize, and identify opportunities for improvement. Adding metrics to this formula can make it even more powerful and effective. And going through the process of putting together a metrics project summary document gives you an excellent record of each project, which can be useful for managers and team leaders in comparing projects and teams and identifying patterns in the future.

Mentoring

Another useful application of metrics is in building or improving a mentoring program in your software development organization. If you already have a mentoring program, or you think you might benefit from one, codermetrics give you a new way to identify those who could benefit from mentoring and those who might be good mentors.

For example, if you notice that a junior coder has trouble finishing tasks as indicated by a high rate of Turnovers, then you might find a coder who has traditionally had a low rate of Turnovers to act as mentor. Or if a junior coder is exhibiting lower productivity (lower Points) or delivering software with lower quality (higher Errors) then you can find coders who are strong in these areas, as demonstrated by their metrics, to serve as mentor.

Alternatively, if you think that the team needs more strength in certain areas you could assign coders who have exhibited those strengths to mentor others. For example, if you have coders who measure strongly in helping others (Assists), handling many areas (Range), or demonstrating innovation or initiative (Tackles), then you could ask them to mentor one or more other coders on the team to try to build more strength in these areas.

Not everyone who is good at something is also good at teaching that to others. Some people are good mentors, some are not. Perhaps you have a fluid mentoring program, where coders themselves identify needs and opportunities for mentoring and pair up based on their own evaluation. Or maybe you have someone, such as a team leader or manager, who assigns or suggests mentor relationships. In either case, metrics can help you identify the people who, from a skills perspective, might be good to mentor others. From there, you will naturally choose those people who seem to have the personal and communication skills to be good mentors.

But metrics can help after the fact, too. By assigning mentors based on prior measured results, you are also establishing an implied criteria for "successful mentoring." The sign of success, in these cases, would be that a coder who is mentored shows improvement in the specific target metrics. If a coder is being mentored to improve coding accuracy, for example, then the coder's Errors should go down. If a coder is being mentored to improve productivity, then Points or Utility should go up. This analysis can be applied to those being mentored and to the mentors, too. As you accumulate more examples, you can identify the mentors who actually produce better or worse results, which may lead to more successful assignment and mentoring in the future. This ability to define goals and measure results is another reason why metrics can be highly valuable in the mentoring process.

Establishing Team Goals and Rewards

In a later section I will discuss using metrics to set individual performance goals. However, in this section I'd like to discuss the idea of using metrics to establish team goals and to determine team rewards. If you are using codermetrics, this is a very effective method you can take advantage of to accelerate team improvement and meet specific goals.

Often in software development, team goals and rewards are based on key project milestones. Meeting specific dates and delivering specific functionality are measurable items, and when dates are met or exceeded, that is often cause for celebration. Software teams have release ship parties or other events. Sometimes there are bonuses or gifts given to team members for meeting these goals, especially if an unusual and demanding amount of effort was required.

These kinds of goals and rewards are valuable, and I am not suggesting you remove or replace them. But if you are regularly gathering and tracking codermetrics, then you have an opportunity to set other types of team goals and to reward the team for important accomplishments, rather than just meeting project dates.

Any measured item—any metric—can become the focus for a team goal and, if warranted, a team reward. Clearly any decision on rewards rests with someone who has authority such as a manager, director, or executive. If that person is not you, but you are an advocate of or participant in codermetrics in your organization, then you might suggest this idea to someone with authority. But setting team goals is something that the team could decide by itself. Part of the advantage of reviewing metrics in regular team meetings is that team members can identify for themselves where they as individuals might need to improve, and where the team can improve. Whether or not rewards will be involved, you might identify specific areas to target for improvement.

The idea is simple. Pick a metric that represents an area where you want the team to focus on improvement, and then set a goal. For example, you might choose a quality-related metric like Errors or Penalties, or a teamwork metric like Assists. If you pick Skill Metrics such as these, which are measured for individual coders on the team, then you would look at the total or the average for the team. Or you might choose a project success metric like Wins, Win Rate, Win Percentage, or Boost. Or you might choose a competitive ranking metric, such as Win Ranking or Capability Ranking.

First, you will need to track the metric for a period of time to establish the team's current level. Next, you will need to determine the target amount of improvement and the target timeframe. The duration may be bounded or it might be open-ended. You might say that the goal is for the team to improve a certain amount in six months, for example. Or you might say that the goal is for the team to improve a certain amount, no matter how long it takes. You also might tie the duration to the timeline for a specific project, in which case the goal would be to improve a certain amount over the course of the project.

How much improvement you should target is something you may determine based on experience, or what you think is achievable. I like using a percentage of the current "normal" level as a target. For example, you might say that the target is a ten percent improvement in Wins, or a twenty percent increase in Boost. Or you might target a fifteen percent reduction in Errors or Penalties, or twenty-five percent more Assists. Ranking metrics can also be very good for team goals. The goal might be to move from second to first in Win Ranking or Capability Ranking.

Like other team goals and rewards, the key is to set the goal, specify the duration (if there is one), and then recognize the achievement (or lack thereof). To recognize an achievement, you could do the same as with project milestones, namely have a party or an event (which is perfect if the team was setting its own goals), or give out rewards. The goal and the level of difficulty in achieving the goal, along with the history of rewards in your organization, will determine what is appropriate. And if specific individuals were especially instrumental in meeting the team goal, then it is appropriate to recognize their special contributions in some manner as well.

The advantage of codermetrics is that once you have established a consistent practice of gathering and sharing the metrics, you are in a much better position to set team goals based on these metrics. The goal becomes clear and the team can then be properly focused. You can set team goals and rewards based on a variety of things, and you can "prove" that the team has met those goals. This is much better than nebulous statements about wanting to improve in areas that are not tracked or measured. Such statements don't often amount to much.

The old management adage that "you can't improve what you don't measure" is often true, although I might say it's actually "you won't improve what you don't measure." Putting a positive spin on it, you could say that "what you measure, you can improve." Codermetrics not only gives you more information about where your team is at, but it gives you a set of tools to improve. One such tool is the ability to set a wider variety of specific goals and deliver appropriate rewards.

Timeout for an Example: The Turn-Around

One difficult challenge for any software development team is to turn things around when they are not going well. I am not talking about ill-conceived or competitively challenged software products, or software products that have simply not found their audience yet. I am also not talking about software development teams that are doing good work but that want to do better. What I am talking about here are specific situations where a software team is clearly struggling to meet goals, work well together, produce high-quality software, and meet its own or outsider expectations. These are the situations that need a real turn-around.

Those of us who have worked in the field for awhile know that sometimes software teams are judged unfairly. Expectations may be unreasonable, or faults of others (such as poor prioritizing) might be blamed on the software team. But in other cases there are legitimate situations where software teams are producing poor software, low quality software, or badly missing reasonable project dates. When a team is struggling, sometimes the members themselves don't realize there is a problem, though sometimes they do.

Having worked in software development for nearly 30 years now, I have seen this situation a few times, and as a manager I've had to address situations like this more than once. I have come to the conclusion that codermetrics can be particularly valuable when you are trying to turn around a software development team.

The circumstance I'll discuss here was at a start-up that already had a product with initial success. The management team, however, was concerned because the software was difficult to use, required extensive hand-holding to get started, and had many major and minor product issues. Since the initial releases, the software team had gotten bogged down in dealing with support issues and it was consistently having to decide between working on important new features and fixing product issues. The management team believed the situation was getting worse and morale on the software team was going downhill. It also wasn't clear whether the members of the software team had an answer. The core team and the leaders had been with the company since inception. They had done a great job delivering an initial product, but they also did not have much experience in dealing with these kinds of issues.

In this case, the software team realized it was struggling, but the team members didn't know what to do. Also, while the team saw itself as struggling, they didn't realize that the management team were concerned that they were failing. In other words, the team members themselves didn't realize how potentially severe the issues were for the business.

On the plus side, the software team had good people with a good mix of skills and experience, everyone had a desire to work hard, and the people generally got along well together. So there wasn't the need to lay anyone off or make other drastic changes to the existing team. But that also meant that the problems were more subtle.

In situations like this, it will help if you can get the software team to see the problems more clearly so that they will be more open to the changes that may be required. It isn't necessary to have metrics from the past for this, but you can begin measuring specific elements and sharing metrics with the team to help focus on problem areas. With this particular team, the following three metrics were particularly applicable and could be measured immediately by taking data from the most recent software release:

Win Percentage
> To show how often prospects who demoed the software were transitioning to customers

Penalties Per Win
> To show the load of customer support issues relative to the number of new customers

Acceleration
> To show the amount of new capabilities delivered weighted by the amount of customer support issues

In this case, as you might expect, the Win Percentage was low, the Acceleration was extremely low (basically zero), and the Penalties Per Win was high. In some sense, the software team already had a sense of these issues. The benefit of metrics is to bring focus to the problem and to help the team establish specific target goals to improve the results.

Once the problematic results were more clearly defined and understood, the next step was to examine the dynamics of how the team was working and the individual contributions that each person was making. The purpose here was not to identify specific coders who were causing all the problems. As I already mentioned, there was no indication that problems were caused by just one or a few people. The goal was to objectively analyze the situation in more detail, which would make it easier to find a solution. While a manager might see or guess the cause of problems without data, there is a benefit in gathering data so that everyone on the team can see the issues as well. This way, the entire team can participate in the analysis and in figuring out a solution. Making the entire team part of the process helps improve team morale and keeps key people engaged during a turn-around.

To analyze the situation, the following four metrics were particularly relevant and meaningful:

Points
> To show how much development or bug fixing work each team member was doing

Range
> To show how many areas each coder was touching

Errors
> To show how many production issues were related back to each coder

Saves
> To show which coders were fixing the more severe production issues

The data for the team over three months (before there were any changes) is summarized in Table 7-2. This data shows some interesting things. First, the Points metric shows that the two most senior coders on the team had consistently low totals. These coders had taken on management and coordination tasks and were spending so much time communicating with customers and support that their coding time had been reduced to about twenty percent. Second, the Range metric shows that everyone on the small team was touching just about every significant system area at least once a month. Everyone was spending some time on a variety of system services and data services, and most coders were also touching the interface services. Third, the Errors metric shows that the production issues were weighted more to the coders who had worked on the user interface. Fourth, and final, the Saves metric shows that the junior coders were fixing a lot of the severe production issues.

Table 7-2. Metrics taken for a start-up software team that was struggling to meet expectations

	Points Per Month	Range Per Month	Errors Per Month	Saves Per Month
Sr. Coder 1	18	4	8	1
Sr. Coder 2	22	5	7	1
UI Coder 1	61	4	34	2
UI Coder 2	49	6	28	0
Jr. Coder 1	55	6	15	3
Jr. Coder 2	53	6	18	2
Jr. Coder 3	46	6	12	2
Average	43	5	17	2

So here we had a team that was struggling to make progress, bogged down with issues, with software that was deemed hard to use. The most senior people on the team were not spending a lot of time coding, and to a certain extent, everyone else was working on everything. The metrics, however, identified where the opportunities existed to re-align and improve, and where the team needed the most help. The metrics not only provided the information to define a potential solution but also the data to explain the reasoning to others on the team. And having the metrics collection underway made it possible to check whether the changes actually had the intended effect after they were implemented. This example shows how codermetrics can help identify the problems and give you the ability to set goals and measure the results.

An analysis of the situation, backed by the metrics, would be as follows:

- The team was far less productive overall than it might have been, because the two most senior coders were spending a large amount of their time doing things other than coding new features or fixing production issues.

- The team was slower and more error-prone than it might have been, because too many people (especially the more junior people) were touching too many areas and working on critical problems.

- The team clearly had a problem with the user interface, both in number of errors and usability.

The team, which I managed, discussed and agreed on this analysis. From there, the solution was clear. First, we unburdened the senior coders so they could spend almost all their time coding, and we asked them to fix a higher percentage of the severe pro-duction issues. I took on the coordination and communication tasks myself and in certain cases we actually asked more junior team members to handle the first investi-gations on customer support issues. Second, we reduced the areas worked on by most of the team, both in fixing production issues and in developing new functionality. This meant that, in certain areas, production issues were fixed or new functionality was added more slowly, but we reached an agreement with the rest of the business that this was best, given that it allowed us to improve our overall speed and quality of output. Third, we hired a great user interface coder to join the team.

With one new hire and no departures, within nine months we turned the team around. The results are shown in Table 7-3, Table 7-4, and Figure 7-7. The product began progressing again at a strong start-up pace, and the team was perceived once again by the management team as over- rather than underachieving. Team morale was high. It really was a great team all along, and the team might have found ways to improve its performance and results in another way, but improved focus and better analysis of the existing dynamics led to better results. Measuring results and measuring activities can be particularly useful in any situation where you need to rapidly improve the perform-ance of an existing team.

Table 7-3. Metrics for the start-up software team after reducing areas of responsibility and adding one new coder

	Points Per Month	Range Per Month	Errors Per Month	Saves Per Month
Sr. Coder 1	74	4	6	4
Sr. Coder 2	65	4	5	3
UI Coder 1	59	2	12	1
UI Coder 2	52	3	10	0
UI Coder 3	72	2	14	2
Jr. Coder 1	55	2	8	0
Jr. Coder 2	53	2	9	0
Jr. Coder 3	51	2	6	0
Average	60	3	9	1

Table 7-4. Metrics showing the improvement in results comparing a release before team changes to a release after team changes

	Win Percentage	Penalties Per Win	Acceleration
Release prior to changes	15%	41	0.5
Release after changes	63%	8	13
Improvement	4X	5X	26X

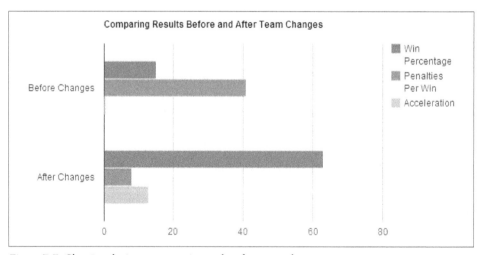

Figure 7-7. Charting the improvement in results after team changes

Using Metrics in Performance Reviews

If you begin to use codermetrics in your software development organization, and if they are appreciated by a large group especially team leaders, managers, directors, or executives, then it is inevitable that you will begin to wonder how to use metrics in performance reviews. As mentioned in earlier chapters, this is an area that should be approached carefully. You do not want the metrics to be seen strictly as grades. If coders believe they are getting graded on specific metrics, they will focus on those areas to the potential detriment of other areas, which will limit the use of a wider group of metrics for mentoring, goal setting, or regular project and team reviews.

In this section, I suggest ways that managers can use metrics to more clearly analyze the contributions, strengths, and areas for improvement for each coder. Then I recommend ways that metrics can be incorporated into the performance review process to increase fairness, enhance communications, and help coders better focus on areas to improve.

Choosing Appropriate Metrics

For each coder, the first step is to decide which metrics you want to include as part of a performance review. Some of the metrics you may review to see what they tell you about the coder's skills and contributions or to check whether they support your analysis of the coder's performance. Other metrics you may want to cite specifically because they identify areas where the coder's skills and contributions are particularly strong and therefore deserve praise, or where the coder's skills and contributions are weak and therefore need work.

Both Value Metrics and Skill Metrics can be relevant and useful for performance reviews. Value Metrics can be summarized for the entire period under review. For example, if you are conducting an annual performance review, you could gather the Value Metrics for each coder on the team for the whole year. If you are normally calculating these metrics quarterly or monthly, this would just mean adding the calculated values.

In evaluating each coder's relative responsibility for the team's successes or failures, Value Metrics can help. Consider reviewing metrics such as these when preparing a performance review:

- Win Shares
- Loss Shares
- Advance Shares

Metrics like these can inform your rating of a coder's performance. You can use these as input to your evaluation, but I don't recommend mentioning these directly in a performance review. If a coder has a high rating relative to other team members in Win Shares or Advance Shares, that means they contributed more than others to key successes. But you shouldn't tell the coder "you got a great rating for Win Shares." Rather, you should focus on finding more details to cite about the coder's key contributions (possibly revealed in Skill Metrics or other Value Metrics) and make sure the performance review reflects the strong contribution. Likewise, if a coder has a high rating for Loss Shares relative to others, that means they have a higher relative responsibility for the loss of existing users. Again, you shouldn't tell the coder "your Loss Shares showed you had some issues." Instead, the Loss Shares rating would be a clue for you to dig deeper for reasons and to include discussion of your findings in the performance review.

To identify a coder's key strengths or weaknesses, you can compare the coder's ratings to peers using other Value Metrics. Consider for review:

- Teamwork
- Fielding
- Pop
- Intensity

With these metrics, where a coder stands out from their peers positively, this finding is notable—though again, it may not make sense to mention the metric value unless the metric has become common terminology within your team. For example, if a coder has a higher Teamwork rating than most other coders, then this signals that they have excelled in the measurable teamwork elements. If you choose to cite this in a review, you might mention the Teamwork metric, or you might just discuss how well the coder exhibited teamwork. In the case where a coder has a lower rating than other coders for any of these metrics, however, you will need to analyze further how much that matters and whether it indicates something worth mentioning in the review. The fact that a coder has a lower Fielding rating, for example, may not be a problem, especially if the coder is strong in other areas such as Pop or Intensity.

To delve more deeply into skills evaluation, I suggest you review the coder's Skill Metrics and compare them to other members of the team. It is useful to look at the trend of the metrics over the course of the review period. For example, if you are conducting an annual review, you might gather a monthly breakdown of the Skill Metrics for the entire team, along with the yearly averages. This will help you analyze relative strengths and weaknesses and see how these may have changed over time.

All the gathered Skill Metrics are worth analyzing, although certain metrics might be especially appropriate for inclusion in performance reviews. Metrics that are particularly useful include:

- Points
- Utility
- Power
- Assists
- Saves
- Tackles
- Range
- Turnovers
- Errors

Where a coder is strong in these measured areas, it is worth citing, and where they are weak, it may be worth noting as an area for improvement. Where a coder is inconsistent, that also might be worth noting and discussing (unless there is a clear reason). Especially relevant is how the coder compares in these elements to his immediate peers, as I will discuss in more detail in the following sections.

One way to select and use appropriate codermetrics in performance reviews is to match them up to the categories that you employ for review ratings. If your review ratings include categories like Quality of Work or Level of Effort, for example, then you could determine the metrics that match to each of these categories and use those to help determine the appropriate rating. For Quality for Work, you could use metrics such as Errors and Efficiency. For Level of Effort, you could review the coder's ratings and consistency in metrics such as Utility, Range, Saves, Tackles, and Intensity.

Selecting metrics to use in performance reviews does not mean you need to change the format of your reviews or any rating system you use. The metrics can simply serve as support in your analysis, to give you more data to provide the most accurate and fair reviews.

Self-Evaluations and Peer Feedback

A common part of the performance review process is to have coders conduct self-evaluations. Sometimes you may also ask peers to provide feedback and input for the performance reviews.

If you are gathering and openly publishing codermetrics, then you can suggest that coders and peers review the metrics when they are preparing self-evaluations or feedback. In self-evaluations this can help coders more objectively analyze their work, since they can compare their own metrics to those of other team members. If you are using metrics in regular team meetings, then they will presumably already have seen some of the comparisons, but it will also be helpful for them to be able to go back to the recorded metrics when they are preparing a self-evaluation for a longer period of time.

For peers providing input on others, it will be helpful to look at the metrics of the coder whose performance they are commenting on. In team meetings, each coder is probably paying more attention to their own metrics, and not as much to peers. By examining the record of a coder's metrics, the peer may be able to compare the data to her opinions, which may result in higher quality feedback. Also, the peer may learn something about the coder being evaluated, possibly even gaining new appreciation for the contributions that the coder made.

Other than suggesting that coders review metrics in self- or peer evaluations, I don't recommend that you provide more specific guidance in how the metrics should be considered or included. By leaving it more open-ended, you enable coders to perform their own analysis and draw their own conclusions, which may lead to findings that managers themselves might not spot.

Peer Comparison

If you are a manager preparing a performance review, in addition to gathering self-evaluations and peer feedback you may also want to analyze each coder versus his peers. For example, you might compare senior coders to other senior coders, junior coders to other junior coders, database administrators (DBAs) to other DBAs, and so on.

Codermetrics can be very useful in helping you make accurate and meaningful peer comparisons. Examining the Skill Metrics and Value Metrics for direct peers, you can spot key differences that you might want to highlight in a review. Say, for example, you see that one junior coder is trailing other junior coders in the consistency of Points produced, or regularly has more Errors. Or on the positive side, you might see that one junior coder is excelling in productivity (higher than peer group in Points or Utility) or precision (lower than peer group in Errors). Or maybe they are leading or trailing peers in other areas that might not be as obvious such as Assists and Teamwork. Any of these might be worth noting in a performance review.

The relative standing of peers may have become clear in regular team meetings and project reviews, but small differences that might have gone unnoticed at the time can actually represent large differences when looked at over six months or an entire year. For example, if one coder is just five percent less productive than peers every month, that might not seem like much, but that can add up to quite a big difference in total productivity over twelve months. Even if you have been reviewing metrics in regular team meetings, revisiting the data as you prepare a performance review and looking at totals over the review period can help you spot key peer comparisons. From there you can decide which comparisons are most relevant to include in each review.

One potential problem is that citing peers by name when conducting performance reviews can have a negative effect on teamwork going forward. If you tell a coder that they are not doing as well as another coder, you are making it personal between the two coders—and the coder doing "worse" may develop personal resentment against the one doing better. Situations like this are somewhat inevitable on any teams, but in the end as long as evaluations are fair, most adults can handle the comparisons (and if they can't, then maybe they aren't suitable members of a team). Still, codermetrics gives you a way to present effective peer comparisons to someone without explicitly naming the peers to whom they are being compared. For example, you can show a coder how their productivity or precision compares to the average, maximum, or minimum values of her peers. If the peer group has only two people, this won't help, of course—but in larger teams you can present the metrics without names, which makes your point without making it too personal.

Setting Goals for Improvement

Codermetrics give you an effective way to establish and track personal goals, very much like the team goals discussed earlier in this chapter,. Whether you are a manager suggesting goals for improvement or you are a coder setting your own goals, with metrics you can define specific goals in terms of specific target numbers and timeframes. Having a real target that is regularly tracked and reported makes it more likely that a goal will be met or at least progress will be made. Goals that cannot be measured are more likely to be forgotten and never achieved.

A manager and a coder who agree in a performance review on any area where the coder will try to improve, can identify the key metric or metrics that apply to the target area. Then they can review the coder's past values for those metrics and decide on a reasonable goal for improvement and a target timeframe. Having established such clear and measurable goals, a manager and a coder will then be able to review the progress and accomplishments in future performance reviews or at more frequent intervals.

Promotions

Metrics can be very useful to identify or justify that a coder is ready for promotion. By looking at Skill Metrics or Value Metrics for a coder and other team members, you can see if the coder's results are consistently above his peer group and in line with a more senior peer group. Such improvement would be a strong indicator that a coder's contributions warrant a promotion. As an example, see Figure 7-8, which charts a coder's progression to the next level of productivity.

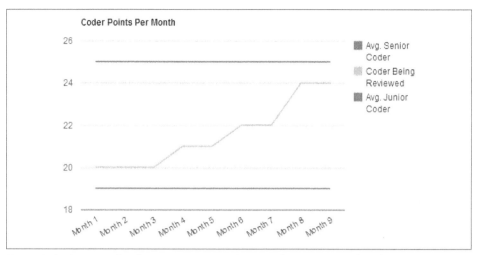

Figure 7-8. An example of progression in productivity for a junior coder that would warrant consideration for promotion

In preparing for a performance review, you can analyze a coder's level to peers on both Skill Metrics and Value Metrics. Increased productivity, precision, responsibility, innovation, or overall contribution to team results are all noteworthy. High and consistent improvements in any of the following metrics might therefore be considered a strong indicator for promotion:

- Points
- Power
- Assists
- Saves
- Tackles
- Errors
- Plus-Minus
- Win Shares
- Loss Shares
- Advance Shares

Improvement in metrics warrants notice in evaluating a potential promotion, although of course this would not be the only criteria. Alternatively, if a coder has not demonstrated consistent improvement in any key measurable area, this might argue against promotion (although a promotion still might be given for other accomplishments).

Taking Metrics Further

In this section I'd like to present a few ideas for how you can take codermetrics further in your organization. These techniques are designed to help you find ways to get more use out of metrics, either by finding new ways to apply them in your processes, or creating new and better metrics, or discovering new and useful insights from the metrics you already have in use.

Create a Codermetrics Council

As you begin using codermetrics, chances are there will be a few "fans" or "boosters" in your organization. These folks, whether they are team leaders or team members, will likely take more of an interest in the ideas, uses, and analysis of the metrics. They might be involved with the initial trials, and they will probably take a role in the data gathering, the calculation, and the storage of metrics. Possibly no one else (or only a few others) in the organization will initially share their interest or see the usefulness of codermetrics. This is a fairly typical way for new ideas to take hold in groups.

Over time, if you integrate metrics into your processes and practices, it is likely that others in the organization will at least gain respect and understanding for metrics. More people will participate— and maybe become fans, too.

At that point, however, it still may be the case that the main responsibility for metrics in the organization rests with a few of the original boosters. Because they were instrumental in starting the use of codermetrics and because they took the most interest, these people may be seen as "driving" or at least "influencing" the strategy and processes for metrics. Others may defer to them to define best practices, changes, and improvements. Maybe they are the ones who are consulted for metrics analysis. If you have forums for discourse on metrics, these folks might be the ones who are seen as the authorities and who do most of the talking.

Again, this is all fairly typical in how ideas spread and then get integrated in groups. The boosters help drive initial adoption and success, then they become the leaders or experts that others turn to going forward.

Granted, it will take some time for you to hit this point. But once you do, I suggest that (unless you have a very small team) you should seek ways to distribute responsibility and "codermetrics leadership" more widely. This is in everyone's best interest, including the original boosters. The methods and techniques for codermetrics discussed in this book are not meant to become static or stale. Codermetrics should and will evolve as you and your teams learn more and as you seek to understand and measure more. By cultivating new boosters and leaders in your teams, you will accelerate your ability to enhance and expand codermetrics and how they are applied.

If you have witnessed the adoption of methodologies or technologies in a software development organization, you have probably seen a similar process. As a new methodology or technology becomes accepted and "institutionalized," it makes sense if the expertise and control spreads beyond what may have originally been a small group. This protects the organization from too much dependence on too few people, and the leadership group benefits if the additional people have good ideas, too.

There are two ways to distribute responsibility and spur growth of your codermetrics leadership team: forcibly or organically. You can probably tell by my choice of loaded terms which one I prefer. Forced growth would be to assign specific people, such as team leaders, to take more responsibility and to become codermetrics leaders. Organic growth would be to let the people who express the most interest and desire join the codermetrics leadership team. The latter works better, since those with the most passion will contribute the most, and they will not feel burdened with extra responsibility even while they continue handling their regular tasks. Also, not all of your codermetric "leaders" should be organization leaders or managers. It's better if there is a mix of seniority and experience so that more junior members are included, too. It brings a wider variety of ideas and perspectives to the council, and it will make it easier to disseminate the council's ideas to a wider audience.

In order to formalize the process and make sure that those interested have a chance to use their energy and get involved, you might consider creating a codermetrics "strategy committee" or "council." The original boosters in the organization would clearly be a part of this council, and then others could be added organically as they express interest. You can put a simple process in place where anyone can apply (and for more junior team members, their manager might need to approve). How large you allow such a group to grow is always a concern—if it grows too large, then it will likely become unproductive. In my experience, however, the number of applicants for such a group will never be that large. You can let people resign from the group when they want, too. Such teams often become remarkably self-regulating to an appropriate and efficient size. If not, if the number of interested people is truly too large, then you might consider dividing into smaller committees each with an area of focus (one group could focus on Skill Metrics and another on Response Metrics, for example).

A codermetrics council might meet once a month or once a quarter, maybe in an informal environment such as over a meal. The council could kick around ideas and observations, and as new ideas worth trying arise, specific individuals on the council could take responsibility for setting up trials. Tests of new metrics or new analyses could be conducted on the side or by coordinating with one or more software teams (the team a council member is on becomes a good candidate for testing a new idea). Depending on the personalities of the council members, they might decide to publish notes or ideas, maybe in an online location or maybe with an email "newsletter." They can also take leadership in ongoing forums and discussions with others in the organization.

Whether you institute a formal council or you simply encourage others to become more involved with codermetrics, you will benefit if you cultivate a larger pool of boosters and leaders. You will be harnessing the natural energy and interest that some team members might have for metrics and process improvement, and put it to good use. Having a healthy and changing group of leaders who interact regularly with each other will increase the chances that codermetrics will stay healthy and evolve within your organization. This will increase the likelihood that the advantages your organization gets from codermetrics will be sustained or increased.

Assign Analysis Projects

Another way to get further benefit from codermetrics is to spend more time analyzing the data you've gathered. Analysis might identify hidden patterns in your organization or in specific teams that could provide useful insights why one team is more productive or delivers better quality results than another, for example. Analysis might spot interesting outliers, such as if one team has a pattern of producing junior coders who advance quickly. If you have collected a year or two of data, especially if you have multiple team tracking metrics, then there could be many hidden gems and patterns that are not being seen or recognized in normal project and management reviews.

The problem, of course, is that no one really has time to do deeper and open-ended exploration and analysis of the data. Maybe managers have some time for this, and maybe some of the metrics fans and boosters in your organization spend some time on advanced analysis, too. But mostly this will be a side activity for team members that already have more than enough to do.

If you have people in your organization who have enough interest and general analysis capabilities, you could consider allowing them a period of focused time to do a metrics analysis project. One way to initiate this would be to let everyone in the software development organization know that they can submit ideas for a codermetrics analysis project to their managers and possibly to the codermetrics council if one exists. If approved, the person would be allowed a period of time, perhaps one or two weeks, to take a "leave" from their normal assignments and work on the analysis project. At the end of the analysis, she would present her findings to the appropriate audience, which might be team leaders, team managers, the codermetrics council—or in some cases, perhaps specific teams or other coders.

Another approach would be to "draft" someone to conduct an analysis project. If a manager has some specific questions or some specific areas that they would like someone to delve into and explore, for example, then that manager might try to find someone in the organization who is interested in and capable of performing the analysis. That person might be one of the codermetric boosters in the organization, or they might just be someone known to have good analytic skills (and might even be someone outside the software development organization) and sufficient time. If the person being drafted agrees and his manager approves, then he would be given a period of time to focus on the analysis project. When complete, he will present findings to the original project sponsor and to others, as appropriate.

Topics for analysis projects might be fairly open-ended or very specific. For example, someone might perform a "General Analysis Comparing Software Teams", or look at "Coder Skills that Correlate with Better Quality." While the topics will vary, in general every project should result in a set of findings that are captured in some sort of document, a set of unanswered questions for further exploration (which might become topics for further analysis projects down the road), and possibly a set of recommendations about how the gathering or use of metrics might be improved to better answer questions and identify patterns in the future. This might include the recommendation for new types of data and metrics to gather.

One thing that everyone should agree on and appreciate is that a codermetrics analysis project may not yield breakthrough findings. Such projects involve research and exploration, and the time and effort allocated should be done with an understanding similar to other research projects—namely that the results may be inconclusive or no more than was already known or guessed. This should not be seen as a failure of the assigned analyst, the project, or of such projects in general. It is to be expected. You spend time searching for more useful patterns and more revealing insights, and sometimes you find them, sometimes you don't. But if you don't try, you may never know.

Hire a Stats Guy or Gal

This is not something I've ever tried, but it's something you see in other disciplines and other fields, and I could imagine it happening someday for metrics-gathering software teams as well. Instead of (or in addition to) assigning internal people to conduct codermetrics analysis projects, you could "outsource" metrics analysis to a consultant: a "stats guy" or "stats girl."

In major sports such as baseball and basketball, with the rise in popularity of advanced statistical analysis of players and teams, this has become fairly commonplace. Teams hire outside consultants who are adept at analyzing data and who help the sports team leverage statistics to develop new strategies.

This is also commonplace in many companies for marketing, sales, and financial data analysis. If the company doesn't possess the skills internally (or there is just more analysis to be done than people have time to do), consultants may be hired on a temporary basis to help with specific projects. The consultants might be highly skilled, focused, and experienced in their particular areas, or they might be working to gain experience (such as summer interns hired from a local MBA program who have basic competencies in statistics and spreadsheets).

If you have accumulated metrics from many coders across multiple projects and possibly multiple teams, and you don't have the time or ability to mine and analyze the data for patterns and new insights, then it is not far-fetched to consider using a consultant or a sufficiently skilled part-time hire or intern. You could possibly borrow an analyst for a short time from another group in your organization, like the marketing department. The analyst wouldn't need a background in software development or codermetrics, just statistical analysis skills. One or more in-house leaders from your software organization could work with the analyst, discussing ideas and questions that could be investigated and deciding on avenues to pursue iteratively as the analyst becomes more familiar with the data and finds more.

As with the internal codermetrics analysis projects, it's not guaranteed that a consulting analyst would deliver great value. But it seems worth considering as an option down the road as you accumulate data—especially if you find consultants who are suited to the task.

Timeout for an Example: The Same But Different

When Billy Beane set out to improve the Oakland A's baseball team, as discussed in Michael Lewis' *Moneyball*, his first step was to learn which player skills or combination of skills and approaches amounted to greater success. Through statistical analysis, he learned that hitters taking more pitches and drawing more walks led to better run production, which led to more wins. He also learned that giving up outs through failed stolen base attempts and sacrifice bunts resulted in worse run production, which led to more losses. Using this data, he was able to focus on drafting players who specifically exhibited hitting traits (good pitch selection and plate discipline) that would translate to success, and he was able to instruct his coaches to teach the valuable hitting traits and to tell his managers not to attempt to steal bases or bunt.

This rational and statistics-based approach to player selection, player development, and coaching brought Beane and the Oakland A's many years of success, even though they had less money to spend on player payroll than most of their competitors. Over the last few years, Oakland has not maintained the same level of success, as competitors started imitating these techniques and Oakland's tight budget resulted in the loss of many successful players that Billy Beane and his team discovered. But that doesn't change the validity and usefulness of the methods. First, you must find the keys to success. Gathering and analyzing data can help you do that more objectively and more accurately. Then you need to apply those keys to find and develop the proven combination of skills and approaches that lead to success. These ideas are applicable to software development teams. Unlike professional baseball, the skills required are not so elite that you have to overspend like the leading baseball teams to consistently achieve (and like Billy Beane, you may be able to apply these techniques to build more successful teams even if you are operating on a tight budget).

Codermetrics can help you identify the patterns of success in your organization. By gathering metrics on multiple projects and multiple teams, you can better see the differences between teams and can better identify the "good" and "bad" patterns of software development teams. This knowledge can be put to use to improve your teams, through mentoring and "coaching" or personnel changes, or to build successful new teams. Some of the patterns and principles you discover may be particular to your organization or to the particular type of software you develop, but some are likely to apply across organizations and software teams of different types.

As an example, let me describe two software teams that I worked with in one company. One of these teams was considered very successful, but became less successful after the departure of a key team member. The other team was considered solid, but actually improved its success after a key team member resigned. Having gone through similar circumstances but with different outcomes, these situations present an interesting case to study and compare.

I'll call the first team the "Red Dog" team. At the beginning of the period, which I'll call Time A, this team had six coders and was working on a software product in its fourth release that was approximately doubling the number of users every year and soundly beating all its competition. The team had two senior coders and four moderately experienced coders. The entire team had been together multiple years. Releases were delivered on time, with high quality, with features and functionality consistently exceeding outside expectations.

At a later time, which I'll call Time B, one of the senior coders resigned to go to another company. This left the team with five coders. The remaining senior coder took over all the key technical leadership responsibilities, and other responsibilities were spread among team members. While the team's performance remained solid and the product continued to succeed, by the following release certain aspects of the team's results clearly began to drop off. The functional improvements, the innovations, and the level of quality all dipped enough to be noticed. Figure 7-9 shows a comparison of the product's Response Metrics from Time A (full team) and Time B (after the senior coder left). Figure 7-10 shows a comparison of the average coder Value Metrics from Time A and Time B.

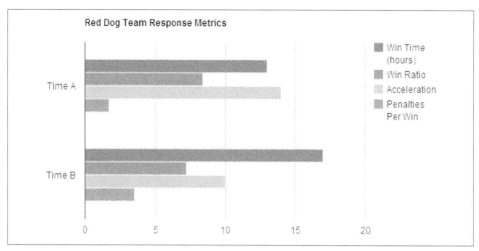

Figure 7-9. Comparing monthly average Response Metrics for Red Dog team's product from Time A and Time B shows that the rate of adoption and acceleration decreased, while quality problems increased

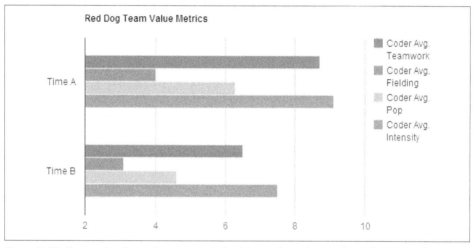

Figure 7-10. Comparing the project average Value Metrics for coders on the Red Dog team from Time A and Time B shows a small but noticeable decline in key metrics

I'll call the second team the "Blue Dog" team. At Time A for this team, there were seven coders working on a software product in its third release that was performing solidly and growing, although it significantly trailed some larger competitors. Like the Red Dog team, this team had two senior coders who split responsibilities. The remaining coders were of similar moderate experience, and like the Red Dog team, the Blue Dog team had all worked together for multiple years.

At Time B for the Blue Dog team, one of the senior coders resigned to pursue other interests. The remaining team had six coders, with the other senior coder assuming full responsibility for architecture and team leadership. At this point, however, unlike the Red Dog team, the performance of the Blue Dog team improved in a few noticeable ways. Not that performance had been bad before, but productivity, quality, innovation, and product advances all became better—to the point that managers and others in the engineering team noticed. Figure 7-11 shows Blue Dog team's Response Metrics and Figure 7-12 shows the coder Value Metrics from Time A and Time B.

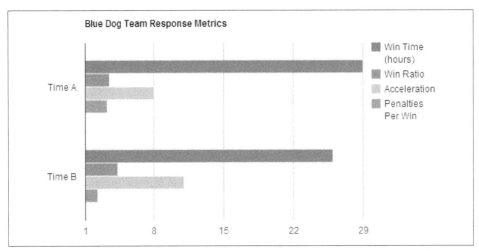

Figure 7-11. Comparing monthly average Response Metrics for Blue Dog team's product from Time A and Time B shows an improvement in adoption rates and user benefits and quality

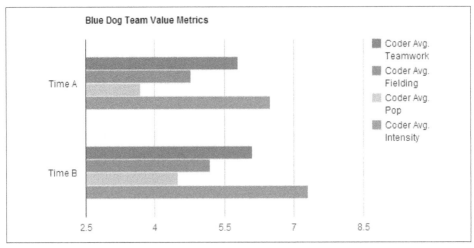

Figure 7-12. Comparing the project average Value Metrics for coders on the Blue Dog team from Time A and Time B shows noticeable improvement in key metrics

So each team had a senior coder leave, but in one case the team's performance suffered a little; and in the other, the team's performance improved. Maybe the senior coder who left the Red Dog team was just better, more important and knowledgeable, and harder to replace. Maybe the senior coder who took more responsibility on the Blue Dog team was stronger, and given more responsibility, simply rose to the occasion.

If you've run across situations like these before, you probably haven't given them a lot of thought. Things change, teams change, as long as the product is doing reasonably well, why worry?

But is there more to learn from a situation like this? With more knowledge and understanding, would it have been possible to help the Red Dog team continue to perform well after the senior coder left? Or would the Blue Dog team still have improved if its other senior coder had stayed on board?

The data in Table 7-5 provides an answer. This is a comparison of the two senior coders who left their teams, showing what percentage they individually contributed to team totals for a set of key metrics. The data shows, for example, that the senior coder on the Red Dog team provided 72% of the total Power rating for the team and provided 81% of the Assists. The senior coder on the Blue Dog team, conversely, only provided 28% of the team's total Power, and handled only 18% of the Assists.

Table 7-5. Comparing how much the departing senior coders on the Red Dog and Blue Dog teams individually contributed to team totals in key areas on an average release

	Red Dog Sr. Coder	Blue Dog Sr. Coder
Team's Total Power	72%	28%
Team's Total Assists	81%	18%
Team's Total Tackles	95%	31%
Team's Total Saves	67%	22%

The metrics are dramatically different. They show that the senior coder who left the Red Dog team handled a much larger share of his team's key tasks and provided a much greater percentage of help to others. This might have been because the senior coder was stronger in those areas, or that the other coders were weaker, but it was most likely because the team established this particular division of labor early on and then continued it. Whatever the cause and reason, the data clearly shows that the departure of the Red Dog senior coder left a much bigger hole to fill.

On the surface, the situations with these two teams look nearly identical, yet codermetrics reveals more detail about the differences and the potential impact. But how can such information and understanding help?

First, with the additional details that metrics provide, you (as a manager or maybe even as a team member) are able to predict much more clearly the potential impact of a departure, and thereby identify strategies to address the potential issues. In this case, for example, you might insist that the Red Dog team spend extra time focusing on how the departing coder interacted with and supported others (Assists), or you might spend extra time to make sure that they learn more about the complex areas (Power areas) that the departing coder handled. Through identification and action, therefore, you might better address a loss to keep a team's performance from declining.

Second, with the extra detail that metrics provide about the level of contributions that a departing coder made, you will be better able to assess how well current team members will be able to step up, or whether the team needs additional personnel. Seeing in this example that the senior coder leaving the Red Dog team provided nearly all the innovation (Tackles), you would know to consider that carefully in your evaluation about whether other team members can fill the gap.

Third, you can also use metrics to help catch such situations earlier. Where one coder is dominant in multiple key and important areas, you could make sure to create better balance in the team, in which case the entire team would become stronger and any subsequent departure would not have as dramatic an effect.

Finally, by understanding the real differences between the situations such as presented here between the Red Dog and the Blue Dog teams, you avoid jumping to incorrect conclusions about whether one situation matches another and the reasons why team performance might be getting better or worse. For example, in the Red Dog case it might be easy to blame the remaining senior coder for the team's declining performance, especially if you think the situation is exactly the same as the Blue Dog case where performance is improving. But in this case the situations were not the same: the teams operated differently before the departures. In the case of the Blue Dog team, responsibility in many critical areas was better distributed, so the team was stronger and one senior coder's departure didn't cause any setback (in fact the team continued to progress, which explains the improvement following the departure). In the case of the Red Dog team, one person had too many key responsibilities—which was not necessarily the fault of any of the other team members, but left them in a much weaker position when that person left.

As codermetrics show you more details about your teams and the differences between your teams, you stand a much better chance to identify ways to improve those teams. Could the patterns and the details be seen without codermetrics? Wouldn't it be possible to know that one senior coder had disproportionate responsibilities on his team and would be more difficult to replace? Yes, although perhaps not as readily or efficiently. Billy Beane, too, might have figured out that hitters who walk a lot are very valuable, and steals and bunts are counterproductive, without statistics. But statistics helped him see the actions that correlated highly with success, which may seem obvious in retrospect—yet before, was anything but. Also, using statistics, Billy Beane didn't need to see every prospect in person and be intimately familiar with the player's situation. In fact, to a large extent he could evaluate many aspects of a player or a team simply by reviewing the statistics.

So sure, statistics or metrics only help you see what's there. But metrics can help make patterns, similarities, and differences more obvious. In the end, the key value of metrics is that they help you more clearly understand the contributions of coders and the dynamics of teams, and they can help you spot key information even if you are not completely familiar with all the coders and teams.

In the movie *The Matrix*, the choice between the red pill and the blue pill represented the choice between ignorance and reality. Working without metrics doesn't mean you will work in ignorance, but using metrics can definitely help you gain a clearer and more accurate view of reality. The situation of the Red Dog and the Blue Dog teams seemed nearly identical, but as the metrics revealed, the reality was that they were quite different.

CHAPTER 8

Building Software Teams

> Coaches can teach players only so much, but they can also learn a lot from veteran players. People look at our team and say we're old, but we're old for a reason. Those guys serve a purpose in our organization. They are there to guide our young players.
>
> —Ken Holland, general manager of the Detroit Red Wings, 1997–present

Aside from people who only like to work alone, everyone wants to be part of a winning team. While there are many definitions of "winning," you would probably agree that for software teams the definition includes producing great software and enjoying the process. But how do you get that? Hiring the smartest and most skilled people possible is always a good starting point, but does that alone produce a winning team?

This chapter presents ideas about how codermetrics can be used to help you make personnel additions and adjustments to build better software teams, and to achieve greater success according to your defined goals. This can apply to new or existing teams. The goal is to create a planned approach to personnel decisions and team building, using metrics to inform and support the process. There are many well-known and proven ideas that work for professional sports teams and that are analogous to the needs of software development teams, so I will draw on those throughout the chapter.

As with all parts of this book, the focus here is on coders. Clearly, there are other people and roles on software development teams, like testers and interface designers. Many of the ideas laid out here might be extended to other roles, but the teams discussed in this chapter are groups of coders, along with their team leaders and managers.

Goals and Profiles

Taking a planned approach to building a software team is very similar to building software itself. First of all, you must determine your business "requirements" and establish a vision of the team you want, just as with software you need a vision that is aligned with business and marketing requirements. Next, you need to develop a design or blueprint of the team you envision, just as with software you need a design. Finally, you need to implement that design to build a team and iteratively improve it over time, just as software gets built, maintained, and enhanced.

Whether you want to build a new team or improve an existing one, the first step is to lay out a vision and a plan. This section describes how you can use metrics to establish targets for new or existing teams.

Set Key Goals

When you want to build a new team or improve an existing team, in a metrics-based approach, the first step is to determine the key "business" or organization goals for the team. The goals should be trackable with metrics you have in place. Once goals are established, you can use them to guide your personnel decisions, and you can track the metrics to analyze the results.

For example, your team goal might be to increase the number of new users or improve the quality of your software. For these goals you could use Response Metrics like Wins or Penalties. Alternative team goals might be to increase productivity or teamwork, in which case you could use Skill Metrics like Points or Assists, or a Value Metric like Teamwork. Whatever metrics you choose, you would define a target value or a target level of improvement. For example, you might say that the team goal is to achieve three hundred Wins per month, or that the goal is to improve the Wins per month by twenty percent.

It is best if the goals are defined within a specific timeframe, such as a number or percentage "per month." This allows you to measure progress at a reasonable frequency. For example, if you are putting together a new team to build a new software product and the organization's goal is to sign up one thousand new users in the first year, rather than setting one thousand Wins (new users) as the goal, I would suggest you set something like three hundred Wins per month as the goal (which, if it takes nine months to reach, would approximately let you reach the organization goal in one year). This will make it easier for you to see on a monthly basis how close the team is coming to the goal, and at what point the team has consistently surpassed the goal.

You can chart how well a team is progressing to its goals, shown in Figure 8-1. Such charts can be shared with the team.

Identify Constraints

Once you have established the goals for a team, you need to identify any constraints and determine if the goals can be met given those constraints. Budget is often a constraint that can limit the number and type of coders you can have on a team. Another constraint for an existing team might be that it's not in your power to make personnel changes and, therefore, any improvement you make must rely on existing team members.

Figure 8-1. Key team goals and progress towards them can be captured in simple charts

Another set of constraints might be current or upcoming responsibilities and commitments. If you already know that an existing team must do certain things in specific timeframes, for example, it may limit the type of changes you can make. Or, if you are building a new team but you know that the team has to deliver software by a certain date, that may limit the amount of time you have to recruit experienced coders. Without enough experienced coders, perhaps the original team goals cannot be met.

If you identify constraints that make the team goals clearly unrealistic, then you need to either reset the goals or eliminate the constraints. This may require business discussions outside the software development team—but better to have these up front than to have unreachable goals that will leave everyone disappointed, frustrated, or worse later on.

In order to proceed with team planning, then, you should identify and evaluate the constraints so you can:

- Define the limits on team size and potential team changes.
- Adjust team goals to realistically account for constraints.

Find Comparable Team Profiles

If you set out to improve an existing team, then clearly it makes sense to examine that team and compare them to other teams to identify specific areas to improve. If you set out to build a new software team, it also makes sense to examine other teams to learn about patterns of success or failure. You might find teams that you might want to emulate, or you might identify patterns that you want to avoid.

Traditionally, people have used personal observations to compare their teams to others, augmenting these observations with informal anecdotes heard from other people. You might have a set of memories or stories about techniques that worked for teams you've worked with or heard about, and you might put those techniques to use going forward. For example, maybe it was your experience that a team had great success with summer interns, so now you are in favor of having summer interns on new teams. Over time, many team-building and management "memes" circulate in various ways and become common practice, in some sense passed down from one "generation" to the next.

Codermetrics gives you the ability to examine teams—both current and past—in new and different ways. By capturing a set of metrics, you can create metrics-based "profiles" of teams. If you gather profiles of multiple teams and determine the relative level of success of each team, then you can begin to compare profiles to identify the key attributes of success. This helps you zero in on key qualities to emphasize on new teams or the most valuable areas to improve on existing teams. Rather than just gathering a set of "best practices" and emulating institutional models for building software teams, therefore, you can gather data in the form of team profiles that give you a more empirical view and that you can use as templates for building better teams.

A codermetric profile of a team for this purpose relies on selected Skill Metrics and Value Metrics. You don't need to include all the detailed metrics for each individual coder. In putting together team profiles, what matters most is getting summary metrics that show the relative distribution of skills and contributions on each team and where the metrics are normalized for comparison. The metrics can be normalized by using averages over a specific time period, such as taking the average Points per coder per month. The profile can be further simplified and normalized by categorizing the team's performance in each area on a simple scale such as High, Medium, or Low. The scale for rating would be based on what you have seen as common over time and across teams. For example, you might say that for average Points per coder per month, one team's value is High and another team is Medium.

When you have enough data, it can also be useful to break down the metrics by category of coder. For example, if you know the averages per month for senior coders and the same for junior coders, it gives you a more detailed and useful profile of a team. See Figure 8-2 for an example team profile that provides both a team summary and a breakdown by type of coder.

It will be straightforward to put together a profile for a team if you are already gathering and tracking codermetrics. In general, three or four months of data is enough to build a team profile, although if more data is easily gathered, that can make the profile more accurate. If you want to profile a team that isn't gathering metrics, however, it can still be done with some data gathering and some estimation. In this case, you would gather the data available from existing systems such as a project-tracking system, bug-tracking system, or a customer support system. Then you might gather additional data estimates by interviewing team leaders, or managers, or team members. Using the data you gather and your experience, you could then estimate monthly averages for metrics to build an estimated team profile. This could be done for current teams but could also be done for teams in the past as long as some data sources or some team members are accessible.

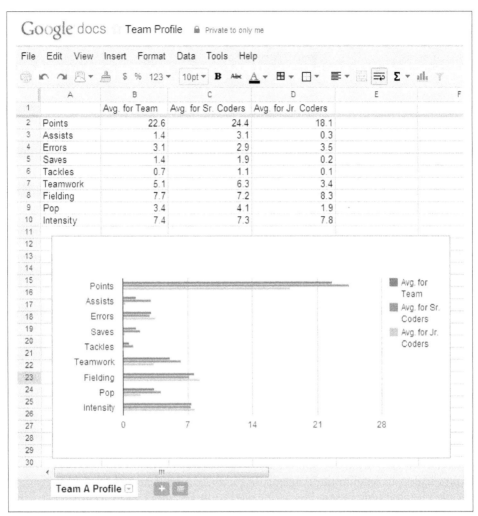

Figure 8-2. A metrics-based team profile shows the average per month values for key metrics and a breakdown of averages by coder categories

Obviously, profiles constructed in this way are less reliable than those built from actively tracked codermetrics, but an estimated profile still can provide useful lessons, so I would argue that it's better than no profile at all.

The other element that every profile needs is a rating of the team's success for the time period covered, which can be derived from Response Metrics. In this case, you want to come up with a common rating system to use across teams. Consider rating success in more than one dimension. Table 8-1 shows an example set of rating categories along with specific codermetrics that you could use to determine the relative success. When actual metrics are not available, you can establish the success ratings through investigation of available data or through interviews.

Table 8-1. Example categories for rating success in team profiles along with codermetrics that can be used to determine success

Success Category	Useful Codermetrics
New user acquisition	Wins, Win Rate, Win Percentage, Gain, Gain Rate
Retaining existing users	Losses, Loss Rate
Adding benefit for existing users	Boost, Acceleration
Improved quality	Penalties, Penalties Per Win
Advances over the competition	Win Ranking, Capability Ranking

In the profile, you can rate each team in each category using a fixed scale. For example, you might rate a team High, Medium, or Low for their level of success in new user acquisition. The actual rating will be based on team or organization goals and how the team did compared to those goals. Such ratings are imprecise and may be somewhat subjective, but since these will be used strictly for categorization and comparison purposes, your main concern is that the ratings are consistent. If, for example, one team achieved fifty percent of the organization goal and you rate that team's success as "Medium," then another team that hits fifty percent of its goal should be "Medium," too.

As you set out to build a new team or improve an existing team, what you want to do is find one or more comparable profiles, or "comps," from existing or past teams that share similarities with the team you envision while taking into account your identified goals and constraints. Through analysis of these comps and the patterns they reveal, you can formulate a more detailed plan for your team.

Professional sports teams do this all the time. If the managers of a budget-constrained hockey team in a small market want their team to be more competitive or more entertaining, they analyze other similarly constrained teams who've had success. They may latch onto the approach of a single successful team as a "blueprint," or blend of techniques and ideas from multiple teams. In baseball, Billy Beane and his managers developed their ideas about building winning teams by analyzing the makeup of successful teams in the past. Then, as teams saw the success that Billy Beane had with the Oakland A's, they began to analyze and copy that approach, while also blending in new ideas of their own.

Using metrics-based profiles of software development teams, you can perform comparative analysis of two or more teams. There are many things you can learn from analysis of these profiles to enhance your planning for a target team. For example, by comparing the profile of a successful team to one that is less successful, you might identify key differences that reveal why one team is more successful—and therefore, where the other team could focus on improving. Or by comparing two profiles of successful teams, you might identify common strengths that another team could emulate to improve its chance of success.

As examples of such comparison and analysis, Table 8-2 and Figure 8-3 show the data from two team profiles. In this case, Team B did a little better in delivering quality and user benefits, so you would say that Team B was better overall. Among the areas measured and listed, Team B was also better in the number of monthly Assists and the level of Teamwork (which is also based on Assists along with Utility and Range). If you were building a new team, you might choose Team B's monthly metric totals as a "blueprint" or a "target" for your new team. Alternatively, if your goal was to improve Team A to try to get results like Team B, you might decide that Team A could improve quality and deliver more benefits if the coders spent more time on helping each other and fulfilling other support requests (which would increase the number of Assists to be more like Team B) and by having some coders diversify their time across more areas (which would increase their Range and thereby the overall Teamwork ratings to be more like Team B).

Table 8-2. Side-by-side comparison of two team profiles; metrics are average per coder per month

	Team A	Team B	Notable Differences
Success: new users	Medium	Medium	
Success: user retention	High	High	
Success: benefits	Medium	High	Team B better
Success: quality	Medium	High	Team B better
Success: competition	High	High	
Avg. Points	22.6 (High)	23.5 (High)	
Avg. Assists	1.4 (Low)	5.1 (High)	Team B better
Avg. Errors	3.1 (Medium)	3.3 (Medium)	
Avg. Saves	1.4 (Medium)	1.6 (Medium)	
Avg. Tackles	0.7 (Low)	0.4 (Low)	
Avg. Teamwork	5.1 (Medium)	9.2 (High)	Team B better
Avg. Fielding	7.7 (Medium)	7.9 (Medium)	
Avg. Pop	3.4 (Medium)	3.1 (Medium)	
Avg. Intensity	7.4 (Medium)	7.6 (Medium)	

One question in analyzing team profiles is whether it's reasonable to compare different teams, especially if they are from different organizations or different time periods. Is it an apples-to-apples comparison from which you can draw meaningful insights—or is it apples-to-oranges, in which case conclusions might be misleading? Logic and common sense can apply. The more similar the situation, the more likely that a comparison can apply, so you should take the situations and circumstances into account. You might consider the type of software worked on, the organization goals, and the size of the team. It is easier to draw meaningful insights from a comparison of two teams that worked on a similar category of software in the same company than it is to draw

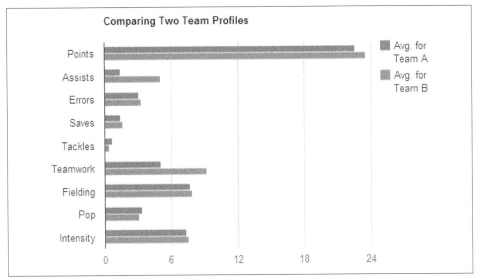

Figure 8-3. A chart comparing the differences between two team profiles

conclusions comparing two teams that worked on entirely different types of software for different companies.

As you set out to lay plans for your team, you should find the most useful comps you can. If you already have a "library" of comps, then you can choose those that best fit your target team and the goals you have set. If you don't have any comps, then I suggest you find at least one team that you believe shares characteristics and has shown success, and develop a profile for that team that you can use as a comp for analysis.

Build a Target Team Profile

At this point you have defined team goals, identified your constraints, and selected a set of comparable team profiles that you can study and use as examples for your team. The final step in "team planning" is to build a target team profile that adheres to your constraints and that you believe, based on your comps and your personal knowledge, is representative of a team that can achieve the goals.

A target team profile is the same as the team profiles discussed in the previous section, but it is a "target" used for planning purposes rather than one based on actual performance data. In this case you define the target success ratings to be in line with your defined team goals, and you define the target monthly metric averages. You may also break down metric averages for specific categories of coders, such as senior and junior coders. Figure 8-4 shows an example spreadsheet containing a target team profile. Analysis of your comps should weigh heavily in building the target team profile. It's not necessary that the target profile exactly copies an existing profile, but it should be derived from the successful patterns observed in other teams.

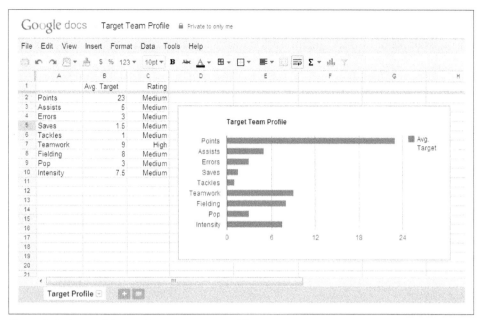

Figure 8-4. A spreadsheet with a target team profile

The theory behind target profiles is that if you build a team that "fits" the target profile metrics (not exactly but within a small margin of error), then the team also stands a much better chance to meet its target level of success (again within some margin of error). This theory is based on the idea that codermetrics can help you identify patterns of success that are not infallible but that increase the likelihood of success and reduce the chance of failure. The approach relies on having chosen good comps, having analyzed those comps, and having applied the analysis correctly to come up with a "good" target team profile. Once you establish a target team profile, you can build a team whose metrics will fit that profile. If you are building a team and the target profile calls for coders to average "High" Points per month and "High" Assists, for example, then shooting for those metrics would guide your personnel, mentoring, and coaching decisions.

With the Oakland A's, Billy Beane and his management team determined that they wanted a baseball team that would be strong in certain statistics that they, through analysis of past teams, determined were consistent with greater success. Among the key metrics they focused on were On-Base Percentage (OBP), On-Base Plus Slugging Percentage (OPS), numbers of strikeouts (SO), attempted bunt sacrifices (BS), and attempted stolen bases (SB). They set a plan to build a team that would have high OBP and OPS while having low SO, BS, and SB. Having established this target "profile," they went about finding new players that already had those skills, and coaching existing players to improve those skills. As a result, at least until the competition caught up, they were able to field a team that fit their target profile and delivered greater success, while operating within their budgetary constraints.

For an example of how this might be done with software teams, see Table 8-3. In this case, you have the current profile of Team A and the profile of a "comp" Team B. These are the same profiles as shown in Table 8-2. Assuming your goal is to improve Team A to have results more like Team B, then according to analysis of the comp, you might focus on improving Team A's Assists and Teamwork. Table 8-3 shows the goals for improvement as you might lay them out in each area, as well as the resulting target team profile.

Table 8-3. Constructing a target profile to improve Team A can be done by adjusting the current profile to be more like that of Team B, which is comparable but has had greater success (metrics are per coder per month)

	Current Profile Team A	Comp Profile Team B	Notable Differences	Target Profile Team A
Success: new users	Medium	Medium		same
Success: user retention	High	High		same
Success: benefits	Medium	High	+ 25%	+ 25%
Success: quality	Medium	High	+ 33%	+ 33%
Success: competition	High	High		same
Avg. Points	22.6 (Medium)	23.5 (Medium)		23 (Medium)
Avg. Assists	1.4 (Low)	5.1 (High)	+ 3.7	5 (High)
Avg. Errors	3.1 (Medium)	3.3 (Medium)		3 (Medium)
Avg. Saves	1.4 (Medium)	1.6 (Medium)		1.5 (Medium)
Avg. Tackles	0.7 (Low)	0.4 (Low)		1 (Low)
Avg. Teamwork	5.1 (Medium)	9.2 (High)	+ 4.1	9 (High)
Avg. Fielding	7.7 (Medium)	7.9 (Medium)		8 (Medium)
Avg. Pop	3.4 (Medium)	3.1 (Medium)		3 (Medium)
Avg. Intensity	7.4 (Medium)	7.6 (Medium)		7.5 (Medium)

Emulating a pattern of success, of course, does not ensure success. It only increases the chances. Whether the end results meet the goals or not, analyzing actual results after you have used target team profiles can be highly instructive and can give you useful feedback for even better team-building in the future. If a team you've built "fits" your target profile but the team's results are worse than the goals, this might indicate that the comps weren't good enough, or that better and more detailed metrics are required. By examining such cases, you can look for ways to improve either the comps, the analysis, or the metrics—any or all of which can help you plan more accurately later on.

Roles

Once you have planned the key goals and focus areas for a team, you need to "design" a team that fits the target profile. This is analogous to the design of software after the target requirements are established. A good design meets the requirements, and a poor design doesn't. A great design will exceed the requirements and deliver unanticipated value.

Every design has constraints. If you are working with an existing team, clearly you are constrained by the reasonable changes and improvements you can make. In most cases you are constrained by budget. When recruiting new team members, you may be constrained by the candidates available at the time in your region. But, within your constraints, you still have many design options from which to choose and many aspects you will need to consider.

A proven approach to good design is to use patterns and templates. That is where roles come in. Roles represent the different parts that coders can play on a team based on their individual qualities and skills and based on the team's needs. Traditionally, you may think of roles as the titles or functions that coders fulfill, such as "architect," or "database expert," or "user interface developer." In this section, I'd like to introduce a very different set of roles that are aligned with the codermetrics introduced in previous chapters and are not dependent on a coder's title or functional role. Again, I use analogies to sports teams in naming and describing these. With a team's goals in mind, you can determine which of these roles need to be filled and how many coders you might have in each role.

Playmakers and Scorers

To some extent, every software team needs to get new work done, although the amount and type of new work will vary based on the organization and the category of software being developed. For example, a start-up setting out to create an exciting new product has a lot of new work to do and that work might call for handling many complex and difficult tasks. Alternatively, a software team that is primarily responsible for maintenance on an existing and long-standing system needs to be productive, but the complexity of tasks handled might be significantly less (although the required level of quality might be much higher).

In your analysis of software teams, think about how much "offensive firepower" the team needs to achieve its goals. Teams creating new products or adding many new features, especially for cutting-edge or highly competitive markets, require a high rate of productivity and must often deal with difficult technical challenges. A software team that needs a strong offense, meaning the ability to handle complex tasks and deal with technical challenges in building new software quickly, needs coders who are "playmakers" and "scorers."

Playmakers are the coders who are highly productive themselves but who also help others get things done. Scorers are the coders who are especially adept at handling complex and difficult tasks without compromising quality. Coders who fit these roles will have high ratings for some or all of the following metrics:

- Points
- Power
- Assists
- O-Impact
- Plus-Minus
- Pop
- Win Shares
- Advance Shares

A team that expects to have high average ratings in these metrics will need to have at least some playmakers and scorers. Most software teams will need at least one coder who falls into this category. The relative number of coders that should be in these roles on a team depends on the needs and goals of the team. Some playmakers and scorers will be very consistent, and some will be sporadic. This should also be considered and taken into account when planning who can fulfill these roles on a team.

Defensive Stoppers

While there are multiple scenarios where a software team might not need a lot of offensive firepower to succeed, every software team must have a "strong defense." On a software team, good "defense" means good quality and fast response to fixing problems. No software team can be successful if it delivers poor quality software or if it can't solve critical issues. And a team is more likely to succeed if it proactively handles problems and comes up with innovative solutions.

Some teams require more defensive strength than others. A team working on software that already has many users cannot afford mistakes and absolutely needs to solve critical problems quickly. A team that is working on a brand new product, however, has a bit more leeway in initial quality, because there may be many fewer users to start. Those users may be more willing to live with certain types of problems, knowing it's a new product, if the software delivers good value. As you analyze your team's situation and goals, you can decide how much defensive strength is required.

Everyone on a software development team is expected to maintain a suitable level of quality and precision, and to this extent everyone is required to "play defense." The following metrics are key measures that should have relatively low values, in line with expectations for every coder, to ensure everyone is making an appropriate defensive contribution. If coders stand out with particularly high values for any of these metrics, then that would be cause for concern and probably an area that requires improvement because it affects the overall defensive strength of the team. These basic defensive metrics for which you want to see low values are:

- Turnovers
- Errors
- Loss Shares

While everyone on a software team needs to perform reasonably well in basic defensive measures, depending on the team's goals, you may also need coders who are particularly strong in these and other defensive measures. These are the "defensive stoppers" on a team, the coders who not only deliver superior quality but who are adept at handling critical issues and, in some cases, take initiative and are innovative in proactively solving important problems. In addition to measuring well for the defensive metrics above, coders who fit this role will have high ratings for the following metrics:

- Saves
- Tackles
- D-Impact

If you need to have a team that is strong in these metrics, then you will either need to ensure that enough coders on the team take on sufficient responsibility, or that you have some coders who are defensive stoppers and take a majority of the responsibility for defense. The relative number of defensive stoppers on a team depends on how much emphasis you want to put here.

Utility Players

Not everyone on a team is a "star." Not everyone gets to handle the glamorous and more complex tasks, and not everyone will be assigned to critical production issues or will provide innovative breakthroughs that solve key problems. Not every coder is a playmaker or scorer or defensive stopper. But the "utility players" who are able to handle multiple types of tasks and are willing and able to fill in development gaps are still very valuable to the success of a team.

A utility player is a coder who does exceedingly well handling a wide range of tasks across multiple product areas. This can be measured and tracked using the following metrics:

- Utility
- Range
- Teamwork
- Fielding

By determining a team's goals and needs and what level of contribution a team will get from the offensive and defensive "specialists," you can decide whether the team needs utility players and if so, how many. Clearly, utility players add value and can strengthen a team's coverage and consistency, which can relate directly to software quality, customer satisfaction, and improved team success. But you could argue that utility players aren't a necessity as long as other coders do a good enough job covering what needs to be done.

Decisions like this on which roles to fill or emphasize on a team will be based on your own analysis, experience, and preferences and can clearly be influenced by the personnel that a team already has or that's available. Personally, I recommend having utility players on software teams because it's my observation that teams strong in these areas and metrics have an increased likelihood of success.

Role Players

What about the coders who are not specifically playmakers, scorers, defensive stoppers, or utility players? Do they have a place on the team? Of course they do. Not everyone has a specific strength identified by the roles already mentioned. You can think of the remaining members of the team as "role players." This means that they do have an assigned role and set of responsibilities on the team, it is just not one of the other identified "specialty" roles. Still, role players are expected to do a good job fulfilling their individual roles.

Not all role players are expected to perform equally. Expectations will be based on each individual's experience and skills. You may not be expecting the role players on the team to rate highly in certain metrics such as Power or Saves or Tackles or Range, but you will expect them to have good ratings for the core Skill Metrics such as:

- Points
- Utility
- Assists
- Turnovers
- Errors

As you build and work to improve teams, you should determine which coders on the team are role players, and the expectations and needs for their contributions and skills. By setting the goals and tracking the metrics, you will be able to identify if the team is getting what it needs from its role players or whether it's an area that needs to improve.

Over time, role players may develop key strengths and may emerge as specialists or leaders on a team. This is something you might enable and encourage through mentoring or coaching. If role players improve their skills, productivity, and precision, then this will show up in improved metrics as well. Such improvements, especially if they become consistent, should only benefit the team and can be factored into ongoing team-building as role players transition to take on other roles in the team, such as scorer or defensive stopper.

Backups

Although it's not related to a separate set of metrics or strengths, I also want to mention "backups." You probably already worry about having backups for key areas in your software or key technologies you use. For example, you might already be concerned that only one coder understands your key classes or how you integrate with a critical third-party subsystem. But I suggest you also think about having backups related to the roles discussed in this section and the types of contributions each coder makes to the team.

If, for example, your software team's success is highly reliant on having a few play-makers and scorers or a few defensive stoppers, ideally you will have backups in case those key coders become unavailable for any reason. If your team's success is dependent on having two scorers, for example, you might decide to have three or four scorers on the team.

Another strategy is to groom coders as backups and have them ready to "step up" if needed. A utility player might be groomed as a playmaker, or a role player might be groomed as a defensive stopper. Over time, you might plan to transition the coders from one role to another, and you would just accelerate the change if there was a sudden need. This strategy of "coder development" is riskier in an emergency than having fully ready backups because coders rushed into new responsibilities may not succeed. But it's a reasonable approach that is also efficient.

Having backups is not something that every team can afford. For some, this will be seen as a luxury or as an "insurance policy" they can live without. If a team loses a coder in a key role or that coder can no longer perform, you can add someone else to the team, so the damage may be small and temporary. But as you build teams that you want to be consistently more successful, it's worthwhile to consciously consider back-ups for each of the key roles identified in this section.

Motivators

Another role that you can consider when building teams is that of "motivator." A person who is a motivator on a team also must have some other role. He might be a playmaker, defensive stopper, or a role player—and a motivator, too.

A motivator is someone on the team who inspires others to work harder and work better through his own intensity and excellence. Some specialists on a team may naturally inspire others through their own good work. Others observe their skill and quality and may be motivated to emulate them and do better themselves. But motivators can come in many packages. They don't necessarily need to be the coders who are handling the most complex or high-profile tasks. A junior coder, a utility player, or a role player may be an excellent motivator if they are hard-working, intense, and do especially well on the tasks they are assigned.

I am not speaking here of a coach or cheerleader, someone who motivates others with words, demands, or encouragement. Instead I'm speaking specifically of team members who exhibit a consistently high level of motivation themselves, as exhibited in their productivity and precision. I call them "motivators" under the belief that one person's commitment may not exactly rub off but tends to motivate others.

Motivators are coders who may exceed in many metrics, but who can be particularly identified by strength in the following metrics:

- Temperature
- Efficiency
- Intensity

As you look at a team, you might ask: who are your motivators? Who will provide a level of intensity that will inspire others? Deciding how much intensity and commitment you want on your team and then identifying where that will come from will increase the team's chance of success. The motivators on the team may shift and change over time, but by paying attention to this particular role you can better ensure that there are a healthy number of higher-intensity individuals on the team at any one time.

Veterans and Rookies

To wrap up this section on roles, I'd like to discuss veterans and rookies. Like motivators, these are adjuncts to the other roles that coders fill on a team. So a coder could be a "veteran scorer" or a "rookie role player."

Sometimes in software development, it seems like "veteran" is a dirty word. People think of veteran as "old," and a lot of people (usually younger people) think of coding and software development as a young person's game. In some organizations, "rookie" is also kind of a dirty word. Some organizations don't want to hire people who have no experience.

Veteran, of course, does not really mean old, nor does rookie always mean young. A veteran is someone who has more experience than others. In a world where software and technology changes all the time, a veteran might be someone who has only two or three years of experience in a technical area if that technology only emerged two or three years ago. A rookie is someone who has little or no experience in a particular area—and again, this has nothing to do with the person's age.

The reason I bring all this up is that I believe it is healthy and worthwhile to look at the makeup of a team in terms of veterans, rookies, and those who are in between. There are also specific implications related to metrics for veterans and rookies that you might want to keep in mind when building teams.

Veteran coders will normally be expected to deliver a higher level of productivity and a very good level of accuracy. In many cases, it might be veterans the on the team who fill key roles such as playmaker, scorer, or defensive stopper. Veterans will also probably be among the most consistent performers. This would mean that the metrics for a veteran coder should not show a lot of ups and downs.

One benefit of adding veterans to a team is that they may be a positive influence on other members, somewhat like motivators, but in this case more through mentoring and knowledge-sharing. Teams that add veterans to work with less experienced coders may see a positive effect in the other coders' performance and metrics. This can be monitored, and if you see such effects, you could take advantage of them in team-building. By adding more veterans to the team, or spreading veterans among smaller groups within a larger team, you may be able to positively affect the performance of other coders as well. The effects can be charted, as shown in Figure 8-5.

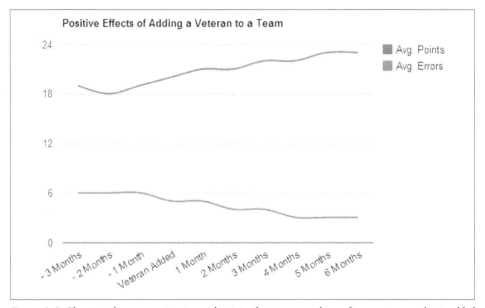

Figure 8-5. Charting the progression in productivity for team members after a veteran coder is added to the team

On the downside, veterans may be more prone to boredom (although it can happen to any coder). If someone has been working in a particular technology or on a limited area of a software product for an extended period of time, then they may begin to lose interest. In this case, their productivity and perhaps even their precision may decline. This is something that metrics could indicate, even early on, with a small but noticeable dip that then levels off. Having spotted the indicators, you could take action by shifting a coder onto a new area or even a new project to re-engage her interest and take fuller advantage of her skills.

Rookies, or very inexperienced coders, don't often become bored. However, unlike the veterans, it is likely that rookies will be inconsistent in their productivity, precision, and overall results. They will have ups and downs, and if you see this in the metrics, there is no particular reason to be alarmed. Over time, however, rookies would also be expected to show a faster rate of growth and improvement than veterans who presumably are already consistent at a more advanced level. A rookie who does not show progression over time, in fact, might need more mentoring or might be cause for concern. Metrics can help spot these situations. See Figure 8-6 for an example.

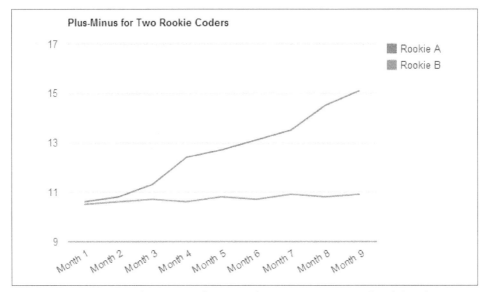

Figure 8-6. Charting rate of progression for two rookies, one progressing well and the other one not progressing

One area where rookies may show initial strength is in their enthusiasm and intensity. This may show up in metrics, and to some extent their excitement and energy may influence others. Adding rookies to a team may influence other team members positively, resulting in increased overall productivity that might also have benefits on overall team success. As you build teams, you might consider adding rookies at regular intervals, not only to add new contributors but also for the positive effect that their energy and enthusiasm can have on a team.

Like other roles on your software teams, making informed and conscious decisions on where to add veterans and rookies (and what percentage of each to have) will help you build better, more sustainable, and more successful development teams.

Timeout for an Example: Two All-Nighters

I admit I am not a big fan of team-building exercises. I like to relax with teammates and do things outside work like going out to lunch, a movie, or a ballgame—but I'm not a fan of "staged" outings where teams work together on artificial projects designed to improve teamwork. There are a variety of ideas and techniques that some organizations use for team-building, from wall-climbing to paintball to making videos. These can be fun, and they may allow teammates to get to know each other better. But in terms of actually improving teamwork or forging closer ties that contribute to long-term sustainable improvement, I am doubtful that such events have any real success.

What I believe does has an effect is when a team goes through difficult and challenging situations together and achieves hard-won accomplishments. While staged events might try to emulate such conditions to create similar effects, there is nothing like the real thing.

One team I worked with at a start-up was a good example. Our product was an on-premise enterprise solution. We spent nine months making major changes to the first release of our product to deliver a much more advanced second release. Those nine months were difficult. We wanted to deliver the second release in six months, but given everything the release included, this turned out to be impossible. Everyone pushed and pushed over that nine months, often working nights or weekends. In the end, we made plans with the entire organization to have the release on a specific date, a Tuesday. The waiting customers were told, a press release was scheduled, and a major change to the home page on our website was ready to go live.

We had been in code freeze for almost two weeks conducting testing on our final candidate build. Only one showstopper bug had been discovered in that time, it was fixed fairly quickly, a new candidate was produced, and testing proceeded. At 10:30 in the morning on Monday (the day before the release), however, another showstopper bug was found. It had to do with integration to another system that many of our customers used. A certain data format encountered when pulling information in from the system would cause our system to crash. We decided we had to fix the bug before release even though the release was less than twenty-four hours away.

By about 2 in the afternoon we had a fix, and we started a new build which took almost two more hours. Then we started testing. At about 7 that evening, however, we realized that a major piece of functionality was missing from the build. Something had gone wrong in the build process.

The entire team stayed while we tried to figure out what went wrong with the build, then having discovered what we believed was the answer, we ran the updated build process (which took another two hours to complete). We got pizza and waited. At the end of all this, after 11 at night, we confirmed that the build was successful. But there was still work to do. We needed to complete more basic regression testing on the build, the build needed to be posted to our various sites for customers to download, and the downloads needed to be tested and confirmed. A few people went home, but four team members including coders and testers stayed on all night to complete the process and make sure the new release was live by 9 on Tuesday morning.

We made it, and everything seemed to be going well after that. We had a nice little party to celebrate (there were less than twenty people in the company) and a number of development team members took a long weekend break. Just a little more than two weeks after the release, however, one of our largest customers had a critical problem in the upgrade process. Our software, which served a very important function for them, was hanging and unusable every time they tried to start it after the upgrade, and there was no way to roll back. Without actually knowing what the problem was or how we could fix it, we promised them a resolution within two days, and the team set out to diagnose and then fix the issue. After one day we figured out what had happened, then it took the rest of that day to make changes and put protections in place in our upgrade code to fix the problem. We realized that the problem could potentially affect many of our customers, so it would require more than just a patch for the one customer. We needed to generate a new release and do a round of testing on the fix and regression testing on the build, plus post all the downloads—and again, we had less than one day left. Once more, the team banded together, with everyone working late into the night and a number of coders and testers staying on all the way through morning to make sure the work got done.

There were other difficult deadlines that the team dealt with, but these were the only two all-nighters that we ever pulled. Successfully coming through the particular challenge and stress of these two situations, however, dramatically boosted the team's sense of trust and confidence in each other and forged a closer working relationship.

That team stuck together and its performance continued to improve for many more releases. Figure 8-7 shows a set of metrics for the team and how it progressed from release to release. The Plus-Minus metric is particularly useful for tracking the combination of productivity and precision, and Intensity is useful for tracking the commitment and consistency of a team. From release to release the team improved, which is something you would want to see with any team. In this case, the two all-nighters, the other challenges, and the increased experience and knowledge were all part of what made the team better and stronger.

Good teams are built, but they usually only become better teams or great teams over time. Whether it's forged through staged events, real events, or a combination of both, if you have a good team you also want to see it improve from release to release, year to year. A team that starts with small wins can build to bigger ones, until a high level of consistent performance becomes ingrained, common, and expected. Tracking and observing metrics for the team will help make sure that it is following a healthy improvement pattern and will help avoid the possibility of performance degradation.

Personnel

Players make the team. As has often been observed in professional sports, there are no great teams without great players. Coaches and managers may help bring out the best in players and help them work well together, but it's the players themselves, the individual team members, who must do the work, solve the problems, and achieve the goals.

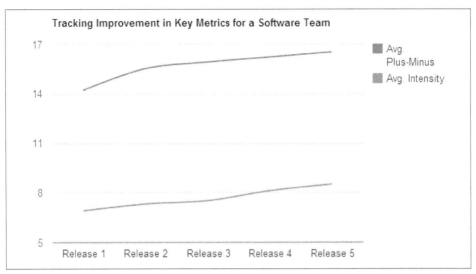

Figure 8-7. The start-up software team improved its performance over multiple releases, as reflected in core metrics

The most important part of any software development team, therefore, are the coders, the personnel. This section covers a set of techniques and concepts for using metrics to help you get the best personnel possible to fit your team goals and team needs.

Recruit for Comps

In the section on team profiles, the idea of "comps" was introduced. Through analysis of current or past performance, you can capture profiles that describe a team's key characteristics. You can then use profiles as "comps" when analyzing an existing team or planning a new team.

You can also create "profiles" for coder roles and use those as "comps" when recruiting new coders. You can create profiles of existing coders from their average metrics, then these profiles can be broken down by roles as defined in the previous section. For example, you might develop a profile for a scorer and another for a defensive stopper by gathering metrics for coders who fill those roles on an existing team. Table 8-4 shows an example of role-based metric profiles, and Figure 8-8 shows a set of charts comparing the core metrics in those profiles.

Table 8-4. Metrics-based profiles of coder roles built from one or more existing software teams can be used as comps for recruiting (metrics are rounded averages per month)

	Scorer	Defensive Stopper	Utility Player	Role Player
Avg. Points	26 (High)	22 (Medium)	22 (Medium)	18 (Low)
Avg. Utility	9 (Low)	10 (Medium)	13 (High)	11 (Medium)
Avg. Assists	6 (High)	3 (Medium)	6 (High)	1 (Low)

	Scorer	Defensive Stopper	Utility Player	Role Player
Avg. Errors	3 (Medium)	1 (Low)	3 (Medium)	3 (Medium)
Avg. Saves	1 (Medium)	3 (High)	1 (Medium)	0 (Low)
Avg. Tackles	1 (Medium)	2 (High)	0 (Low)	0 (Low)
Avg. Range	3 (Medium)	3 (Medium)	6 (High)	1 (Low)

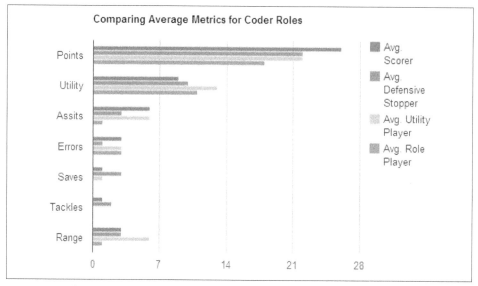

Figure 8-8. A chart comparing the profiles of coder roles built from one or more existing software teams

To build comps for recruiting, you can gather metrics for the coders on your team, but you can also look at other teams in (or outside) your organization. Over time, you might build a library of coder comps. Then, when you set out to recruit a new coder to join a team, you can determine which comps best match the skills and contributions you are seeking to add to the team. Having determined the comp that matches the role you are trying to fill, you will be able to more clearly communicate what sort of experience or skills are required for the position, and you will be in a better position to evaluate candidates in the interview and reference-checking process.

This process is very common to the way professional sports teams analyze prospects and decide on players they want to add. Today, in many sports, the scouting team will have defined profiles based on supporting statistics that define the types of players they are looking for. But they also have summarized these in terms of comps. They might say, in other words, that they are looking for a basketball player like Current Player X, or they might say they are looking for a "shooter" or a "rebounder." If scouts see a prospect that they decide to analyze, they might describe the prospect in terms of a comp. For example, they might say that the prospect reminds them of Current Player Z, or that the prospect is a "prototypical point guard."

Knowing the comp profile during recruiting can help you write a better job description. If you know you are looking for a scorer, for example, you can specify that the coder must have a proven ability to handle complex tasks efficiently. If you are looking for a utility player, you can make it a key point of the job description that candidates need to be comfortable and have proven experience dealing with a wide variety of tasks and responsibilities.

In the interview process, you can focus on exploring the areas that are important according to the role and your target comp profile. If your comp calls for someone who will have a high number of Assists, for example, you can ask candidates how they helped others in past jobs, or if you are looking for a high number of Tackles, you can ask questions related to initiative and innovation. You can explore these questions with references, too. In the end, through interviews and references, you can build at least a mental profile for each candidate and how they rate in key skill areas (if you were reviewing a lot of candidates, you might actually want to document these profiles, too). Clearly, much of this will be estimated, and you will probably focus on rating them High, Medium, or Low in skill areas, as opposed to assigning them numeric values. For example, you might determine through the interviews and references that you think a candidate will produce a high number of Points and Tackles, or a low number of Errors. The ratings will be based on what you believe a candidate has done in the past, and what you project that she would do on your team.

Having constructed an estimated profile for each candidate based on their interviews and references, you can compare each to the comp(s) that you decided best match the ideal candidate. Table 8-5 shows an example of a target comp (Defensive Stopper) for an open position, along with the estimated profiles for three candidates constructed during the recruiting process. In this case, you can see that the data indicates Candidate B is the best fit for the role, because that candidate is closest to the Defensive Stopper profile in the key areas of Errors, Saves, and Tackles.

Table 8-5. A comp profile identifying the ideal qualities for a new recruit (Defensive Stopper) and the constructed profiles of three interviewed candidates

	Defensive Stopper Profile	Candidate A Profile (estimated)	Candidate B Profile (estimated)	Candidate C Profile (estimated)
Avg. Points	22 (Medium)	Medium	Medium	Medium
Avg. Utility	10 (Medium)	Medium	Medium	Medium
Avg. Assists	3 (Medium)	Medium	High	Medium
Avg. Errors	1 (Low)	High	Low	Medium
Avg. Saves	3 (High)	Low	High	Medium
Avg. Tackles	2 (High)	Low	Medium	Low
Avg. Range	3 (Medium)	Medium	Medium	Medium

The advantage of comps and using metrics in this way in recruiting is to bring more definition and clarity to the process, which increases the chance that you will find and choose the best coders to fit your team's goals and needs. While other factors like personality, character traits, and salary requirements will clearly weigh into recruiting decisions, using comps can help inform your decisions and help you avoid mistakes.

Establish a Farm System

Another idea you can borrow from professional sports teams is to establish a "farm system" for personnel development. The analogy of a "farm" is used because these are systems where young players are nurtured and cultivated until they are ready for "harvest," the same way that crops on a farm are cared for and grown. In professional baseball and hockey, there are teams that young players can join the minor leagues to compete and develop their skills. These leagues are less demanding, so players can focus on improving (with lower stress) until they have proven they are ready to join the major league teams. In basketball and American football, teams use a different trial method. They sometimes sign players to temporary contracts in which they are invited to practice with a team and "try out" for a permanent roster spot.

There are a variety of ways to build a farm system for your own organization. One would be to have teams that are working on less critical software projects and use them to develop coders who might eventually be promoted to teams with more critical responsibilities. Another way is to have an intern program, where you let university students work in your organization for a period of time as part of existing teams, working on real tasks and projects. A third way you could build a farm system is by using contractors on a temporary basis, which allows you to evaluate their performance before deciding whether to hire them full-time.

Metrics and comps can be used to evaluate how coders in a farm system are developing and whether they are ready to "move up" to a permanent position on a target team. Using comps, you can determine the level of productivity and precision of coders on a target team and you can compare these comps to the farm system coders. If you are using interns, you might have different expectations and different comps than if you have established internal teams for coder development or if you are using contractors. For example, for interns you might define a comp profile for a rookie role player and then analyze how well interns fit the rookie comp. For contractors, you might have higher expectations, so you could compare their performance to the profile of more veteran members of a team.

Building a farm system is a reliable and proven method for finding good coders to add to your software development teams. It's a "try before you buy" approach. It requires you to make the extra effort to establish the farm system, but it makes the eventual personnel placement decisions easier and less prone to error. Metrics can help ensure you carefully and accurately analyze the coders in your farm system, and can help increase your confidence determining if and when they are ready for the "big leagues."

Make Trades

When a team isn't meeting its goals, or one or more team members are struggling, you have a variety of options. You can recruit new team members or bring up new members from your farm system. You can "cut" (let go) team members who are struggling if you don't feel their performance can be developed and improved, or if you don't have time to wait for them to improve.

Another option that can be a faster road to improvement is to "trade" one or more coders between two teams in your organization. One benefit of this approach is that it doesn't require you to cut coders who might still have value to your organization. Also, you don't have to wait while you recruit new candidates, nor do you have to take the risk that comes with new hires. If there is a better fit for coders on other teams, presumably you can make the move without a lot of risk because the coders are already "known quantities" in terms of skills, strengths, and weaknesses. Another potential benefit is that you might improve the performance of two teams with a single move. If you have multiple teams that are not succeeding as well as you like, swapping certain coders between the two teams might be an excellent option to consider.

Professional sports teams do this regularly. If a team wants to improve its roster, it may trade for a player from another team who has a sought-after skill set. In order to obtain a player in a trade, a team will sometimes trade back one or more other players. In this case, they will send players to the other team to fit that team's needs. The players that a team trades away are either those who weren't working out or those who are deemed less critical and more replaceable. The target outcome in any trade is that a team upgrades its roster, meaning that the gains of players received in a trade are believed to outweigh the losses of those players traded away. As with any personnel changes, there is still risk that the results will not turn out as expected or desired, so part of evaluating whether or not to make a trade is determining whether the risk is worth taking. But certainly, many sports teams have quickly improved themselves through trades.

In a software development organization, a trade simply involves moving a coder from one team to another where the coder's skills are determined to be a better fit for the target team. Multiple coders and multiple teams might be involved. It is actually easier than with sports teams, because in this case the internal teams are not competing and so the two teams are not trying to get the better of each other in a trade. You can make trade decisions that are meant to be in the best interests of the organization.

Metrics can be very useful in helping you identify which teams and coders are good candidates for trades. For example, see Figure 8-9. Team A has a strong "offense" (Points and Power) while Team B has a strong "defense" (Saves and Tackles). If you wanted to create better balance on these two teams, you might consider trading one or more scorers from Team A for one or more defensive stoppers on Team B. Analyzing coders' metric profiles would help you identify which coders are most appropriate to include in the trade.

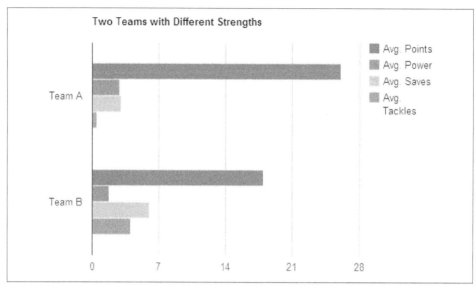

Figure 8-9. Team A and Team B have different strengths and weaknesses that might be better balanced by trading coders from one team to the other

Coach the Skills You Need

It is always worthwhile, of course, if you can find ways to improve the performance of personnel that you already have on a team. In addition to the normal evolution that occurs through experience, you can also accelerate improvement with targeted mentoring and coaching.

As discussed in previous sections in this book, metrics can help you identify the weaknesses of a team and the characteristics of individual coders. Examining metrics, combined with your firsthand observations, you can pick out the areas where the team can improve, determine which coders might best deliver that improvement, and then coach the coders in the target areas.

For example, you might determine that a team needs more defensive strength. Perhaps the team has too many production bugs in critical areas, or critical production issues are not getting solved quickly enough. Or maybe the software has key difficulties that make it hard for users, but no one has time to solve them. You might, therefore, decide that you need to add one or more defensive stoppers to the team. One approach to fill this role would be to coach one or more current team members to become defensive stoppers.

If you are using metrics regularly as part of your development process, and if you are sharing and discussing them in team meetings, then the process for coaching improvement in target areas is fairly simple. You can:

- Choose the coders to coach by identifying those who have already displayed strength (perhaps sporadically) in the needed skills.
- Identify target metrics and the values that you want each coder to reach.
- Make sure that each coder reduces other responsibilities as necessary in order to focus on the new areas.
- Track the coders' improvement in key metrics and review with the coders on a regular basis.

It may help to identify other coders, possibly on other teams, that a coder can study or talk to, so they can learn more about the skills and techniques to emulate. Formal mentoring, as discussed in "Mentoring" on page 175, may also be used as part of the development process. In that case, you would assign a mentor to each coder that you are coaching.

Coders can often improve in specific areas just through increased focus and dedication to those areas. Metrics allow the coaches and the coders to track progress. If sufficient progress is not made in an acceptable timeframe, you may need to choose other candidates for coaching or to take another approach to improve personnel (such as recruiting, trades, or using a farm system).

Coaching is an important technique in building and maintaining successful teams. As with other techniques for building software teams, metrics used intelligently can help improve the efficiency and results of the coaching process.

Timeout for an Example: No Such Thing As a Perfect Team

Is there such a thing as a perfect team? Unless your definition of "perfect" is pretty loose, you would have to say no. In sports we know there are no perfect teams or even perfect seasons. The 1995-1996 Chicago Bulls with Michael Jordan had the best record ever in professional basketball, winning seventy-two games in the regular season, but they still lost ten times. Even the 1972 Miami Dolphins, the only American pro football team to go through an entire season undefeated and win the Super Bowl, had multiple flaws and four of its seventeen wins were by less than four points.

The best software teams I ever worked on definitely weren't perfect. Our software wasn't perfect, that's for sure. But I remember these teams fondly and I think of them as good, maybe even great, because we accomplished the goals that were put before us and that we set for ourselves. We delivered software that impressed and sometimes delighted our users. We improved over time, and we had fun along the way.

The closest I ever saw a software team get to perfect was, ironically, a team that worked on a product that never shipped. After a year of development, with a product already in beta and one month shy of the ship date, the project was cancelled for business reasons (the company had to cut back in areas because overall profits were declining). I was a member of the team, so I'm biased, but I believe the software was revolutionary and would have been a huge success. Needless to say, I didn't agree with the business decision to cancel the project and throw away the work. My teammates and I got "traded" to other teams in the company.

What made that team so good, so close to perfect in my mind? I think it's the fact that everyone on the team had a defined role, that we all embraced our roles, and that our roles were sufficiently complementary to create a strong and well-balanced team. Everyone on the team was highly skilled and capable, and probably each of us could have taken different roles. However we each took on the role that best fit our skills and preferences, and we were happy to focus on that and leave other roles to our teammates. On a team of seven coders, we had what I would call:

- One playmaker (a high level of Points and Assists)
- Two scorers (a high level of Power and Pop)
- Two defensive stoppers (a high level of Tackles)
- Two utility players (a high level of Utility and Range)

And in this mix we had three veterans, one rookie, and two motivators.

The result was a team that had a great mix of offensive firepower and defensive strength, with excellent attention to detail. Because of the complementary mix of skills and because everyone fully accepted their role, we were highly efficient and had no conflict. Granted, we were not perfect. Individually we each had flaws, so as a team we had flaws. We made mistakes in the software—undoubtedly, if it had ever been released there would have been issues to solve. But while no team is perfect, it is possible to have teams where the makeup of the team is nearly ideal—where the structure of the team, the roles, and the mix of experience couldn't be much better. Take a team with a near-perfect makeup, with teammates committed to excellence, and then give it a worthy goal. That's a formula for success—not perfection, but success.

In my lifetime, I've never seen a perfect sports team (although the UCLA Bruins basketball teams in the late 1960s and early 1970s, which I saw firsthand, were pretty close). But the teams I think of as the greatest had a superior mix of offensive skill, defensive determination, hustle, resilience, and a commitment to teamwork and winning that was superior to any individual pursuit of recognition. The players on those teams had well-defined roles that they gladly accepted, even the back-ups who sometimes only helped in practice and never played in real games. Those teams also exhibited a joy that appeared to not only come from winning, but from the knowledge that they were working hard and helping each other to become the best they could be.

There's no such thing as a perfect team, and it's impossible to say which team was the greatest. But you know an excellent team when you see one. With planning and thought, the patterns of successful teams can be identified and good teams—even great teams—can be planned and built, if that's what you want.

CHAPTER 9

Conclusion

Good is not good when better is expected.

> —Vin Scully, the voice of the Brooklyn and Los Angeles Dodgers

In the last 25 years, computers and the Internet have forever changed the way that professional sports teams go about their business, giving them the ability to gather, store, share, and analyze a vast amount of statistics on their own players, prospects, and competitors. There is so much money involved in major sports that they can afford the best technology and software, and they can pay to have analysts whose sole job is to review statistics and help the team find an advantage. Computers and data analysis play an integral part in evaluating talent, player development, and competitive strategy. Coaches and players study tape and detailed statistics to improve their own performance and to find ways to beat the competition.

Advanced statistical analysis is no longer optional for teams that want to win in the NFL, NBA, NHL, and MLB. It is required. Every team invests heavily in gathering and analyzing statistics to arm their player personnel departments, their coaching staffs, and their players. Teams no longer think it's enough to just work and try harder, they want to be smarter. Statistics help teams make more informed personnel decisions. Statistics help coaches and players identify better competitive strategies and focus on the right things.

How do statistics help teams make better decisions? Statistics help them analyze productivity, skills, strengths, weaknesses, patterns, and trends, which leads to greater understanding. With more understanding, they have a greater chance to accurately analyze a situation. Then, with the data to support their analysis, they have a much better chance that a group of decision-makers will reach a good consensus. In the absence of such data, people fall back on their preconceived notions, and groups are disproportionately influenced by the members that argue the best or hardest for their preferred solutions. Statistics make the decision-making process more rational, more objective, more informed.

The value of statistics or metrics, therefore, is real and proven, although using metrics doesn't mean that every decision will be right or optimal. Sometimes you'll still make bad decisions or have disappointing outcomes. While the use of metrics and the knowledge they can provide won't ensure that you make the optimal decision or pursue the optimal path every time, good metrics will increase the chance that you make a better decision or choose a better path than you might have otherwise. Over the course of many choices and opportunities, the effect of better decisions, implementing better processes, and getting better results can be dramatic.

For example, imagine that you have a software team with twelve coders. Suppose that two of those coders already perform at their highest capacity. In other words, there really isn't anything they can improve. But suppose that the other ten coders all have room for improvement. If you were to gather metrics for those coders and review and discuss those metrics regularly, you could imagine that you might identify specific areas—specific metrics—that each coder could focus on improving. Then you could measure each coder's progression, so again you could imagine that using the metrics would increase the likelihood that some or all of them improve. If, on average, the ten coders became ten percent more productive and ten percent more accurate in their work as a result of the increased focus, then multiplied across the team, that would be the equivalent of hiring another full-time coder.

Metrics, however, are not a solution in and of themselves. That ten percent improvement for each coder is not going to happen just because you start putting numbers in spreadsheets. But if you've decided that you want to be better and that you are willing to do the hard work to improve, metrics are an extremely useful tool to help you choose the right path to get there. And metrics are very useful to help you define an ongoing process for continuous improvement and for maintaining a high level of performance over time.

When it comes to a team—whether it's a sports or a software development team—there are many areas where metrics can help create opportunities. The number of these opportunities is basically multiplied by the number of people you have on a team. As has been discussed in this book, metrics can help software teams in recruiting, coder and team evaluation, goal-setting, and progress analysis. The self-awareness that metrics provide can also be highly valuable. You can see this in sports. Many sports players increasingly use statistics to help them figure out how to improve their own skills, by identifying areas to focus on and develop. They don't necessarily focus on statistics during a game (although some do), but they use analysis between games to help them better prepare. Coders who review metrics at regular intervals can achieve similar benefits.

Iterative improvement is the nature of our field. Metrics can be used by coders and software teams in a cycle of review, adjust, review. Likewise, you may iteratively improve the metrics themselves or the way that you use them. As you include metrics in your development process, you'll learn more not only about your teams but about the metrics and their use. I firmly expect that a year from now, I'll have new ideas about metrics and how to use them for software teams—and if you put codermetrics in practice, I'm sure you will too.

Part of the reason that metrics and the way we interpret them or use them must evolve is that the "game" itself changes. In American professional football, rule changes have vastly altered the way offenses and defenses can operate, which has directly affected which statistics matter more. In software development, new technologies come along all the time that may change what you do or the way you work and, therefore, can affect how you would use metrics. Developing a software application ten years from now might require a different set of skills, and those skills might be measured in a different way than they are today. The continued advance of telecommunications may also affect the makeup of teams and the way they work, which again might require different metrics or analysis. For many years now, the Internet has fueled the formation and growth of open source development teams, which clearly have different dynamics, and could use specific metrics and analysis tailored to such teams.

Over time, I hope that we can have discourse in our industry to turn codermetrics into something even richer and better than what I've originally laid out here, continuing to evolve codermetrics as our industry changes. To gather feedback and facilitate the sharing of new ideas, I am setting up a website at *http://www.codermetrics.org*, where I invite you to contribute your own stories and thoughts. The site will be regularly updated with new information supplied by colleagues, as well as new developments or ideas. I hope that other writers and websites will emerge on this subject as well. There are many participants in software development beyond coders that I haven't touched on in this book—such as testers, designers, and managers—and metrics for those participants are additional areas for further thought.

As a final story, since I've focused so much on sports analogies in this book, I'd like to discuss a great sportsman who epitomizes what it means to be a great teammate: Jack Roosevelt "Jackie" Robinson, who was born in 1919 in Cairo, Georgia, and died in 1972 at the age of 53. Jackie Robinson was arguably one of the greatest all-around athletes in the United States in the twentieth century. He was a standout in football, basketball, and track at UCLA (he was the national long jump champion). Baseball, for which he became famous, was perhaps his "worst" sport. After college he played baseball in the Negro Leagues, then he was drafted into the Brooklyn Dodgers' farm system—and then in 1947, Branch Rickey asked Jackie Robinson to break the major league baseball "color barrier," which he did.

He played ten years for the Dodgers. As their undisputed leader, he helped the team to six World Series appearances and one world championship (in the prior 25 years, the team had only had one World Series appearance and no championships). By modern sabermetrics-type statistical measures, he was one of the top hitters of his time (he walked frequently, so his on-base percentage was very high), and he is rated as one of the top defensive second basemen ever. In both team and personal statistics, therefore, he was a success.

But the statistics only tell part of the story about how great and valuable a teammate he was. By all accounts, Jackie Robinson was a great competitive leader, and a man of great integrity and endurance—which he had to be to survive and succeed, given the pressure he came under for breaking the color barrier. There were also many other great players on his Dodger teams: you can't win a world championship in baseball with just one player. But there was no one who could lay claim to being a better teammate than Jackie Robinson, no one who brought any more skill and effort to each ballgame to help his team win, no one who conducted himself in a more dignified way, no one who spurred his teammates on as much or motivated them more.

In many sports, to honor a former player, a team will "retire" that player's number so that no future player will wear that number again. It is no accident that there is only one player in baseball who has his number retired by the entire league, by every team—Jackie Robinson and his number, 42. It is not only a testament to what he took on to advance the sport, but how he did it, how he played the game, and what he stood for.

Jackie Robinson was not just a great ballplayer, he was a great teammate—and he helped make the Dodgers great. Great teams are made up of great teammates. You don't get one without the other. Jackie Robinson had many great teammates on the 1955 Brooklyn Dodgers, including star hitters like Duke Snider, pitchers like Don Newcombe, and role players like Don Zimmer. Some of the things that go into being a great teammate are tangible and measurable, but some are not. Skills like hitting and fielding can be measured. Character traits like integrity, honesty, and competitiveness are very hard to quantify.

When using metrics, therefore, you should measure and analyze the tangibles, but remember the intangibles, too. The general managers on professional sports teams have realized this. Living without metrics in today's competitive environment would be stubborn and foolhardy. But to rely solely on metrics without appreciating and evaluating a person's character would be a mistake, too. Teams with players who have the winning combination of strength in the measurable skills that fit their roles and strength in character (players like Jackie Robinson), are the ones who have the greatest and most consistent success.

It is a trait of great teammates that they want themselves and their teams to be better than good…they want to be great. Metrics are not everything, but they can help a software development team and individual coders improve. Whatever your role, if you are a person who wants yourself and your team to be better than good—to be great—then I encourage you to consider the "competitive edge" that metrics can provide in that regard. Be like Jackie Robinson. Be dignified, be a great teammate, play with honor and integrity. But play to win.

Codermetrics Quick Reference

The following is a table of all the metrics introduced in this book.

Table A-1. Codermetrics quick reference

Metric	Description	Formula
Points	Measure the overall productivity of each coder on assigned tasks	Points = Sum (Complexity for all completed tasks)
Utility	Measure how many assigned tasks each coder completes	Utility = Number of tasks completed
Power	Measure the average complexity of the tasks that a coder completes	Power = Points / Utility
Assists	Measure the amount of coder interruptions and how much a coder helps others	Assists = Sum (Interrupts) + Sum (Helps)
Temperature	Measure how "hot" or "cold" a coder is at any given time	Start with Temperature = 72; thereafter Temperature = Previous Temperature × (Current Points / Previous Points)
O-Impact	Provide a single "Offensive Impact" number that summarizes the contributions of a coder in moving projects along	O-Impact = Points + Utility + Assists
Saves	Measure how often a coder helps fix urgent production issues	Saves = Number of Product Issues with the highest Severity that a coder helps fix
Tackles	Measure how many potential issues or opportunities a coder handles proactively	Tackles = Number of Pluses where coder demonstrates initiative or innovation
Range	Measure how many areas of software a coder works on	Range = Number of Areas Worked by a coder
D-Impact	Provide a single "Defensive Impact" number that summarizes the contributions of a coder in helping to avoid large problems	D-Impact = (Saves + Tackles) × Range
Turnovers	Measure the complexity of assigned tasks that a coder fails to complete	Turnovers = Sum (Complexity for all completed Tasks)

Metric	Description	Formula
Errors	Measure the magnitude of production issues found related to areas that a coder is responsible for	Errors = Sum (Severity for each Product Issues × Population Affected)
Plus-Minus	Measure the amount of positive contributions versus negative issues for each coder	Plus-Minus = Points - Turnovers - Errors
Wins	Measure the number of active users added	Wins = Sum (User Activations)
Win Rate	Determine the average amount of time it takes to get a win	Win Rate = (Time Elapsed / Wins)
Win Percentage	Measure the percentage of trials that successfully convert to active users	Win Percentage = (Successful Trials / Trials Completed) × 100
Boost	Measure the amount of additional user benefits delivered	Boost = Sum (Population Benefited for each User Benefit)
Losses	Measure the number of active users lost	Losses = Sum (User Deactivations)
Loss Rate	Determine the average amount of time it takes to accumulate each loss	Loss Rate = (Time Elapsed / Losses)
Penalties	Measure the overall urgency of customer support issues	Penalties = Sum (Urgency for each User Issue)
Penalties Per Win (PPW)	Measure the overall urgency of customer support issues relative to the number of new users	Penalties Per Win = Penalties / Wins
Gain	Measure the number of Wins minus the missed opportunities and Losses	Gain = Wins - ((Trials Completed − Successful Trials) + Losses)
Gain Rate	Determine the average amount of time it takes to accumulate each Gain	Gain Rate = (Time Elapsed / Gain)
Acceleration	Measure the ratio of user benefits delivered to urgent user issues created	Acceleration = (Boost / Number of User Issues with the highest Urgency) × 100
Win Ranking	Establish ranking versus key competitors based on number of new user activations	Win Ranking = Numeric position based on New Users vs. Competitors
Capability Ranking	Establish ranking versus key competitors based on breadth and depth of software features	Capability Ranking = Numeric position based on Features vs. Competitors
Influence	Measure the percentage of positive contributions by each coder relative to others on the team	Influence = Individual (O-Impact + D-Impact) / Team (O-Impact + D-Impact)
Efficiency	Measure the percentage accuracy of each coder relative to others on the team	Efficiency = 1.0 - (Individual (Turnovers + Errors) / Team (Turnovers + Errors))
Advance Shares	Assign a relative level of credit to each coder for user advances	Advance Shares = Acceleration × Influence
Win Shares	Assign a relative level of credit to each coder for new users	Win Shares = Wins × Influence × Efficiency

Metric	Description	Formula
Loss Shares	Assign a relative level of responsibility to each coder for lost users	Loss Shares = Losses $\times$ (1.0 - Efficiency)
Teamwork	Establish a relative rating for team-oriented contributions	Teamwork = Assists + Saves + Range - Turnovers
Fielding	Establish a relative rating for the range and breadth of work successfully handled	Fielding = (Utility + Range) - (Turnovers + Errors)
Pop	Establish a relative rating for the amount of complex work, innovation, and initiative	Pop = Power + Tackles
Intensity	Establish a relative rating for heightened productivity and dealing with demanding issues	Intensity = Saves + Tackles + (Avg. Temperature - 72)

Bibliography

The following books and articles were used in the preparation of this book:

Brooks, Jr., Frederick P. *The Mythical Man-Month: Essays On Software Engineering, Anniversary Edition*. Boston, MA: Addison Wesley, 1995.

DeMarco, Tom, and Lister, Timothy. *Peopleware: Productive Projects and Teams, 2nd Edition*. New York, NY: Dorset House, 1999.

Gladwell, Malcolm. *Outliers: The Story Of Success*. New York, NY: Little, Brown and Company, 2008.

Grady, Robert B. *Practical Software Metrics For Project Management And Process Improvement*. Upper Saddle River, NJ: Prentice Hall, 1992.

James, Bill. *The Bill James Gold Mine 2009*. Skokie, IL: ACTA Sports, 2009.

James, Bill. *The Bill James Handbook 2011*. Skokie, IL: ACTA Sports, 2010.

Lewis, Michael. *Moneyball: The Art Of Winning An Unfair Game*. New York, NY: W. W. Norton and Company, 2003.

Lewis, Michael. "The No-Stats All-Star." *The New York Times Magazine*. February 2009.

McConnell, Steve. *Software Estimation: Demystifying The Black Art*. Redmond, WA: Microsoft Press, 2006.

Oram, Andy, and Wilson, Greg, eds. *Making Software*. Sebastopol, CA: O'Reilly, 2010.

Spolsky, Joel. *Joel On Software*. Berkeley, CA: Apress, 2004.

Spolsky, Joel. *More Joel On Software*. Berkeley, CA: Apress, 2008.

Spolsky, Joel, ed. *The Best Software Writing I*. Berkeley, CA: Apress, 2005.

Stelman, Andrew, and Greene, Jennifer, eds. *Beautiful Teams: Inspiring And Cautionary Tales From Veteran Team Leaders*. Sebastopol, CA: O'Reilly, 2009.

Surowiecki, James. *The Wisdom of Crowds: Why The Many Are Smarter Than The Few And How Collective Wisdom Shapes Business, Economies, Societies, And Nations.* New York, NY: Doubleday, 2004.

Surowiecki, James. "It's The Workforce, Stupid!." *The New Yorker.* April 2007.

Taleb, Nassim Nicholas. *The Black Swan: The Impact Of The Highly Improbable.* New York, NY: Random House, 2007.

Also used were other writings, articles, and statistics from Bill James Online (*http://www.billjamesonline.net*).

Index

We'd like to hear your suggestions for improving our indexes. Send email to *index@oreilly.com*.

About the Author

Jonathan Alexander has over 25 years experience in software development. He is currently VP Engineering at Vocalocity, a leader in cloud-based business telecommunications. Previously he built and managed software teams at vmSight, Epiphany, and Radnet. He studied computer science at UCLA, and began his career writing software for author Michael Crichton.

Colophon

The animal on the cover of *Codermetrics* is a whitebar surgeonfish (*Acanthurus leucopareius*). All species of surgeonfish and other members of the *Acanthuridae* family (such as tangs and unicornfish) are distinctive for the sharp spines on either side of their tail fin—and in fact, *Acanthurus* is derived from the Greek for "thorn tail." The common name of surgeonfish also arose due to these scalpel-like appendages, which the fish can use for defense with a rapid side sweep of their tail.

The whitebar surgeonfish is subtropical, and can be found in coral reefs around Pacific islands, Australia, and Southeast Asia. They grow to be around 8–9 inches long, and are primarily beige in color with iridescent blue spots and a dark brown face. Their eyes are set high in their face, directly in front of a white bar that runs from the top of their head down toward their throat. These fish also have a white bar on their tail. Their small mouths have one row of teeth that they use to scrape up algae, their sole food source.

Whitebar surgeonfish are popular in saltwater aquariums, and widely commercially available for that purpose. However, some species of surgeonfish tend to grow quickly (and to a large size) in an aquarium setting, so it's advisable to do some research before adding them to a tank.

The cover image is from *Cuvier's Animals*. The cover font is Adobe ITC Garamond. The text font is Linotype Birka; the heading font is Adobe Myriad Condensed; and the code font is LucasFont's TheSansMonoCondensed.

Have it your way.

Get even more for your money.

Join the O'Reilly Community, and register the O'Reilly books you own. It's free, and you'll get:

- $4.99 ebook upgrade offer
- 40% upgrade offer on O'Reilly print books
- Membership discounts on books and events
- Free lifetime updates to ebooks and videos
- Multiple ebook formats, DRM FREE
- Participation in the O'Reilly community
- Newsletters
- Account management
- 100% Satisfaction Guarantee

Signing up is easy:

1. **Go to: oreilly.com/go/register**
2. **Create an O'Reilly login.**
3. **Provide your address.**
4. **Register your books.**

Note: English-language books only

To order books online:
oreilly.com/store

For questions about products or an order:
orders@oreilly.com

To sign up to get topic-specific email announcements and/or news about upcoming books, conferences, special offers, and new technologies:
elists@oreilly.com

For technical questions about book content:
booktech@oreilly.com

To submit new book proposals to our editors:
proposals@oreilly.com

O'Reilly books are available in multiple DRM-free ebook formats. For more information:
oreilly.com/ebooks

O'REILLY®

Spreading the knowledge of innovators   oreilly.com